everyday
sexism

LAURA BATES

**SIMON &
SCHUSTER**

London · New York · Sydney · Toronto · New Delhi

A CBS COMPANY

First published in Great Britain by Simon & Schuster UK Ltd, 2014
This paperback edition published by Simon & Schuster UK Ltd, 2015
A CBS company

3 5 7 9 10 8 6 4

Simon & Schuster UK Ltd
1st Floor
222 Gray's Inn Road
London WC1X 8HB

www.simonandschuster.co.uk

Simon & Schuster Australia,
Sydney

Simon & Schuster India,
New Delhi

A CIP catalogue record for this book
is available from the British Library

ISBN: 978-1-47114-920-7
ISBN: 978-1-47113-158-5 (ebook)

The author and publishers have made all reasonable efforts to contact
copyright-holders for permission, and apologise for any omissions or errors
in the form of credits given. Corrections may be made to future printings.

This publication contains references to the Everyday Sexism Project website,
www.everydaysexism.com, and the Project's Twitter account. The publishers
do not accept any responsibility for the contents of websites and Twitter feeds
which they do not own.

Typeset in the UK by Nick Venables
Printed and bound in Italy by L.E.G.O SpA

Contents

Foreword by Sarah Brown

One of the mysteries of becoming a parent is how you can simultaneously grow up and regress at the same time. Having children drags formative ideas, long submerged, violently to the surface and forces women to consider how they moved from the girl they were to the woman they are. For me the transition to motherhood was the catalyst for an almighty showdown with my own assumptions, memories, hopes and disappointments: all parts of me profoundly shaped by my early – and lifelong – experiences of everyday sexism.

If you want to understand what I'm talking about, go and ask your nearest small friend what they want to be when they grow up. It doesn't need to be your son or daughter; it can be a cousin, nephew or niece, a friend's child or neighbour's little one. Chances are, if you ask them what they see in their future, you'll get an answer of boundless confidence. On our small island we have enough aspirant Marie Curies to cure cancer 1,000 times over, enough Andy Murrays-in-waiting to win every Wimbledon until the end of time. And sufficient ambitious aspiring heads of LEGO – male and female – to make the current CEO a little nervous about his long-term future. Witnessing that limitless self-belief in my own boys for the first time threw me back to what I used to believe as a girl: that there's nothing really beyond somebody with the courage to try and the patience to practise.

Children, in other words, are not optimists *in spite* of the odds; they don't really understand that there are such things as odds. The idea that some things – whether that's an Oscar, Olympic gold or an Oxford degree – might not be for 'the likes of us' simply does not compute.

Then something terrible happens. Some children learn the word 'no'. Not the no of a loving parent introducing boundaries and keeping their kids from eating too many sweets or not sleeping enough or running out near roads or walking too close to a fire. But the harsh, horrible *no* of '*know your place*'. The *no* that, for some of us, gets more and more deafening with age, but which seems, like a dog whistle, to be completely inaudible to others who don't simply fail to respond; they don't even know it's there.

It's the *no* that says skipping ropes are for girls and science kits are for boys. It's the no that says that nice girls don't and that plain ones better watch out in case they get left on the shelf. The no that says it doesn't matter whether you've a Cambridge professorship, an OBE or your own BBC series: you're still just an object to be appraised by cyber judges more interested in your body than your brain.

The most dangerous effect of that *no* is that it gets so deeply internalized you start saying it silently to yourself. You get so used to extra hurdles being put in your way that it becomes too exhausting to even think about clearing them – and then you forget you even can clear them.

Well, I've had enough of that *no*. And so has Laura Bates.

Laura's Everyday Sexism Project gives women the power over our own no. The power to say no to street harassment, to being discriminated against at work, to being patronized by companies more interested in pinkwash than serving real women's needs.

Through her online activism Laura has already inspired 50,000 of us in to #ShoutingBack – and to asking men to shout along in tune just by tweeting out on @EverydaySexism.

When I spoke at a blogger's conference a few years ago I shared a little of my own experience of being trolled and said there's nothing more cowardly than a bully with a BlackBerry. That triggered a massive response of tweets and posts of sympathetic outrage, but I realize that this is as nothing compared to what is happening now. Today's online campaigners are getting something far, far worse – rape threats from people whose shame should go with them to the grave. The only consolation I took from that horrible summer of 2013 was just how many men were disgusted to discover that this is something that happens and whose own feminism was awakened by their sudden glimpse of what women go through every day.

This, for me, is one of the most exciting aspects of what Laura has done with Everyday Sexism and is doing with this book. Neither are verdicts *on* men, but resources *for* men – things that will help them understand the structure of patriarchy, which they can either replicate or resist in their own lives. The genius is that the project also serves as a brilliant, sparky, welcoming haven for girls and women who have suffered daily acts of vile sexism, grown too used to it for their own comfort and relish the chance to share, speak up and talk back.

That spirit of empathy – of helping each of us to understand what happens to all of us – is what gives Everyday Sexism its dynamism and what I hope will inspire all of you holding this book now to take action on behalf of some girls whose names you will never know and faces you will never see.

When Laura and I first started discussing her project, she explained that part of her hope was that giving women a place to log their experiences would render them visible and, therefore, important. My own work on getting kids who miss out on the chance to learn into school has a similar aim – to make the global education emergency as visible and as important as previous catastrophes like slavery and apartheid. I have always believed that speaking up, and gathering together like-minded voices to amplify the message works – that this reaches decision-makers and government leaders and holds them to account. I believe this because I have seen it work. We have all understood that it works from winning women the vote at the start of the twentieth century to the end of apartheid in South Africa to global campaigns to drop Third World debt in more recent years. It is what Laura was reaching out for as she started the project and, as she reviews and acknowledges past legislative wins for feminism, highlights the continuing desperate need for social and cultural change. Laura calls it our 'international collective purpose'. So nicely put, I think.

With the opening up of Everyday Sexism as an online platform to share stories about the regular, run-of-the-mill, taken-for-granted, daily sexist moments that women encounter, the floodgates have opened. Each act needs to be called out, each act can be shared and common understanding between women used to restore both self-confidence and a constructive righteous indignation. Feminism's new, mostly younger sisterhood is taking back control and calling it out.

This model of twenty-first-century feminism is one of global sharing and of claiming its own online space away from the trolls and lurkers and shining a spotlight on their dark spaces. This version reaches out and includes those who might be the most vulnerable of all: our youngest sisters, daughters and friends. Laura rightly identifies the huge challenges that girls face today as they forge their own identities and establish their place in an image-complex world. Girls and young women have been held back in both big and small ways for too long, and the emerging feminist groups across campuses, workplaces and online blogs are taking this on. What Laura's book does is take a good look at three things: how the push back on sexism is global; how it is taking place online; and how it has a big part to play in getting it right for younger girls. This pretty much guarantees that this book will immediately form a central part of all Women's Studies courses.

The bigger prize in knocking back the daily acts of sexism is to build a picture as to how we transform our attitudes to girls so that they do in the end get to realize their potential. Around the world there are 31 million girls who don't get a single day at school. More than 10 million girls are married off as child brides every year. Millions more are forced to lose their education and chance of better future employment as they are sent out to work as cheap child labour or kept at home to serve as carers. The evidence is clear that providing universal education in developing countries could have huge impact on economic growth ... and the results are starkest of all when it comes to educating girls. As ever it makes both big and small sense to invest in girls, and it is time to close that gender gap.

This book provides plenty of stories and evidence that will shock and enrage you. But it will also, I hope, reaffirm your belief that change can happen and we can win it if we try.

One of the best places any woman who wants to change the world can start is with picking up a book. If we look at women who have held leading positions in every continent around the world – from Graca Machel to Dilma Rousseff to Julia Gillard to Joyce Banda – they all have one thing in common. They all have an above-average level of education. It isn't true in every single place but, as a general rule, remember this: women who lead, read.

So, read on to find out about the reality of everyday sexism. And then lead on to play your part in ending it. Laura has given us the tools, but it is up to all of us to finish the job.

Sarah Brown
@SarahBrownUK

Everybody Has a Tipping Point

The funny thing is that when mine came, in March 2012, it wasn't something dramatic or extreme, or even particularly out of the ordinary. It was just another week of little pinpricks: the man who appeared as I sat outside a café, seized my hand and refused to let go; the guy who followed me off the bus and lewdly propositioned me all the way to my front door; the man who made a sexual gesture and shouted, 'I'm looking for a wife' from his car as I walked wearily home after a long day. I shouted back, 'Keep looking!' but as I trudged home I started for the first time to really think about how many of these little incidents I was just putting up with from day to day.

I remembered the university supervisor who was rumoured to wear a black armband once a year to mourn the anniversary of my college admitting women. I thought about the night that a group of teenage boys had casually walked up behind me in the street before one of them grabbed me, hard, between the legs, forcing his fingers upwards against my jeans. I recalled the boss who'd sent me strange emails about his sexual fantasies and mysteriously terminated my freelance contract with no explanation almost immediately after learning I had a boyfriend. The university supervisor whose email suggesting we meet for our first tutorial said, 'I'll bring a red rose and you bring a copy of yesterday's *Telegraph*...' The senior colleague who, on my first day working as an admin temp – aged just seventeen – propositioned me via the company's internal email system. The guy who sat next to me on the bus and started running his hand up and down my leg – and the other one who sat opposite me and began masturbating under his coat, his confident eyes boring into mine. I remembered the men who cornered me late one night in a Cambridge street shouting, 'We're going to part those legs and f*ck that c*nt!' and left me cowering against the wall as they strolled away cackling.

And the more these incidents came back to me the more I wondered why I'd played them down at the time – why I'd never complained, or even particularly *remembered* them until I sat down and really thought about it.

The answer was that these events were normal. They hadn't seemed exceptional enough for me to object to them because they *weren't out of the ordinary*. Because this kind of thing was just part of life – or, rather, part of being a woman. Simply, I was used to it.

And I started to wonder how many other women had had similar experiences and, like me, had simply accepted them and rationalized them and got on with it without really stopping to protest or ask why.

So I started asking around – among friends and family, at parties, or even in the supermarket. Over the course of a few weeks I asked every woman I met whether she'd ever encountered this sort of problem. I honestly thought that, if I asked twenty or thirty women, one or two would remember something significant from the past – a bad experience they'd had at university, perhaps, or in a previous job.

What actually happened took me completely by surprise. Every single woman I spoke to had a story. But not from five years ago, or ten. From last week, or yesterday, or 'on my way here today'. And they weren't just random one-off events, but reams and reams of tiny pinpricks – just like my own experiences – so niggling and normalized that to protest each one felt facetious. Yet put them together and the picture created by this mosaic of miniatures was strikingly clear. This inequality, this pattern of casual intrusion whereby women could be leered at, touched, harassed and abused without a second thought, was *sexism*: implicit, explicit, common-or-garden and deep-rooted sexism, pretty much everywhere you'd care to look. And if sexism means treating people differently or discriminating against them purely because of their sex, then women were experiencing it on a near-daily basis.

The more stories I heard, the more I tried to talk about the problem. And yet time and time again I found myself coming up against the same response: sexism doesn't exist anymore. Women are equal now, more or less. You career girls these days can have your cake and eat it – what more do you want? Think about the women in other countries dealing with real problems, people told me – you women in the UK have no idea how lucky you are. You have 'gilded lives'! You're making a fuss about nothing. You're overreacting. You're uptight, or frigid. You need to learn to take a joke, get a sense of humour, and lighten up...

You really need to learn to take a compliment.

How, I wondered, was it possible for there to be so much evidence of the existence of sexism alongside so much protest to the contrary? Gradually, as I became more aware of the sheer scale of the problem, I also began to understand that it was an invisible one. People didn't want to acknowledge it, or talk about it – in fact, they often simply refused, point blank, to believe it still existed. And it wasn't just men who took this view; it was women, too – telling me I was getting worked up about nothing, or being oversensitive, or simply looking for problems where there weren't any.

At first, I wondered if they were right. People weren't exactly falling over themselves to share my 'Eureka!' moment. This could be like my ill-fated but *utter* conviction, aged eleven, that it was actually 'helicockter', not 'helicopter', and everybody else was just pronouncing it wrong. Perhaps I was just overreacting and women really were equal now, more or less. I thought I'd take a look at the statistics, to see if we really had finally reached a level playing field.

I found that in this supposedly 'equal' society, with nothing left for women to want or fight for, they hold less than a quarter of seats in parliament, and only 5 out of 22 Cabinet positions. That just 7 out of 38 Lord Justices of Appeal and 19 out of 106 High Court Judges are female. That it's been more than 14 years since a female choreographer was commissioned to create a piece for the main stage at our Royal Opera House. That in 2010 it was reported that the National Gallery's collection of some 2,300 works contained paintings by only ten women. That our Royal Society has never had a female president and just 5 per cent of the current Fellowship is made up of women. That women write only a fifth of front-page newspaper articles and that 84 per cent of those articles are dominated by male subjects or experts. That women directed just 5 per cent of the 250 major films of 2011, down by nearly half from a paltry 9 per cent in 1998. That a Home Office survey as recently as 2009 showed that 20 per cent of those polled thought it 'acceptable' in some circumstances 'for a man to hit or slap his wife or girlfriend in response to her being dressed in sexy or revealing clothes in public'.

Then I looked at the crime statistics and found that on average more than 2 women are killed every week by a current or former partner, that there is a call to the police every minute about domestic violence, and that a woman is raped every 6 minutes – adding up to more than 85,000 rapes and 400,000 sexual assaults per year. That 1 in 5 women is the victim of a sexual offence and 1 in 4 will experience domestic violence.

Those stats did very little to convince me that everything was OK and I shouldn't be worrying my pretty little head about it. Actually they had the opposite effect. I started wondering whether there might not be a connection between ours being a society in which so many women become so accustomed to experiencing gender-based prejudice that they almost fail to even register it anymore, and the fact that men dominate political and economic spheres and a fifth of women suffer some form of sexual assault. The figures certainly didn't allay my fears and convince me I was just making a mountain out of a molehill – far from it. To me they suggested an urgent and essential need to pay attention to the 'minor' incidents – each and every one of them – in order to start joining the dots and build up a proper picture of what was going on.

I didn't for a moment think that the problem of sexism could be solved overnight. But nor did I see how we could possibly even begin to tackle it while so many people continued to refuse to acknowledge that it even existed. I thought if I could somehow bring together all those women's stories in one place, testifying to the sheer scale and breadth of the problem, then perhaps people would be convinced that there was, in fact, a problem to be solved.

At least that would be a start.

So, in April 2012, I started a very simple website where women could upload their stories – from the niggling and normalized to the outrageously offensive – and those who hadn't experienced the problem first-hand could read them and, I hoped, begin to realize what was really happening on a daily basis.

Without any funding, or means to publicize the project beyond my own Facebook wall, I thought perhaps fifty or sixty women would add their stories – or that I might be able to persuade a hundred or so of my own friends to add theirs.

Stories began to trickle in during the first few days. Within a week, hundreds of women had added their voices. A week later, the number had doubled, then trebled and quadrupled. I started a Twitter account, @EverydaySexism, and found that people were keen to discuss the phenomenon there too. In exactly the same way that raising the subject in a roomful of people led to more and more women chipping in with their own examples, the idea spread through social media like wildfire, snowballing and gathering momentum as it travelled.

Suddenly stories began to appear from America and Canada, Germany and France, Saudi Arabia and Pakistan. Tens of thousands of people started viewing the website each month. Before two months had passed the website contained more than 1,000 entries.

There were people who said I might be making it all up – or that it didn't prove anything because the stories couldn't be independently verified. And that's true (the verification part, not the making it up) and applies to the project entries quoted in this book. This is important, so while we're here let's clear it up. The project was only ever intended to be used as a qualitative source, just like many other highly respected social studies and research projects that rely on reported evidence. Yes, we should be aware of the possibility that an entry has been fabricated. But really there's no incentive for anybody to make things up. Firstly, the project consists of so many accounts that there's no fame or attention to be gained from adding a false story – each one is just a drop in the ocean. Secondly, because IP addresses are automatically submitted with the entries, we're immediately alerted when anyone submits more than one story. On the few occasions when trolls have posted a small batch of sarcastic and over exaggerated entries, it has been easy to spot and remove them. More importantly, though, now that tens of thousands of women have added their experiences, the stories are corroborated by each other – they're repeated and echoed by those of other women, of different ages and backgrounds and from different countries, with the same themes arising again and again. These accounts are also supported by the thousands of girls and women I have met at schools and events over the past years, by women who have emailed me in confidence and women I have interviewed for this book. They're all saying very similar things. It would have to be an awfully big coincidence for so many of them to be making up the same story.

So, the stories kept coming. Then one day a journalist from *The Times* contacted me, asking about running a feature on the project. Other papers and magazines swiftly followed, then radio and television programmes. I began to write regularly for the *Independent* and later the *Guardian* and other media, chronicling the accounts as they streamed in and highlighting common themes. Articles about the project appeared around the world, from *Grazia South Africa* to the *Times of India*, *French Glamour* to the *Gulf News*, the *LA Times* to the *Toronto Standard*. Every time the project was featured in the foreign press I'd receive emails from women in those countries asking if we could start a version of the project for their country too. Within eighteen months we had expanded to eighteen countries worldwide.

Hundreds of women and girls wrote to me about their own experiences, describing not only what had happened to them but also how they'd felt guilty or unable to protest – how they'd been made to feel that whatever had happened was their fault, or that they shouldn't make a fuss. The first time the true scale of what I had started to uncover really hit me was when one woman wrote to me saying: 'I'm 58 so I have too much to say in a small box. Here are some highlights arranged in decades.'

The stories came from women of all ages, races and ethnicities, of different social backgrounds, gender identities and sexual orientations; disabled and non-disabled, religious and non-religious, employed and unemployed. Stories from the workplace to the pavement, from clubs and bars to buses and trains. Of verbal harassment and 'jokes', of touching and groping and grabbing and kissing and being followed and sworn at and shouted at and belittled and assaulted and raped.

This is why the project, while it initially set out to record daily instances of sexism, quickly came to document cases of serious harassment and assault, abuse and rape. In the early days, as the first stories of this kind were recorded, I wondered why people were coming to us – why they weren't sharing and being supported elsewhere. And then I started to realize that there wasn't anywhere else. Thousands of these stories had never been told. Thousands of these women had grown up in the confident assumption that these violations were their fault; that their stories were shameful; that they should never tell anybody. And their experiences weren't 'out of place' among the tales of daily, niggling, normalized sexism any more than the violets 'don't belong' in the same spectrum of colours as the oranges and greens. You can't separate one out and look at it without the others, because together they create a full picture. Our experiences of all forms of gender prejudice – from daily sexism to distressing harassment to sexual violence – are part of a continuum that impacts on all of us, all the time, shaping our selves and our ideas about the world. To include stories of assault and rape within a project documenting everyday experiences of gender imbalance is simply to extend its boundaries to the most extreme manifestations of that prejudice. To see how great the damage can be when the minor, 'unimportant' issues are allowed to pass without comment. To prove how the steady drip-drip-drip of sexism and sexualization and objectification is connected to the assumption of ownership and control over women's bodies, and how the background noise of harassment and disrespect connects to the assertion of power that is violence and rape.

And so we accepted all these stories, and more, until in April 2015 – just twenty months after the project was launched – 100,000 entries had poured in. This is their story. This is the sound of a hundred thousand women's voices. This is what they're telling us.

Chapter 1

Silenced Women: The Invisible Problem

'Even though I am an experienced businesswoman, I feel I can't say anything. It's my choice: tell him to please not touch me and create a fuss, making things awkward with my clients, or stay quiet. I stay quiet'
Everyday Sexism Project entry

Vital Statistics

After experiencing workplace sexual harassment only 27 per cent of women reported it to someone senior
Slater & Gordon, 2013

Of women seriously sexually assaulted during their time at university, only 4 per cent reported it to their higher-education institution and only 10 per cent to the police
National Union of Students (NUS), Hidden Marks survey, 2010

50 per cent of those students seriously sexually assaulted who didn't report it said it was because they felt ashamed or embarrassed
NUS, Hidden Marks survey, 2010

90 per cent of victims of the most serious sexual offences know the perpetrator
Ministry of Justice, Home Office & Office for National Statistics (ONS), 2013

Only 15 per cent of female victims of the most serious sexual offences reported it to the police
Ministry of Justice, Home Office & ONS, 2013

28 per cent of women who are the victims of the most serious sexual offences never tell anybody about it
Ministry of Justice, Home Office & ONS, 2013

It's something I just always accepted as a reality since I was young. No one told me that it wasn't my fault or that I could/ should speak up. I was told to be passive and not to stir things up.

Being told I have no sense of humour when comments are made about my breasts, vagina or behind.

I joined a dating site. Got one message instantly. 'I'd pay to ram you up the ass.' And guess what his excuse was when I argued with him? 'Chill out love, it's just banter.' It really isn't.

Dismissal of arguments or thoughts because 'she's just pms-ing' or hormonal.

I was raped by 2 men at the age of 14 and my family normalized it by ignoring it ... I was confused ... I was sure it was wrong.

Called a prude for objecting to Porn Fridays where female colleagues' faces were photo-shopped onto porn pics.

Sexism is an invisible problem. This is partly because it's so often manifest in situations where the only witnesses present are victim and perpetrator. When you're shouted at in a deserted street late at night. When a senior colleague with wandering hands corners you in the empty copy room. When a man presses his erection into your back on a tube so crowded nobody could possibly see what's going on. When a car slows down as you walk home from school and the driver asks you for a blowjob then pulls away up the road as smoothly and silently as he arrived. When your boss casually mentions as she passes you on the stairs that you need to arrive with a lower-cut top and more make-up on tomorrow if you want to keep your job. When a pair of hands moves you aside in the queue for the bar and slides down to grope and feel your bottom. Moments that slip like beads onto an endless string to form a necklace that only you can feel the weight of. It can drag you down without another person ever witnessing a single thing.

It's not easy to take something invisible and make people start to talk about it. There's a lot of wariness and caution at first – people sneakily giving each other the side-eye because they don't want to be the one to admit they see it if everyone else is going to carry on pretending not to. Nobody wants to be *that* guy. So at best the person who's experienced the sexism is left jumping up and down with their arms in the air pointing out the patently obvious, while everybody else scratches their chins and gazes earnestly into the middle distance.

At worst the victim doesn't say anything either.

In this, sexism is a bit like climate change. Human beings tend to cling to convenient obliviousness – 'I haven't seen it, so it can't really exist!' – in spite of embarrassing, burgeoning bodies of evidence to the contrary. In order for this comfortable bliss of ignorance to be maintained, it follows that any flagging up of the problem will be met with denial: so naturally you get accusations of lying, or exaggeration. These aren't always intentionally unkind

– I think they're as often motivated by a horrified inability to accept the severity of the problem as by a deliberate attempt at dismissal.

But, whatever the motive, such reactions come as a secondary blow on top of the initial injurious experience. As girls grow up, these responses start to impact on their own judgement of situations – they learn not to trust themselves and not to make a fuss. Society teaches them that they don't have the right to complain. One way or another, women are silenced.

One girl who wrote to the Everyday Sexism Project described just such a 'learning experience':

▸ When walking to a friend's house on Saturday at about 6.30pm, two drunk men started following me. One grabbed my hair and said 'you are too pretty to be out alone' – they had been shouting at me for the last 100m. I felt violated and arrived shaking. I told my boyfriend the next day; he said my 'story' was unlikely as I was just being attention seeking. I began to feel like I myself was exaggerating and should just remain quiet. We are both 15.

Disbelief is the first great silencer.

The incidents that go unwitnessed definitely help to keep sexism off the radar, an unacknowledged problem we don't discuss. But so too do the regular occurrences that hide in plain sight, within a society that has normalized sexism and allowed it to become so ingrained that we no longer notice or object to it. Sexism is a socially acceptable prejudice and everybody is getting in on the act.

The past year alone has given us some stonking high-profile examples. During this time the Russian conductor Vasily Petrenko helpfully announced that in his profession men will always be superior because orchestras are distracted by a 'cute girl on a podium' and German artist Georg Baselitz declared that 'Women don't paint very well. It's a fact.' Meanwhile London Mayor Boris Johnson 'joked' that women only go to university because 'they've got to find men to marry' (hilarious, no?) and the Canadian literature professor and author David Gilmour blithely revealed that he's simply 'not interested in teaching books by women'. (I expect Zadie Smith, Toni Morrison, Maya Angelou and Margaret Atwood could set him straight on their relevance, were they not so busy winning more awards than Gilmour has ever managed to scrape nominations for.)

In November 2012 Labour MP Austin Mitchell directed a sexist tirade at his former colleague Louise Mensch after she disagreed in an interview with something her husband had said. In a message that appeared on his Facebook and Twitter pages as well as his official website, Mitchell wrote: 'Shut up Menschkin. A good wife doesn't disagree with her master in public and a good little girl doesn't lie about why she quit politics.' He later showed his great amusement at the ensuing public anger, first telling those who protested to 'Calm down, dears', and later asking: 'Has the all-clear siren gone? Has the Menschivick bombardment stopped?'

Clearly none of these men feared repercussions. In fact Mitchell's 'Calm down, dears' just couched his 'prejudiced and proud' stance firmly within the political context of a prime minister who publicly silenced a female MP with the same words the previous year.

Against such a backdrop it's little wonder other politicians feel so confident wearing their bigotry like a badge of honour.

From highbrow to lowbrow these attitudes are rife across the board of celebrity. In the same week as Mitchell's outburst, and with the earnest air of a Radio 4 consumer phone-in about synthetic versus feather duvets, BBC Radio Cumbria produced a segment that cleverly managed to combine both sexism and racism, asking: 'If you could have a Filipino woman, why would you want a Cumbrian one?'

In 2012 US radio talk-show host Rush Limbaugh managed to keep his job and his show despite launching a misogynistic barrage of abuse at law student Sandra Fluke, whose only 'crime' was to be invited to testify to Congress on the importance of including contraceptive coverage in health-insurance plans. Limbaugh attacked her repeatedly on air, labelling her a 'slut' and a 'prostitute', suggesting that her parents should be ashamed of her and saying she was 'having so much sex, it's amazing she can still walk'. With all the unimaginative persistence of a dog with a chew toy, he seemed unable to drop the subject – later adding: 'If we are going to pay for your contraceptives, and thus pay for you to have sex, we want something for it, and I'll tell you what it is. We want you to post the videos online so we can all watch.'

Over in Hollywood actor Seth MacFarlane decided that the best possible way to celebrate the combined talents of actresses attending the 2013 Oscars ceremony was to sing a song entitled 'We Saw Your Boobs'. (No prizes for guessing what it was about.) Apparently the fact that several of the breast-baring scenes he gleefully referenced explored rape or abuse passed MacFarlane

by. (As did, it seems, the abilities and, you know, *humanity* of the women themselves.) That this was presented as a hilarious piece of entertainment at one of the most widely watched media events of the year speaks volumes.

Back in the UK, television critic (and noted Adonis) A. A. Gill was busy veering into wildly irrelevant sexism in his review of *Meet the Romans*, a series presented by Cambridge Classics professor Mary Beard. Rather than critiquing Beard's credentials or presenting skills he chose to condemn her looks and style, branding her 'too ugly for TV' and suggesting that she 'should be kept away from cameras altogether'. In a column for the *Daily Mail* Beard responded with the dry observation that Gill had 'mistaken prejudice for being witty' – which excellent riposte frustratingly gave rise to the common excuse that sexism isn't a problem because 'women can handle it'. Yes, some can, but the point is that they shouldn't have to! (In this instance who knows what incisive historical revelations would have occupied that week's column had Beard not been forced to waste her time responding to Gill's puerile snot-flicking?)

During the London Olympics the *Telegraph*'s Andrew Brown pronounced a breathtakingly patronizing and pompous censure on the female athletes daring to represent their country in the martial arts. 'I realize this will probably sound appallingly sexist,' he wrote, and then carried on regardless. 'It's disturbing to watch these girls beat each other up...' – his condescension was spectacularly misplaced when you consider how easily the 'soft limbs' he was wringing his hands over could have taught him a swift lesson about respect for equal rights had he strayed into the Olympic arena.

In each of these situations – which together represent just a tiny sample from an extensive daily stream – we have women being openly lambasted, dismissed or objectified on the simple basis of their gender. Nothing more. From our politicians to our national broadcasting corporation, from the biggest media event in the world to the most famous sporting contest. It's partly sheer normalisation that leads to such widespread acceptance of gendered prejudice. We're so immersed in sexism that we find it impossible to see it, even when it stares us in the face. Rashida Manjoo, UN Special Rapporteur on violence against women, visited Britain in 2014 and said: 'Have I seen this level of sexist culture in other countries? It hasn't been so in your face in other countries.' Yet despite her (lengthy and detailed) assessment, commentators immediately dismissed her expert findings out of hand. On one radio programme, sceptically asked to defend Manjoo's view, I had to reply that, while I strongly agreed that sexism was a huge and under-acknowledged problem in Britain, I wasn't in possession of enough concrete data to make a decisive global comparison. If only, I was very tempted to add, there was an international expert we could ask whose job was to do precisely that. Sexism seems to occupy a ludicrously acceptable position when it comes to public discourse, with a general willingness to laugh and ignore it rather than define it as the prejudice it is. And this makes it particularly difficult to fight, allowing objectors to be ridiculed and dismissed as 'overreacting' while perpetrators like Mitchell can take up cowardly defences behind the poor shield of 'humour' or 'irony'. Consider, by comparison, the fate of his contemporary and namesake Andrew Mitchell, who was forced

to resign from his position as Chief Whip at around the same time amidst allegations (denied by him) that he called policemen 'plebs', voicing offensive class prejudice.

One woman's project entry read:

▸ It's amazing that many of us feel so resigned to something which if directed at any other group of people would be considered very offensive.

So, women are silenced both by the invisibility and the acceptability of the problem. And perhaps the most powerful evidence of all for the public acceptance of sexism is the ever-growing number of major daytime television programmes taking issues around women's safety and assault as topics for 'debate'.

The very fact that it is necessary in 2013 to explain why it's not OK to publicly debate whether or not women are 'asking' for sexual assault is mindboggling. Yet the refrain has become so common that it seems difficult to open a newspaper or turn on the television without hearing the issue being discussed, as if it is a perfectly valid question with interesting points to be made both for and against.

In February 2013 the ITV morning show *Daybreak*, with an average of 800,000 viewers, ran a segment asking 'Are women who get drunk and flirt to blame if they get attacked?' The discussion was introduced with: 'Some of you think so ... others vehemently disagree...' Then: 'Keep your thoughts coming in – it's really interesting to hear what you think.'

The words 'horrifying', 'depressing' or 'painful' would have

better described what it was actually like to hear what some of the *Daybreak* viewers thought. Comments were aired from interviewees on both sides of the debate, including one young man who said that 'if you want to be treated with respect, you've got to dress with respect' and a studio panellist who – when discussing *sexual assault!* – used the phrase 'It takes two to make a decision about something'. The presenters later announced the results: 'One in six people in the *Daybreak* poll think sexual-assault victims are to blame if they're drunk or flirtatious with the offender.' No comment was passed on this statistic as it was presented.

It's the topic of the day, with one TV presenter musing over whether 13-year old girls walking past building sites in crop tops are 'asking for it', while online community Debate.org is running an ongoing poll on the topic: 'are rape victims who dress provocatively "asking for it"?'

In the very same week as the Daybreak poll, the BBC 3 current-affairs programme *Free Speech* ran a segment posing the question: 'Are young women in this country putting themselves at risk of being abused by going out clubbing and wearing provocative clothing?' Once again, the ensuing debate showcased points made for and against. One panellist put herself firmly in the camp of agreement: 'Absolutely ... You should not be going out dressed like a hussy, quite frankly. There's no other word for it.' She later added: 'You are putting yourself at risk. And, as women, we need to understand we are vulnerable.'

Yes, for the love of God young women, come along – *learn your limits*. Or, rather, know society's limits. How dare you think you have the right to go out wearing whatever you like – how *foolish*

and *ignorant* of you to expect not to be assaulted, you *brazen hussies*! What do you think this is? A free country?

There has been a long string of similar public declarations in all corners of the media. In the *Telegraph* Joanna Lumley urged young women to behave properly: 'don't be sick in the gutter at midnight in a silly dress with no money to get a taxi home, because somebody will take advantage of you, either they'll rape you, or they'll knock you on the head or they'll rob you.' In an interview soon afterwards Conservative MP Richard Graham appeared to support her: 'If you are a young woman on her own trying to walk back home through Gloucester Park, early in the morning in a tight, short skirt and high shoes and there's a predator and if you are blind drunk and wearing those clothes how able are you to get away?' (Actually, as one young woman shrewdly pointed out to me, you're generally much more able to run in a short skirt than in a long one...)

It is notable that, in the main, these sanctions seem to be coming from adults of a particular generation – they are a natural reaction, some might argue, to a series of societal shifts that have seen youth culture change dramatically over the past twenty-five years. But, while this might slightly mitigate the *intention* behind some of the comments, it neither excuses nor explains their intense focus on young women's behaviour to the near-exclusion of all else. If anything, those who grew up in a generation with rigid and sexist gender roles and expectations of young women's dress and behaviour are, sadly, only perpetuating such oppression by projecting it afresh onto girls operating within a new, freer youth culture. But to see such young women as 'brazen hussies' is to entirely miss the point – the focus instead should surely be on the

fact that society is dictating to young women that this is the only way for them to win acceptance and approval. Miley Cyrus is the perfect recent example of this. Yes, her 2013 VMA performance (which saw her near-naked, grinding sexually with a much older male singer and sticking out her tongue provocatively) stirred strong emotions, but the resulting censure was reserved entirely for her choices as a young female – not for the man standing behind her, nor the rigidly gendered industry that led her so compellingly down that particular path while her male contemporaries are free to peddle their pop in suits and ties.

It is in this focus on young women's behaviour while utterly failing to analyse the actions and impact of the society around them that we encounter the greatest silencing method of all: the blaming of victims.

Let me immediately make two important points. First, the idea that women's dress or behaviour is in any way to blame for sexual assault or rape is *utter nonsense.* Second, to publicly debate such a notion is to give it credence, to spread the idea; it is to send perpetrators the message that they can act with impunity – and to remind victims they may be blamed if they speak up.

The victim is *never* to blame.

The 2013 UK government figures on sexual offences state that the vast majority of rapists are known to their victim: 'Around 90 per cent of victims of the most serious sexual offences in the previous year knew the perpetrator.' According to Rape Crisis (England and Wales), 'women and girls of all ages, classes, culture,

ability, sexuality, race and faith are raped. Attractiveness has little significance. Reports show that there is a great diversity in the way targeted women act or dress.' Rape is *not* a sexual act; it is not the result of a sudden, uncontrollable attraction to a woman in a skimpy dress. It is an act of power and violence. To suggest otherwise is deeply insulting to the vast majority of men, who are perfectly able to control their sexual desires.

The same inaccurate conclusion is drawn about pretty much every form of assault and harassment you can think of. Popular television show *The Wright Stuff* (where female viewers are frequently addressed as 'you girls', making me want to claw my own eyes out – but that's beside the point) ran a jaunty segment asking whether men pinching women's bottoms in nightclubs was 'just a bit of fun'. The question arose in response to a campaign by women in London to encourage nightclubs to expel men who groped them uninvited. This time the healthy side order of 'they're asking for it' was thrown in by panellist Lynda Bellingham. 'Oh for God's sake, it's just a bit of fun,' she opined. 'Have you seen what women wear in clubs these days? If they bend over you could see their knickers.' So once again a direct line of causation is drawn between women's dress and sexual assault.

Setting apart the euphemistic description of groping and physical assault as a cheeky 'bum pinch', the fact that such efforts are immediately met by cries of 'aren't you making a fuss about nothing?' from such high-profile platforms shows the uphill battle women are fighting to even *begin* to object to sexism and harassment. What we are really hearing is the suggestion that if women dare to leave the house they simply must expect to

be manhandled and touched by strangers against their will. If something happens to a woman when she's in a club, or when she has dared to dress up (in the way, incidentally, dictated and demanded by the media with which she is constantly bombarded), then she certainly shouldn't have the audacity to complain.

These three powerful silencing factors – the invisibility of the problem, the social acceptance of it, and the blaming of victims – are corroborated loud and clear by the reports we received, particularly from young women who are learning such lessons hard and early. They said they felt unable to complain about incidents, either because they wouldn't be taken seriously or, sometimes, because they didn't even think they'd be believed.

🐦 I tried to tell family about harassment or assault, but they'd almost always imply I'd done something to make it happen.

🐦 Pretty much told it was my problem or that I was 'too sensitive'.

One woman explained how her family's attitudes towards victims in the public eye spilled over into their indictment of her.

▸ Just watching BBC Look North. Story about a woman who was raped in a park at night. My mother: 'Stupid woman, what on earth was she doing walking in a park?'

Incidentally, when I came home and told Mum I'd been raped by my boyfriend, she replied: 'That's what you get if you behave like a slut.'

Often the social acceptability of sexism and harassment is so ingrained that the abuse itself appears to come second in importance to the family's desire to avoid a scene. As one girl explained:

▶ When I was about 13, a friend of the family used to grab my bum or my breasts whenever we saw him (which sadly, was quite a lot). He would do it right in front of my mum, sister and his WIFE and nobody ever said anything. It made me feel really uncomfortable (obviously), but at the time I was far too young to understand what was going on and it's only very recently that I've come to understand that he was actually assaulting me. I have felt so confused and unhappy about this for years, I'm so angry that his wife and my own family never questioned the fact I was being inappropriately touched right in front of them. I want to bring up the subject with my mum and sister, but I'm afraid that they won't take it seriously.

We've received endless accounts reflecting this theme of young girls learning early and even from their parents that responsibility for sexual harassment falls on their own shoulders.

🐦 Harassed in the street aged 12 (by an adult man), told by my mum it was my own fault for wearing a short skirt.

It is significant that the silencing starts early. One woman's entry highlights how the impact of learning such 'truths' from the people you trust the most can cause them to become very deeply

ingrained – making it much harder for women to realize that what is happening to them is wrong, or to speak up about it later on:

🐦 My father told me it's impossible to rape a girl, it's the girls fault. I was 16 & a virgin when I was raped several times – I was 30 when I realized it was rape thanks to dad.

Sadly many women describe similarly belittling comments from their own partners:

▸ Had a frightening experience with a drunk man muttering threats while sitting across from me on a train, and then following me off and throughout the station, until I literally had to run and hide to lose him. When I later told my boyfriend what happened he said: 'well I'm glad you're home safe now' and completely dismissed it.

▸ I told my husband [about a sexual assault] but he didn't believe me and said it must have been a mistake.

Such dismissal is not limited to an 'out of touch' older generation; it is reported just as frequently coming from young people. After somebody she knew had been sexually assaulted, one young woman heard her acquaintances discussing the case, saying: 'She's an attention whore; she should have seen it coming.' Young people repeatedly reported their peer groups silencing and policing victims who tried to speak out:

▸ At a nightclub at my uni a guy walked past me and put his hand right up my dress, at the front, very violently, and then walked past. I was SO shocked, furious and confused. Went back over to my group of friends and told them what happened; general apathy and no surprise. One male in the group said, 'Well, you are wearing a really nice dress tonight...'

The crucial thing to understand is that dismissive patterns learned from an early age become internalized, which in turn begins to prevent women from even trying to speak out should the need subsequently arise. One young woman describes an experience that took place at a house party when she was just sixteen. The end of her account starkly reveals how strongly society had already programmed her not to report what happened:

▸ One guy kept calling me a bitch... 'excuse me bitch', 'oi bitch, what's your name?' I thought he was a bit weird – and had a terrible sense of humour. I kept away from him and chatted to my friends for the rest of the night.

Later on I was so drunk I went upstairs to sleep in a spare bedroom of my friend's house.

I woke up later, it was quiet and it sounded like everyone had gone home – except that guy from earlier who was on top of me, having sex with me, one hand covering my mouth and the other round my throat.

I knew that, being drunk, no one would believe me.

Another young woman reported a case where the man who

harassed her went on to sexually assault another girl. Her description of the public reaction to the case perfectly illustrates why so many girls believe they will not be taken seriously from the outset:

▶ I was waiting at a bus stop late at night and a drunk, leering man was also waiting for the same bus. He intimidated me into a conversation with him. I tried to be polite as I was scared not to talk to him. He said he'd get off at the same stop as me, which filled me with fear.

Once the bus arrived I let him get on first to not sit near him. I rang my Dad who thankfully met me a few stops early. Sadly, a few months later I was reading our local newspaper online and saw the photo of the same man and an article – he was convicted of sexually assaulting a 14-year-old girl on the same bus by groping her bottom. I can imagine how frightening this was for her after encountering him myself. The worst thing was the comments people left regarding the 14-year-old girl – saying she had 'over reacted' was a 'drama queen' and 'had been wearing a short skirt', and that 'it was harmless touching – a bit of fun.' How must she feel reading that? What must she make of our society, and her place as a young woman in it? So many people dismissed what he had done.

Even for those who do find the courage to speak out, often after a long period, being dismissed, disbelieved or silenced by their own family or friends can be a devastating experience. The refusal to believe that something has happened – from minor sexist incidents all the way up the scale to more serious harassment,

assault or violence – is re-victimization. It silences the victim and often prevents them from reaching out for help. For one woman, the response she got from a friend was as much of a blow as the horrendous experience of domestic violence she had survived:

▶ A friend of mine who I told my story to decided to tell everyone. And then he had the nerve to tell me that he didn't believe me. That I just wanted attention. That I just wanted people to feel sorry for me. And that something like that couldn't have happened to me because I have a family and a house and I go to a good school. I guess the worst part of the whole thing isn't even the betrayal, but the desperation that I felt. Not only had I experienced the abuse, but when I tried to trust someone with my feelings, they were dismissed as a lie.

There is a triple bind here. Media coverage in which victims are blamed sends insidious messages to young people, causing them to criticize and doubt themselves; the dismissive responses of those closest to them make them question their own experience; and the abject normalization of it all makes them wonder what the point is in speaking out anyway. In short, society, the media and those close to the victim collaboratively demonstrate such extensive doubt that they simply stop trusting themselves…

▶ Once at a party when I was 16 I was lying half-asleep and drunk on a sofa when I felt a boy I barely knew put his hand up my skirt and touch me. I was too embarrassed to confront him when I realized what he was doing, I just moved away. I told my

boyfriend and he didn't believe me. I had been sleepy and drunk so I decided not to tell anybody else because I thought it seemed implausible although I was certain it had happened.

The impact of these multiple methods of silencing is immense. Heartbreakingly, the women who have finally shared their stories with the Everyday Sexism Project have often already suffered the effects of keeping their stories to themselves for months or years.

▶ I haven't told anyone else about it six years later. I still feel ashamed and dirty, and some part of me resents myself for not doing anything – I still feel like it's my fault.

▶ Once I found the Everyday Sexism Project, I felt (in a bizarre way) relieved to see other women with stories similar to mine. It also made me realize that these and other incidents in my life was sexual harassment, not just me overreacting.

▶ Reading through the stories on this site has been both painful and healing. I have admitted more here than I have to my dearest friends.

One of the saddest things about the silencing of women through shame, normalization, dismissal, disbelief and blame is that it has become so common that it is used as a controlling tool by abusers themselves.

▶ My neighbour raped me when I was 16 – he said I was a slut and was asking for it and no-one would believe me if I told anyone.

As long as we as a society continue to belittle and dismiss women's accounts, disbelieve and question their stories, and blame them for their own assaults, we will continue to provide perpetrators with this powerful and effective threat.

▶ In hindsight, I probably should have reported him but due to previous experience I felt like no one would have done anything about it [...]

This is an all-too-common refrain.

There is another, final and widespread silencing tool: the defence of 'humour'. The backlash against feminism has played a significant role here, in its portrayal of all criticism as 'humourlessness' and its veiling of harassment and abuse under the protective shield of 'banter'.

▶ Colleague just used the term 'lady logic'. Another colleague then said 'Oooh heads down chaps' meaning that I was about to kick off. My attempts to halt the sexist banter have become part of the joke for them now. I'm being silenced.

▶ My twenty-year-old brother recently revealed to me that he didn't see the point of my university education, as I am 'only a baby machine' anyway. Hurt, I tried to protest, while he and his friends loudly laughed at me, told me to get back into the kitchen and to stop being so publicly 'menstrual'.

▶ In a club a group of guys watched me and my then-boyfriend for a few minutes before coming over to me and putting their arms round my waist and asking for a blowjob the second my boyfriend left me to go to the toilet. I told them to have some respect for both me and my boyfriend, a bouncer overheard the whole thing, burst out laughing and told me to lighten up 'because it's only banter'.

▶ Two weeks ago at work my manager came up behind me and slapped me very hard on my bottom. I spun around and confronted him, then reported the incident to a manager in a higher position. The man in question phoned me the following day [...] he said 'I didn't realize you couldn't take a joke'.

The correlation between humourlessness and people trying to talk about sexism is strong in the public consciousness – since starting the Everyday Sexism Project I've become painfully aware of it. There's an almost absurd lack of questioning on this subject: people who have known me for years have suddenly refused to tell jokes in front of me in case I'm 'offended'; others have expressed sympathy with my husband on the basis that he probably now has to 'watch what he says'.

The irony is that I've never needed my sense of humour *more* than when facing the daily barrage of sexist incidents reported through the project, and the constant stream of online insults and attacks. It's often the strongest line of defence – and frankly the only way I've held onto my sanity. When people like to write to me on Twitter, for example, telling me that writing about these issues is a pathetic waste of time when I could be concentrating on more important things, I find some light relief in replying that while they may be right I'm quietly confident it's a better use of time than writing to other people to tell them what they shouldn't be wasting their time on! It's the wry smile that keeps me going when I receive an email like the recent ironic missive that began: 'Sexism doesn't exist [...]' but ended: '[...] so why don't you get off your high horse and change your tampon?' Or the tweet from a man who felt I was misguidedly barking up the wrong tree in trying to expose sexism where it didn't exist. Obligingly, he helped to solve the problem by writing: 'Still not seeing the sexism, you daft cunts. Go back to the kitchen, you slags.' You have to laugh.

Over the last year or so I've come up against this insistence on equating feminism with humourlessness a lot. Perhaps the most revealing example, though, was when I took part in a televised debate on the issue of the *Sun*'s Page 3. It was to be me and a glamour model discussing our points of view. The driver taking me to the studio was kind, welcoming and loquacious, chatting away and cracking jokes. We had a great time until I incidentally revealed which side of the debate I was on. He stammered, stuttered and stopped talking – he apologetically explained that he'd assumed I was the Page 3 girl. Sadly the stream of conversation quickly died away after that. It really brought home to me how firmly cemented in the public consciousness was the idea that a young blonde woman couldn't possibly be talking about feminism and women's rights – particularly not if she also had a sense of humour and the ability to chat happily away about frivolous topics! It was as if I had morphed terrifyingly before his startled eyes into a green-skinned, horn-sprouting monster FEMINIST with not only a capital F but all shouty letters after it too.

This idea of the humourless feminist is an incredibly potent and effective silencer. It is used to isolate and alienate young girls; to ridicule and dismiss older women, to force women in the workplace to 'join in the joke' and, in the media, to castigate protest to the point of obliteration. Former News International employee Neil Wallis's weak attempts to discredit the No More Page 3 campaigners by branding them whining 'Wimmin' is a classic recent example, where the ridiculing of the women as out-of-touch harpies was used as a smoke screen to cover the fact that he had not a single actual argument to make to counter their cause. It's a pernicious and cowardly silencing tool, which uses baseless bullying as an excuse to avoid engaging intellectually with the issues at hand, and it has been used to shut down feminist campaigners for decades. Most sad of all is the impact it has on really young girls, who are faced with a barrage of objectification and abuse, yet told to lighten up and find their sense of humour just for voicing tentative objections.

▶ I'm 16 and in my last year of school. Constantly the guys (and girls) in my friendship circle make sexist remarks. Most of the time they don't realize they're being offensive, most of the time it's just 'banter'. For example, the other day my male friend said to me if I wear shorts to this Halloween party he will 'rape me, oh but it won't be rape because I will like it'. I responded telling him you shouldn't say things like that and I got called uptight [...] What is wrong with the world so that this is deemed OK? I am scared of going to university when I am older. Not because of exam stress but because of the horror stories I have heard from friends and

family. The horror stories of girls that have been subjected to
assault for 'banter'. I am scared. I am actually scared of being a
female.

So, there's a lot to overcome if we're going to start talking properly
about sexism, sexual harassment and assault. The invisibility; the
social acceptability and normalization; the dismissal, disbelief and
blaming of victims; and the accusations of being a Humourless
Feminist Bore™. The good news is that the stereotype is starting
to shift, as more and more people stop scratching their chins and
finally admit to being able to see sexism. But in the meantime,
as one woman wrote in her project entry, victims navigating this
maze of denial can feel like they're caught between a rock and a
hard place:

▶ You complain, they try to silence you. You shout so as not to be
silenced, they roll out the mad-woman clichés. Lose lose.

Chapter 2

Women in Politics

'I think if you're going to lead a country you've got to be powerful and have a loud voice'

Eleven-year-old schoolgirl interviewee

Vital Statistics

Women make up just over one fifth of MPs in the UK
Parliament (147 out of 650)
www.parliament.uk, 2013

Just 5 out of 22 Cabinet Ministers are women (23 per cent)
www.gov.uk/government/ministers, 2014

The UK comes 57th in the world for gender equality in parliament
Inter-Parliamentary Union, 2013

Only 23 per cent of members of the House of Lords are women
(182 out of 779)
www.parliament.uk, 2013

The percentage of women in the Cabinet has decreased by
43 per cent since 2000
Guardian, 2013

At the current rate it will be more than 150 years before
an equal number of women and men are elected to English
local councils
The Centre for Women and Democracy, 2011

🐦 I love her, but when I first told mum I wanted to go into politics, she said 'Oh yes! You'd make a WONDERFUL politician's wife.'

🐦 Guy in my politics class told the teacher he didn't think women had the right to vote. His reason: 'it doesn't seem right'.

🐦 I was on a busy train reading my Comparative Government textbook (I'm a politics student) when the man opposite me commented 'That looks a bit complicated for you love, why don't you try something a bit simpler?'

🐦 At school, a teacher said it was good that 'masculine' girls like me wanted to go into politics because most women were only there because men let them, to 'shut up the feminists for a bit'.

🐦 I was told 'if you want to be in Politics, you could be an MP's secretary'.

🐦 Recently told by stranger I'm 'too pretty to be involved in politics'. Reply: 'Good thing I was blessed with a brain, then.'

In the heat of the Paris summer, the minister for housing takes the floor in France's National Assembly to begin an address. A deafening chorus of hooting and catcalls drowns out the words. She is wearing a dress. Her male colleagues – her fellow politicians – are sexually harassing her, publicly, openly, in Parliament. For wearing a dress. (For the fashion record, it's a modest below-the-knee number in blue floral buttoned up nicely – perfectly suited to the formal occasion. But we know that's not the point.)

Does this sound like an exaggeration? Like a bad film? It was the experience of Cécile Duflot in July 2012.

Bishkek, Kyrgyzstan. A packed audience eagerly hangs on the every word of the interviewee on stage, the US Secretary of State. This is a once-in-a-lifetime opportunity for students of the University of Central Asia to put their questions to her, and for the Kyrgyzstan Public TV and Radio to grill her on her foreign policy. 'Which designers do you prefer?' asks the moderator. 'What designers of clothes?' the Secretary of State replies. 'Yes,' the moderator confirms. 'Would you ever ask a man that question?' she responds. The moderator pauses to reflect. 'Probably not. Probably not.'

This was a question asked of Hillary Clinton during a 'townterview' in Bishkek in 2010.

The House of Commons, London. The Labour and Co-operative MP for Walthamstow steps into a lift with a female colleague. Suddenly they are confronted by a Conservative MP demanding to know what they're doing in the lift. Obviously, he says, they must be unable to read, 'because this is a lift for MPs or disabled people and you're clearly neither'. When the young blonde woman informs him that she is indeed an MP, *as well* as a woman, he remains incredulous enough to demand to see her Commons pass as proof.

This was 2011, and one of Stella Creasy's early experiences of Westminster.

Giving a stump speech as a mayoral candidate and being interrupted to be asked: 'Just what are your measurements?' – Sam

Bennett, Pennsylvania, 2001. Trying to speak in Parliament as male MPs made breast-jiggling gestures – Jackie Ballard, Liberal Democrat MP, 1997. Described in media headlines on her death as 'a better politician than wife and mother' – Margaret Thatcher, former prime minister, 2013.

The list could go on and on. Over and again, female politicians are subjected to ridicule, criticism and dismissal on the basis of their sex – from their colleagues, the media and the general public alike. It is a catalogue of prejudice that takes many subtle forms, and its impacts are enormous – on individual women in office, on the political aspirations of younger women, on the gender balance of government and on political outcomes that affect women everywhere. Even when it doesn't outright prevent women from achieving political success, it doesn't mean that they are able to operate free of ongoing and pernicious discrimination.

First, there's the irrational obsession with political women's appearance, despite this being completely immaterial to their job performance...

Angela Merkel, Chancellor of Germany, is one of the most *influential* and authoritative world leaders, named by *Forbes* magazine as the most powerful woman in the world. But that didn't stop that very same magazine running an article on her 'silly pageboy haircut' and 'ill-fitting suits'.

Failing to realize that one of the leaders of the free world might have a few things on her mind other than leafing through the latest copy of *Vogue* for fashion tips, they went on to deal her possibly the most condescending backhanded compliment ever given. 'Merkel's frumpy style', they said, may in fact have 'proved an asset to her career'. The author draws this brilliant conclusion from the observation that: 'The dull outfits for which she became famous demonstrated consistency and prudence, two qualities generally prized in German politics.'

At best, this is just silly. Merkel has been consistent and prudent in her policies. Isn't *that* (rather than, say, the tailoring of her trousers) quite a lot more likely to be the reason why German voters saw her as a consistent, prudent politician?

'Oh yes, Merkel's leadership is exemplary – she's effectively led Europe through the recent financial crisis while keeping domestic policy on an even keel with outstanding results and continues to head one of the strongest economies in the world, completely bucking the local trend, but somehow I'm still just not... WAIT, A FRUMPY SUIT?! Where do I vote?!'

From 'Hollande's Honeys' to 'Blair's Babes' and 'Cameron's Cuties' (a cringe-worthy attempt by the *Telegraph* in 2010 to coin the painful 'Brown Sugars' thankfully failed), the advent of a new Parliament has long been the cue to examine the political stance and voting history of male politicians while analysing the heels and hairstyles of their female colleagues. Witness the *Sun*'s feature comparing the cleavage of various MPs, under the headline 'The Best of Breastminster'; the *Mirror* piece on the fashion faux pas of 'Cameron's Cuties', and countless column inches devoted to Theresa May's shoes. (I mean actually countless. I tried.)

Next, there's the scrutiny of female politicians' 'femininity'...

Hillary Clinton's experience shows that women in politics are fair game for an arbitrary lambasting purely on the basis that they are either *too* feminine, or not feminine *enough*. Her 'unfeminine' laugh has been commented on so many times it has been dubbed 'the Clinton Cackle'.

(Sarah Palin, conversely, was repeatedly attacked for being: 'Too Sexy for Vice President', 'Too Sexy for the Left', 'Too Sexy for the Whitehouse', 'Too Sexy to be President', 'Too Sexy for National Office' and even, bizarrely, 'Too Sexy for her Feet'. She was eventually immortalized as a blow-up doll.)

Yet in 2007 the *Washington Post*, in a piece whose title was phrased to sound uncannily like an actual piece of political commentary – 'Hillary Clinton's Tentative Dip into New Neckline Territory' – condemned Clinton for daring to let slip the awful secret that she had female anatomy. Straining desperately to spin an entire 800-word article out of an irrelevant observation, the *Post* resorted to phrasing the revelation in bulletin-like sentences as if it were the latest breaking news in a tensely unfolding political situation:

She was wearing a rose-colored blazer over a black top. The neckline sat low on her chest and had a subtle V-shape. The cleavage registered after only a quick glance. No scrunch-faced scrutiny was necessary [...] there it was. Undeniable.

That five sentences were required to confirm that the cleavage was, in fact, there, is less surprising when you see the pictures and realize that Clinton was smartly dressed, with all of about one centimetre of visible cleavage on display.

When American actress Ashley Judd considered running for office in 2013, media outlets exploded with consternation at the fact that she had previously performed *outraged stage whisper* *nude* scenes in movies. Would Judd be 'the first potential senator who has – literally – nothing left to show us?' they fretted. Eventually, citing her responsibility to her family, Judd chose not to run. (Meanwhile Anthony Weiner blithely continued his run for the New York mayoral office, blissfully unconcerned that his junk had been pinged around the internet more times than a Grumpy Cat video.)

Then, there are the sexist tropes (mother, virgin, whore, harpy, ballbreaker, bitch) into which political women are neatly and arbitrarily pigeonholed, and from which their wherewithal as candidates is irrationally extrapolated...

When Sarah Palin's vice-presidential candidacy was announced in August 2008, CNN debated the breaking news under the headline: 'VP Pick: Teen Daughter Pregnant'. One pundit loudly declared that 'the facts are this: what kind of mother is she? Is she prepared to be the vice president? Is she going to be totally focused on the issues?' (None of which, it's worth noting, were actually facts.)

When male MPs disagree, it's described as just that – a disagreement. When Nadine Dorries and Louise Mensch failed to see eye to eye on policy, the papers dubbed it the 'catfight' of the Tory 'blondes', playing on negative stereotypes of bickering women and raking Mensch for being 'undignified'.

When Australian prime minister Julia Gillard was accused of being a hard-hearted harpy for not having a husband and children, the suspicion of her 'unwomanliness' somehow carried over into an irrational questioning of her political ability. (New South Wales senator Bill Heffernan famously claimed Gillard was unfit to lead the country specifically because she was 'deliberately barren' – not a charge likely to be levelled against any male politician.)

And when Home Secretary Theresa May made a mistake in timing in the case of the deportation of Abu Qatada in 2012, the *Metro* newspaper headline screamed 'It only takes a minute, girl' above a photo of her and Qatada captioned 'Dating game'. Gleefully embracing the archetype of a befuddled old dear, they had her as 'Muddled May' – destroying any fears of subtlety with a cartoon portraying her, complete with headscarf and tortoiseshell glasses, clutching her handbag and saying, 'I'm having one of those days'. (See also the Republican-leaning *Boston Herald* attacking 63-year-old Elizabeth Warren's 2012 Senate bid by repeatedly dubbing her 'Granny' in front-page headlines.)

Of course it's quite right that all politicians should face media criticism and scrutiny. But here the focus was not on May's disorganization or error, where it should have been; it was on her gender and age – or rather the implication that she had a feeble, unreliable woman's mind. And with this single, lazy, sexist stereotype they attempted to call into doubt her entire suitability for political office.

So these stereotypical and restrictive female tropes are used as the justification to find female politicians wanting – whether because they will be too authoritative or not firm enough, too stylish or too unfashionable, distracted by partners and children or hard-hearted for lack of them.

This idea that women simply can't be good politicians is worryingly persistent. I spoke to three current female Parliamentarians to ask how they felt sexist typecasting affected women in political life. Stella Creasy MP, who has championed the flourishing UK women's movement, spearheading the UK's celebration of the One Billion Rising campaign, told me: 'Too often women aren't being considered as capable leaders because our concept of what leadership is is defined by our history rather than our future. So it's defined by a sense of people gone past and the role they played.'

So, she concludes, since historically so many more men than women have been leaders, we tend towards the assumption that leadership is an inherently 'male' role, requiring 'male' qualities and attributes.

It's not hard to see where she's coming from. On a recent school visit, talking to a mixed class of eleven-year olds, I asked the pupils to guess how many out of just under 200 countries in the world had a female leader. I assumed they'd make a guess of around 60 or 70, allowing me to shock them with the actual figure of just 19. But the real shocker turned out to be the guesses themselves – 'less than 10 per cent' ... 'about 9' ... '3 per cent' ... The first estimate was almost exactly on the money. Intrigued, I asked them why they thought so few women were political leaders.

'I think men have more leadership than women,' replied one boy – not rudely or antagonistically, but as if it was a simple, non-contentious statement of fact. And, in a group where the girls had angrily and vocally responded to an earlier claim that 'Sports is for boys' with cries of 'No it's not!' not one person contradicted him. In fact, the girls seemed to agree.

'I think if you're going to lead a country you've got to be powerful and have a loud voice and men are associated more with that and girls are usually more quiet,' said one. Another articulated Creasy's fears almost to the letter: 'I think it's because they think men have more leadership and men can be more controlling – they just don't think it's a woman's thing.'

Sitting at her desk under a large banner reading 'Well-behaved women rarely make history', Caroline Lucas, MP for Brighton Pavilion, voices almost identical concerns: 'Most people's concept of what a leader is has been a male stereotype of somebody who is having power over rather than empowering people.'

She believes the stereotype of the loud and shouty male leader goes hand in hand with other stereotypically 'male' ideas about the very nature of politics. The common perception that success requires 'being good at clever putdowns in order to shut somebody up because that's kind of how Westminster works [...] The *Punch and Judy* of Prime Ministers' Questions.' She explains: 'People see PMQs as a kind of high point – they think that's what the rest of it is like and the trouble is quite a lot of it *is* like that: what's valued is the person that can have clever putdowns and shout the loudest.' The result, she says, is a 'kind of "bear pit", which is in so many ways so deeply frustrating and inimical to good policy making.'

Kezia Dugdale, Member of the Scottish Parliament for Lothian, recalls the old question: 'What's the point in electing women to Parliament if they have to act like men to survive?' She says: 'We want more women in our parliaments to represent women's voice and women's issues, but sometimes they have to change who they are and how they behave in order to make progress and deliver on the things that they believe in so there's a compromise that's made there just by the culture of how politics is done.' Not to mention the double frustration that many women are perfectly capable of demonstrating such supposedly 'male' traits as assertiveness and tenacity through their character alone, not because they are intentionally 'acting like men'. But sadly in such cases the assertiveness mysteriously becomes 'shrillness' and tenacity morphs into 'nagging', or 'hysteria'.

All my interviewees agree that female leaders are treated differently than their male peers by the press. Creasy cites the media analysis in the wake of Baroness Thatcher's death as a recent example of tired sexist stereotypes being applied to female leaders: 'Last week on *Question Time* they were talking about Baroness Thatcher. You had a panel of four men and one woman talking about women in politics and how they should behave and what was "a good temperament" or a "bad temperament".'

She is tired, she says, of 'seeing mainly men defining what is acceptable for women [...] Too often, women in public life are caricatured – you've got to be a harridan, or a bitch, or somebody's mother.'

If you take each example individually, it might be difficult to gauge the negative impact of media sexism on female politicians. There are articles written about male politicians' appearance, children and family lives too, of course. But (setting aside the fact that the incidence of such coverage is vastly less frequent) there is a simple way to appreciate the absurdity and definite difference in tone of the commentary faced by their female peers. Simply pluck some lines at random from the press they receive and try to imagine the same quotes being included in articles about David Cameron or Nick Clegg:

As she expounded her tough stance on immigration she stood in shoes worthy of the front row at Paris fashion week.
Guardian, on Home Secretary Theresa May

Even at the rather early hour of 8am for our interview, she is, as always, perfectly groomed...
Daily Record, on Deputy First Minister of Scotland Nicola Sturgeon

Though aged 60 (and counting), she teeters up to the Despatch Box in high heels, grinning girlishly at the Opposition benches before hesitantly lisping a few opening apologies for losing her place or some such calamity.
Daily Mail, on Equalities Minister Lynne Featherstone

What's worse is that this sexism doesn't come from the media alone. Often political women find their male colleagues exacerbate such prejudice, or try to use it as political capital. Examples are many, and can be drawn from all levels of politics.

As if by magic, as I write these words a news story pops up on my Twitter feed – a Conservative councillor has suggested in a public council meeting that Labour should recruit 'better-looking' female members. Really this kind of find is not serendipitous: there's just an awful lot of it about. When seventy-six-year-old MP Glenda Jackson spoke passionately about Thatcherism during a debate in the House of Commons, another Conservative councillor publicly branded her a 'rotting pork chop on a stick'. When former Liberal leader Lord Steel's wife voiced differing views to his on the topic of Scottish independence, MSP Murdo Fraser tweeted: 'Is he not master in his own house?' When photographs emerged of Nigella Lawson seemingly being throttled by her then-husband Charles Saatchi, MEP Nick Griffin tweeted: 'If I had the opportunity to squeeze Nigella Lawson, her throat wouldn't be my first choice.' And so on.

Like Austin Mitchell's vitriolic outpouring about 'good little girls' obeying their 'masters', each of these instances serves as a painful and weighty reminder of how steeply sloped the political playing field is – and how willing some male politicians are to use gendered prejudice to attack and debase their female peers.

Perhaps this willingness to put the boot in stems partly from male MPs' lack of understanding of what their female colleagues are dealing with. Both Lucas and Creasy describe personal experiences it is difficult to imagine male MPs ever having to contend with. Lucas started her political career at Oxfordshire County Council when her youngest son was three months old ('They were practically all men – there was no crèche or anything like that...'). So she tried to make the best of a difficult situation: 'I had some girlfriends outside who were helping me juggle the baby around. But at a critical time, he needed a feed; I needed to be in the Chamber and so there wasn't an easy way around it.'

The outcome? 'I was asked to leave the Council Chamber – it sticks in my mind forever – because by breastfeeding the child I was "bringing the council into disrepute".'

The horrifying rape and death threats Stella Creasy received for supporting women's campaigns have been well publicized and rightly so. I interviewed her before that time and it seemed she was subject to unacceptable lines of attack even then. 'I've had quite violent tweets about what people would do to me,' she told me. The deluge of terrifying and violent communications she has since received is appalling. One such tweet contained a photograph of a masked man in a darkened room wielding a long kitchen knife, with the accompanying message 'I'm gonna be the first thing u see when u wake up'. I wonder how many male politicians have faced anything remotely comparable.

You might think – given these and other really quite extreme examples of sexism in politics – that it should be relatively easy for female leaders to fight back. It isn't. One of the cleverest and most insidious twists in the whole sorry tale is the way in which women are double bound by a gender-biased definition of professionalism and the threat of being labelled 'whining'. For an archaic method of silencing, it remains depressingly successful in preventing complaint. A perfect example of this phenomenon emerged in 2012, when Australian prime minister Julia Gillard stopped the international press with a passionate, eloquent skewering of the opposition party's open misogyny towards her in Parliament and elsewhere. The video of Gillard's speech quickly went viral. In it she ran through a whole catalogue of sexist tripe thrown her way by the leader of the opposition, Tony Abbott (this included photographs showing him alongside signs saying 'Ditch the Witch' and branding her a 'man's bitch'). She declared that he had subjected her to 'misogyny' and 'sexism' – 'every day, in every way'.

And yet – despite international public acclaim for Gillard's strength in standing up against the abuse to which she'd been subjected – media commentators and politicians alike were quick to brand her melodramatic and oversensitive. One *Telegraph* writer accused her of 'gratuitously' betraying her 'emotional sensitivity' and (perhaps oblivious to the irony in the statement) suggested that she simply needed to 'man up'. Opposition politicians similarly sought to shame Gillard into silence. One described her pithy, intelligent refutation of months of misogyny as 'playing the gender card' and claimed that she had 'demeaned every woman in this Parliament'. (Ah, so *she* was the real threat to women in politics? Of course!) Finally he came to his illogical and unoriginal conclusion: 'if you can't stand the heat, get out of the kitchen'.

This unimaginative attempt to silence Gillard (with a kitchen-related metaphor, no less!) perfectly illustrates the irrationality of sexism in politics. She's the victim of a vast range of misogynistic abuse so she chooses to confront it, clearly and deliberately, sending a firm message that she won't tolerate such prejudice. And yet this very response is then cited as proof of her unsuitability for the political environment. Thus the power remains firmly in the hands of the perpetrators, for whom gender prejudice serves both to underpin the initial line of attack and undermine any subsequent rebuttal.

These patterns are so hard to break because they are so self-perpetuating. When the basis of the prejudice itself makes protest near impossible without facing a backlash almost greater than the initial injury, female politicians are left, once again, between a rock and a hard place.

Both Creasy and Lucas have stood up against gender prejudice in politics and faced an astonishing backlash, so can attest to the weight of this double bind.

Creasy describes an incident when a Labour colleague, Kate

Green MP, complained about the Houses of Parliament stocking a beer 'called Top Totty, advertised by a woman wearing bunny ears and a bikini'. (Creasy pauses, aside: 'I'm sorry, did we forget something about the twenty-first century and the fact it's happened?')

When Green complained, Creasy says, she was 'deluged with people being abusive – people in other political parties who said couldn't she take a joke and wasn't she being po-faced? And I was one of those people who stood up and said, "You know what? Sorry, no: this is the twenty-first century and you're going to go to the wall for a picture of a woman wearing bunny ears and a bikini? Really? Is that really the kind of argument you want to be having?"'

Lucas tells a strikingly similar tale. In this case SNP MP Eilidh Whiteford had allegedly been told during a committee meeting by Ian Davidson, chairman of the Scottish Affairs Select Committee, that he would 'give her a doing'. Lucas protested but, she says, 'Other people came and criticized me for having stood up for her. It really felt like the men were closing ranks – you don't point this out and you certainly don't make public complaints about it.'

It seems this double bind is somehow strong enough to overrule clear workplace sexual-harassment legislation. As Lucas succinctly pointed out in a *Guardian* article at the time, 'such language is not tolerated in normal workplaces – why should it be excused in the Commons?'

She also references other archaic hangovers (unsociable working hours, for example) that allow Westminster to drag its feet like a stroppy public schoolboy in its reluctance to embrace true gender equality. When I asked her whether politics is still a boys' club she said: 'You still get the sense that they haven't quite come to terms with women being here.'

So why does all this matter?

It matters because, around the world, women are enormously underrepresented in politics. According to information compiled by the Inter-Parliamentary Union in February 2013, just 20 per cent of parliamentary seats in the world are held by women. The UK figure is only slightly above that average at 22.5 per cent, bringing it in at an underwhelming fifty-seventh in the world for gender parity. This means that, in terms of achieving gender equality in Parliament, the UK ties with Pakistan and trails behind other countries, including Iraq, Sudan, Afghanistan and Tunisia. Just 5 out of 22 Cabinet posts under the Conservative and Liberal Democrat coalition government are held by women. The House of Lords was barred to women until as recently as 1958, so it doesn't come as much of a surprise that women hold only a fifth of the seats there too. Bishops also sit in the House of Lords, creating an extra 26 places that cannot be occupied by women, since the Church of England refuses to allow women to reach those lofty heights. (When the issue was recently debated, one wry tweeter succinctly summarized the issue: 'This week the Church of England General Synod will be discussing "women Bishops", or as I call them, "Bishops".')

According to the Center for American Women and Politics, in the USA women hold only 18 per cent of seats in Congress, 20 per cent of Senate seats and 18 per cent of seats in the House of

Representatives. Four states (Delaware, Iowa, Mississippi and Vermont) have never sent a woman to either the Senate or the House. Only 2 women of colour have ever served in the US Senate and only 47 in Congress. Just 24 per cent of state legislators are women and only 5 out of 50 states have a female governor. And, according to Name It, Change It – a new organization set up to combat sexism in US politics – just 31 women have ever served as governor, compared to 2,317 men.

At the time of writing, just 19 of the world's 196 countries have female leaders. (Such figures are occasionally debated on the grounds of disagreements about the number of countries in the world and how the term is defined, but nonetheless should give you some idea of the vast gender gap in political representation worldwide.) Between 2010 and 2012 there was a fleeting period when an unprecedented total of 20 female world leaders served simultaneously.

We're still struggling to make it beyond 10 per cent.

So, while we're still fighting for equal representation, the issues of sexism in politics and in the media portrayal of politicians are hugely important – because they play a major role in creating and maintaining that gender gap.

Accounts sent into the Everyday Sexism Project certainly suggest that these attitudes about the 'unsuitability' of women for political roles are trickling down from the media and political environments to impact strongly on girls' ambitions from a very young age.

▶ I took A-level politics [...] I had worked hard to prepare for a debate in which I was the only female in my team. While providing a counter-argument my teacher stopped me and asked the males in my team whether they were going to let a woman do all the talking.

▶ Told I should be a 'porn star' and that I look like a 'prostitute' when talking about what we wanted to do when older, after I said that I wanted to get involved in politics.

A little later on, when girls start to consider the possibility of studying politics at university, they are frequently met with the assertion that it isn't a 'suitable' subject for women, or that they don't have a natural aptitude for it.

One student recalls being told:

▶ Oh, you're doing a politics course? You must be very smart, things like that are really hard for girls!

Sadly these ideas sometimes come from the least likely of sources.

▶ Went on a trip to the Houses of Parliament as part of our Government & Political Studies A-Level [...] We were given a tour [...] The guide said, 'There is a book shop over there, there are recipe books for the girls.'

▶ During a tour of the Houses of Parliament this week an official male guide commented that MPs were not allowed to change their minds once they had entered the voting lobby and he added 'surprisingly the rule was not changed [...] even when women became MPs'.

Everywhere you look, the idea that women simply aren't suited to politics seems to be deeply ingrained, with even direct evidence of strong female leaders being twisted to fit the stereotype instead of debunking it.

▸ I was discussing politics with a guy I know who began to say how much he admired Margaret Thatcher [...] This guy later told me, in the same conversation, that women shouldn't ever be leaders. I said, 'Well what about Thatcher?' He then told me 'she was basically a man anyway [...] she had a male brain'. So obviously women don't owe their success to hard work and have to hope they have masculine qualities to make up for it.

One frustrating consequence of women being underrepresented in politics is that often *any* woman is seen first and foremost to represent *all* women, as if she speaks and advocates for them, and can be judged as if all womankind stands or falls by her actions. Creasy says: 'The notion that I could represent all women: that's a thing that really annoys me. As though women aren't very diverse – as though we're quite homogenous really in what we care about. Somehow, men are multifaceted and talented and represent all sorts of different things, but women? The prime minister can have *a* woman to advise on women – job done!'

This is particularly pertinent when you consider the enormous political underrepresentation of women of colour, disabled women and LBGTQ women – none of whom are miraculously 'included' in the debate simply by the introduction of a white, middle-class female voice.

And, just as in business, the visibility of women lower down the rungs of political power is often used as a veneer of equality, to ignore even greater gender imbalance higher up. Even the aforementioned eleven-year-olds seemed satisfied by it, commenting: 'There are quite a few women in politics but they're not like the president or prime minister, because men rule.'

In addition, argues Kezia Dugdale, the underrepresentation actively discourages female politicians from taking up the mantle of 'women's issues', lest they become 'labelled' with a reputation for 'softness'. She says this doesn't stop her fighting for the issues about which she feels passionate, but: 'You do have that thought in the back of your head of not just wanting to be seen as somebody who's constantly raising issues around domestic violence or gender inequality or everyday sexism [...] I can sense it – *Oh, there she goes again...*'

And indeed the very notion that there is such a thing in politics as a 'women's issue' is deeply damaging – not just to the women fighting for those causes but also to society at large. The political marginalization caused by labelling problems such as domestic violence 'women's issues' is inestimable. Here women are ostracized from mainstream policies by the implication that their focus should be only on those that affect them directly – which of course in turn mutes their voices in other debates. To boot, the suggestion that such things are women's messes to sort out immediately reinforces the wrong message: that victims are to blame. To call gendered violence or domestic abuse a 'woman's issue' is to absolve perpetrators of responsibility while equally alienating and discounting male victims. This inevitably means that we lack the focus on perpetrators' motivations and actions, which is so desperately needed for meaningful progress to be made. The attitude trickles down from politics into other areas: to the media running stories about domestic violence under the 'women' section of the paper, which many men are unlikely even to read, or to schoolboys being sent out of the classroom altogether while the girls are given a talk about 'how to avoid being raped'. The approach is completely backwards at every stage.

On the subject of other so-called women's issues Creasy is clear: 'When people talk to me about the childcare debate as a women's issue, I say, "No, the childcare debate is a parents' issue", because actually lots of men want to spend time with their children.' She describes the 'unconscious expectations about women – about whether women can do economic issues, or whether we can do defence' – as 'even more damaging' than the 'overt references to looks or breasts, the "Calm down, dear" stuff'. That, she says, 'is just embarrassing, but even if that stuff were to go, unless we challenge those unconscious expectations about what women are capable of, we won't get any further forward'.

She describes how, on Louise Mensch's resignation, she was deluged with phone calls from the press, asking whether she thought this woman 'couldn't have it all' and what she thought it meant for women in politics.

'I had to say to all these journalists – men and women – "I have to stop you there,"' she says. '"Number one, I don't have kids. Number two, my partner doesn't work overseas. Number three,

I don't write novels. Why are you calling me? Why do you think I share an affinity for Louise and what she stands for? We're in different political parties. Is it just because we were both blonde and elected at the same time? Because I can't see anything else here."'

Apparently Creasy offered up the names and numbers of five of her male colleagues 'who all have young families, who understand much better what Louise is going through and the difficulty of balancing family and work commitments right now'. None of them got a phone call.

Within such an environment can it be a coincidence that the policies coming out of Westminster often seem to hit women so much harder than men?

Women comprise around two thirds of public-sector workers, so the huge cuts made in this area have a disproportionate impact on women's jobs. The *Guardian* reported that unemployment among women aged between 50 and 64 rose by 39 per cent from 2010 to 2012, and unemployment among all women by 11 per cent, compared to an overall increase of just 5 per cent among all over-16s. And, according to the Fawcett Society, with the majority of carers for children, disabled people and the elderly being women, around three quarters of all cuts to benefits come out of women's pockets. Finally, because public services such as childcare and social services tend to be used by women more frequently than they are by men, budget cuts here also impact disproportionately. The Fawcett Society has dubbed this combination of disadvantages 'Triple Jeopardy'. Lucas agrees: 'A major injustice is being done to half the population – the fact that the cuts are demonstrably damaging women far more than men – that's something fundamental and unjustifiable.'

Is it possible then, that the underrepresentation of women in the UK Parliament, where these policies are debated and decided, could be linked to the fact that women are the hardest hit?

'I think there's something in it,' Lucas replies. 'Obviously you can't just draw a simple link [...] but at the very least one could say that, if more women were here, it would be more likely that the issues that are demonstrably unequal in terms of their impact on women would be picked up and stopped, essentially. Perhaps they'd never even get as far as the statute books or proposals in the first place [...] I think there's a much stronger chance that the policies coming out of this place would be fairer to women if we had more women in here, just as I think it would be the case when it comes to black and ethnic minorities as well.'

Creasy agrees: 'I certainly think that there are connections. I'll give you a very practical example of what I mean on a day-to-day level of making policy. I was talking to some of my colleagues here, who were involved in the debates around tax credits. When tax credits were first proposed there was a suggestion that they would also go to the main earner in the household. And it was women in the treasury, women in government, saying, "Hold on a minute: have you realized the different lives that women lead and the implications that that would have in terms of tackling child poverty, in terms of social justice?" That meant they went to the main carer. It is frightening to me that [we can] fast forward twelve, thirteen years and we're having exactly the same debate around universal credit – where again that's going to go to the main earner in a household, which potentially sees 300,000 women losing what is their basic income.'

If Creasy is right, then speeding up the rate of progress towards political gender equality is vital – not just for female politicians themselves but for women everywhere.

Lucas firmly believes that one vital step towards this goal is to encourage younger women into politics: 'I always make it a real priority to speak at schools – I think that's really important – there's nothing more powerful than the example of people actually doing it so I think it's important MPs get into those places early on and demonstrate that not only can we do it but we can actually do it bloody well as well!'

Dugdale firmly agrees about the importance of reaching out to girls. She's currently planning an empowering Next Generation Feminists event in the Scottish Parliament; this will get teenagers inside the Parliament walls, where they'll be encouraged to start their own campaigns on issues they care about – perhaps setting some on a pathway that will lead them back to the very same building.

Meanwhile, Creasy is rallying young women up and down the country with plans to mark next year's One Billion Rising event, encouraging volunteers to take on new roles of leadership and responsibility that could provide them with a stepping stone into further democratic engagement.

There is hope for the future. But, for now, Creasy notes that the number of women in Parliament seems to have stalled at around 20 per cent – roughly the same figure, she points out, as we have 'in TV, the judiciary, in academia […] women on boards'. She dubs this phenomenon the '80–20 society', emphasizing that the problem is by no means limited to politics. ('If it was just about this 650 people, that'd be easy to tackle. Actually what we've got to tackle are all the barriers across British society that mean that we're in that position.')

But it strikes me that, for all its archaic quirks and elitism, politics in many ways serves as a kind of microcosm, demonstrating the impact of so many of the wider issues described within the Everyday Sexism Project – stereotypical notions of gender, sexual harassment, the portrayal of women in the media, the objectification of women, workplace imbalance – and perfectly demonstrating how they combine to create the perfect storm.

One of the clearest messages to emerge from the Everyday Sexism Project has been that everything is connected: inequality is a continuum, with the minor and major incidents irrevocably related to one another as the attitudes and ideas that underlie one allow the other to flourish. This isn't to say that one directly leads to another; rather that the culture created and sustained by each incident is part of the fertile ground from which the others spring. Perhaps this is particularly pertinent in politics, where a barbed sentence in a newspaper article, or the simple insertion of the qualifier 'mother of two', or the 'lighthearted' sniggering of a male MP, or an inappropriate 'slip of the tongue' on the part of our prime minister can all add to the subtle, insidious ideas that prevent female politicians from being taken seriously and succeeding both among their peers and with the public.

And, just like the conclusion I have drawn from the Everyday Sexism Project – that it is essential to challenge all forms of gender imbalance and prejudice, no matter how small, in order to tackle the overall problem, the same must be true in politics.

When I spoke in Parliament and referenced the two project

entries we had received describing sexist comments made by Parliamentary tour guides, the head of the House of Commons Diversity and Inclusion team contacted me in horror afterwards and took immediate steps, contacting the current guides, to ensure it would never happen again.

Lucas shows me a Bill she presented before Parliament: the 'Micro Businesses and Energy Contract Roll-Over Bill'. Near the very end is a tiny phrase, inconsequentially hidden away in the 'Interpretations' section. It reads: 'without the customer actively indicating his or her desire to do so'. This was the first ever non-gender-specific Parliamentary Bill to include the wording 'his or her' rather than the male pronoun alone. In 2012, Lucas and her team still had to battle to be allowed to make this tiny, historic change.

Like Green and Creasy's stand against 'Top Totty' in the Parliamentary bar, these may sound like minor issues, but tackling each one is part of the vital process of dismantling the invisible and interconnected barriers still preventing us from achieving gender parity in politics.

It seems inevitable that politics must both lead and benefit from the charge against sexism – we need political change to ensure practical change, from flexible working hours and parental leave to more comprehensive education on the subjects of sex and relationships. But, equally – as these political women make clear – a cultural shift in attitudes towards women is desperately needed to give younger women traction in gaining political positions, and established politicians greater impact, allowing them freedom and opportunity to wield their power in the service of equality.

Chapter 3

Girls

'If you don't have a thigh gap you NEED to get a thigh gap'

Fourteen-year-old schoolgirl interviewee

Vital Statistics

Girls as young as 5 are worrying about their weight
UK All-Party Parliamentary Group on body image (APPG)
report, 2012

By the age of 14 half of girls have been on a diet to change their shape
UK APPG report, 2012

87 per cent of teenage girls are unhappy with their body shape
Bliss magazine survey, 2004

1 in 3 girls aged 16 to 18 have experienced unwanted sexual touching at school
YouGov, 2010

33 per cent of girls aged 13 to 17 have experienced some form of sexual abuse
NSPCC, 2009

1 in 2 boys and 1 in 3 girls think it is sometimes OK to hit a woman or force her to have sex
Zero Tolerance, 1998

Over 20,000 girls under 15 are at high risk of female genital Mutilation in England and Wales each year
Forward, 2007

My father's reaction when he learnt I was a baby girl: 'They are twins, and GIRLS to boot?!'

My 2-year-old daughter given toys/books all based on beauty and getting her prince. My son given cars and trains.

My mom told me repeatedly that men won't like me because I was too opinionated [...] it started when I was 3.

We were asked what we wanted to be. I wanted to say a doctor but didn't because I thought girls couldn't be doctors. I was 4 years old.

Aged 5, man leaned over the garden wall where I was playing, asked me to twirl so he could see my knickers.

6 years old, as a bridesmaid, took my cardigan off at the reception and got WOLF WHISTLES from adult men nearby. Straight back on.

In Brownies (age 7) sang songs about potential careers. One verse I remember went: 'typing letters, sitting on the boss's knee'.

Got told by a friend of mine to suck his cock, in the street. We were both 8, and his dad laughed.

Being told by age 9 that getting catcalled, whistled, honked at were to be taken as compliments.

🐦 When I was 10, my 50-year-old neighbour telling me he wanted to be the first person to know when my breasts started to develop.

🐦 When I was in 1st year (age 11), my form teacher held a beauty contest – asked the boys to vote for the girls, ranked us on blackboard.

🐦 Age 12, at KFC, some guy hands me a note with crap handwriting, but reads pretty much as 'I want to fook you'.

🐦 13 years, told teachers I wanted to be an engineer: 'Too complicated, women don't do that usually.' I was the best pupil in my maths class.

🐦 Told I was pretty and then asked my age. Said I was 14 and he asked me to sit on his lap.

🐦 Men shouted at me from their car 'get your tits out you fucking slag'. I was 15.

🐦 When I was 16, a boy forced me into closet, said he 'wanted to get to know me' and wouldn't let me go. I fought my way out, was called a tease.

🐦 At my careers interview aged 17 I said I wanted to be a barrister. She laughed in my face. I was a straight A student.

🐦 Working in a bar aged 18, collecting glasses, man waits until both my hands are full then grabs my boobs from behind.

You can trace an entire childhood in sexism through the entries sent in to the Everyday Sexism Project. The flashes of realization and first, painful moments of learning a woman's place. Often the memories are so vivid women carry and are shaped by them for the rest of their lives.

I've been asked in countless interviews what has shocked me the most since starting the project. I think journalists expect me to tell them that it's the stories of rape, or the most appalling accounts of violence. Those stories have certainly angered and devastated me, of course, but nothing has shocked me more than the thousands and thousands of entries from young girls under the age of eighteen. When I started the project, I thought adult women would share their stories. The torrent of harassment, abuse, violence and assault being faced by children was a horribly unexpected surprise.

People in the UK often talk about the terrible struggles faced by children in other countries around the world. Meanwhile we are ignoring the increasingly desperate situation faced by girls right under our smug noses.

One day, in the very early months of the project, I read two or three entries in a single week from girls who had been subjected to leering and shouting from men in the street while walking home from school in their uniform. Dismayed, I posted a question on Twitter: surely, I asked, this couldn't be a common occurrence? By the end of the day a deluge of hundreds of tweets had confirmed that the experience was not only common but almost ubiquitous.

Some were memories recounted by older women, but many came from current pupils, and have been borne out since by painful conversations with girls at schools around the UK, who describe the phenomenon as simply the norm. One entry read:

▶ At the age of 15 I was recently greeted with 'hello sexy' on the street by a creepy man [...] it was only about 5 in the evening. I have also had men say things like 'hello darling' and 'sexy lady' whilst walking home from school IN MY UNIFORM.

As the weeks went past the problem was reported so frequently that it became rare for a day to go by without a 'schoolgirl harassment' entry.

🐦 I was 12, and a guy in a car followed me, saying he wanted to fuck me.

🐦 Age 14, walking to school, in uniform, man on a motorbike reaches out and grabs my breast as he passes me.

▶ Between the age of 12 and 14 me and all of my friends have been followed home at least once. I'm told it's because of what I wear, but I have had people talking to me when I'm wearing my school uniform with a below the knee dress. Whose right is it?

▶ I am only a teen, and I was in my school uniform walking home from school, and even then men in a car drove past me, yelled obscene things and whistled and called me sexy bitch and stuff! I mean, I'm only 15!

There were several occasions during those early days when something like this stunned me almost into denial. A great sadness of running the project is that almost nothing surprises me anymore. Gradually, as time went on, I started to build up a picture of what children are facing – from their first experiences of toys and tantrums ('Don't cry like a girl') through nursery and primary school and into their early teens, with all the incumbent pressures and bombardment of sexualization, and finally to near-adulthood – all the while learning, learning. But, rather than acquiring the skills and knowledge that would open up the world to them, girls appeared to be seeing it close down at every turn, constantly being taught harsh lessons about all the restrictions and insults and petty categorization that being a woman brings. It starts so young, and once it has started, it never stops...

One of the earliest manifestations of childhood sexism is in the almost surreal segregation of children's toys. The absolute separation along colour, type and aesthetic lines has now become so complete that the briefest glance around almost any children's toy store reveals a bizarre battleground. Bright hothouse pinks face off against defiant blues across a strip of notably empty no-man's land. Soft and cuddly on one side; sporty and energetic on the other. Cooking and domesticity here; science and exploration there. No toy so neutral as to defy categorization. The outright lack of gender neutrality gives pause for thought when imagining the contortions of the poor shelving staff – where best for a purple tractor, one can't help but wonder, or a gun that fires bubbles?

With the overt segregation of our children's playthings, as with sexism in many other forms, we become so accustomed to the norms that it can take a shock to jolt us into realizing how ridiculous they are. A good case in point was the infamous hijacking of hundreds of talking Barbies and G.I. Joes by the Barbie Liberation Organization, who switched the dolls' voice boxes and took them back to the shelves. Barbie lisping 'Vengeance is mine!' while the macho action figures proclaimed that 'The beach is the place for the summer!' forced us to acknowledge the real absurdity of such over exaggerated lines.

It has been suggested that to protest against the categorization of 'boys' and 'girls' toys is an over-the-top feminist reaction to a harmless marketing decision. Yet when you actually look at the divide – with science, exploration, construction, engineering, discovery, adventure – for all intents and purposes, creativity itself – cordoned off as 'boys' only', you really start to realize what an impact these apparently arbitrary definitions could be having on children's skill development and aspirations. As one woman wrote on Twitter:

Each time a girl sees science toys under a 'boys' sign, she is told science is not suitable for her.

Similarly of course, this absurdly exaggerated separation sends the message to boys, loud and clear, that cooking, shopping and playhouses are not for them, nor the 'girly' compassion of caring for dolls – and that theirs is the domain of aggression, sport and technology.

My daughter was never keen on playing with dolls – she had one baby doll, and a little pushchair, but never really played with them. My son, however, loved pushing the doll around in the pushchair.

I lost count of how many negative comments this received – from my mother, other kids' mums, etc. I always simply said, 'He's playing at being a Daddy'. How odd that we're comfortable for a girl to 'play Mummy', and even think it odd if she doesn't, and yet society is freaked out by a little boy playing Daddy.

But, while it is true that both boys and girls are denied access to much of the contents of the others' toy chest, the breadth of choice available to boys, from building sets to sporty games, LEGO to woodwork, remains markedly wider than that presented in pink. Girls are not only being denied access to scientific and adventurous toys; they're also presented with such a narrow range of options that domesticity and stereotypically 'female' duties are shoved down their throats before they've even reached the age of five.

🐦 When I was 2 years old I had a toy vacuum cleaner, at 3 I had a toy iron and ironing board and at 4 a toy oven.

Or, as one woman wryly remembered:

🐦 In primary school we had a playground wedding. I was the 'bride' and my wedding present from my 'groom' was a saucepan.

Oh the romance!

It's clever, this childhood gender imbalance, because it hides in the things we take for granted and consider most innocuous and integral to infanthood.

Take, for example, children's films and television. Although there have been laudable attempts to subvert the stereotypes in recent years, with films like *Tangled* and *Brave* showcasing strong female heroines rather than the typical 'damsel in distress' formula, they remain stubbornly problematic in other ways. The heroines are still unrealistically thin, for a start. Meanwhile Rapunzel's power comes from her glossy long blonde hair – and, although she spunkily knocks out the male hero with a frying pan on their first meeting, her story still ends with the 'happily ever after' of marriage.

Elsewhere just the briefest glance at the shelves of any newsagent carrying children's magazines is enough to reveal the bombardment of media messages bulldozing young girls towards pretty pink pliancy. I'm not talking about teen magazines, like *Bliss* and *Shout*, but titles explicitly targeted at *children*.

For boys, a wide variety of activities and interests are represented, from Doctor Who to building, dinosaurs to architecture. There is choice, and with it a platform on which boys may build their own identity. But for girls the shelves overflow with pink, and all that pink represents.

In my tiny local newsagent alone, the magazine options include: *Tinker Bell*, *Princess Kingdom*, *Fairy Princess*, *Princess Friends*, *Pretty Princess* and *Disney Princess*. Judging by the type of activities included ('What colour is the princess's dress?' 'Point to your favourite colour fish!') it's pretty clear these mags are aimed at young children. Of the eleven titles I buy (the man behind the counter looks at me like I've taken leave of my senses) only one doesn't include free jewellery or make-up (the most common choice being a pink lipstick).

Between them these eleven magazines offer six separate stories or articles about weddings – from Princess Aurora, who 'dreamed many times that a handsome prince would find her', to Ariel and Cinderella, who had 'perfect wedding days'. Between just *seven* titles there are thirty-seven images of a princess embracing, kissing, dancing with or otherwise striking a loving pose with her handsome prince. Almost every princess is white with long blonde hair and blue eyes. Their waists are smaller than their heads, their legs matchstick thin. When they're not busy planning their weddings, they engage in such other engrossing activities as dressing up, finding their missing lip-gloss, counting their lipsticks, trying on new lipsticks, getting their lipsticks muddled up, searching through mazes to find hidden lipsticks... You get the picture.

There is a smattering of stories in which the princesses are allowed to be active, but even here the 'weakness' of their sex seems to let them down – whether in losing races to boys because they are too 'busy bickering', or in dropping their tiaras while swinging in the trees.

It feels a bit like a punch in the stomach every time I read an Everyday Sexism entry about girls being told, unequivocally, at such a young age that they are somehow by definition inferior to their male peers. Marked out – sometimes even at their very moment of success – as if they're somehow defective on the basis of sex alone.

One mother tweeted to tell us:

🐦 My 11yr old just won a cross country race. As she passed the boys, a teacher shouted 'Come on, don't be beaten by a girl!'

And, while these magazines push the idea of feminine allure and make-up as the ultimate achievement to their young readers, the parameters of the 'beauty' they present are stiflingly narrow. While interviewing two young mixed-race girls, I ask them what they think of the magazines. They tell me:

It's a bit weird because they're all white skinned [...] none of them have black skin – I think that means if people are looking at this and they're dark skinned, they'll think, 'Oh my gosh, I really wish I looked like this.'

There is one, the Frog Princess, but all the most famous ones are like Cinderella [...] a typical princess – blonde hair, white skin, blue eyes, pink lipstick – perfect girls. It makes it seem like black people aren't as popular. You don't see a punk princess, you don't see a princess with tattoos, you don't see a black princess, or a Goth princess [...] It'd be really fun if you saw a princess with baggy jeans on and a normal jumper and normal weight, but then people would say that's not a princess!

Fast-forward a couple of years and the magazines segue into a similarly narrow fixation with real-life male idols and female beauty. *Top Model* magazine – placed in the 'Primary Girls' category by Newstand.co.uk and aimed at nine- to fourteen-year-olds – features waiflike cartoon 'models' with torsos barely the width of their heads, prominent collarbones, and enormous eyes with dilated pupils. A cartoon entitled 'The Perfect Girl' describes the trials and tribulations of a top model unable to attract the attention of a cute guy, despite trying all the *obvious* methods ('I've tried everything: colourful outfits, basic look, curly hair, straightened hair [...] he ignores me.').

'Mascara alone is not enough!' wails an article on the magazine's website... 'You need more to achieve a radiant look...'

Did I mention it's aimed at nine- to fourteen-year-olds?

Another online section, entitled 'Fight against cellulite', offers this pearl of girlhood wisdom: 'Have you tried pinching?' Great news, girls: 'pinching yourself with a twisting hand movement [...] every day for 5 minutes will prevent cellulite from forming.' Hallelujah! You no longer have to wait to hit your teens before you can start inflicting pain on your own body because it doesn't match up to the pictures in a magazine!

Enter Monster High, a new franchise aimed at tweens, based on a world inhabited by makeup-caked, miniskirt-clad ghosts and skeletons who provide the perfect excuse for a litany of (literally) bone-thin characters. (You almost wonder if there was a meeting in there somewhere where the producers were scratching their heads over how to promote utterly unrealistic and unattainable body shapes to children without attracting criticism – answer: skeletons!) The character descriptions on the website quickly reveal their deepest concerns...

Clawdeen Wolf is a 'fierce fashionista [...] gorgeous, intimidating'. Her major 'flaw' is her hairy legs but, though 'plucking and shaving is definitely a full-time job [...] that's a small price to pay for being scarily fabulous'. Her favourite activities are 'shopping and flirting with the boys'. Meanwhile Draculaura has the terrible defect of not being able to 'see my reflection in the mirror' so 'I have to leave the house not knowing if my clothes and make-up are just right'. Monster High is supposed to be a horror story. I'm just not sure its creators realize just how well they've succeeded.

One parent summed it up when she wrote:

🐦 My 7-year-old daughter told me 'Barbie is fat' when she compared it to her Monster High doll.

Of course, in isolation none of these things is a disaster. Of course, there's nothing wrong with girls taking an interest in fashion or beauty or boys. But the sheer saturation of tween culture with these characters and images creates a powerfully dictatorial consensus about who girls should be (princesses, fashionistas, girlfriends), what they should be interested in (boys, make-up, clothes) and how they should look (thin, white, made-up). And these influential cultural mores are having a profound effect on the way our daughters see themselves and the shape of their futures.

In the words of one ten-year-old interviewee:

It's more important for girls to be pretty. Girls are meant to be used as models, but boys are more clever so they don't have to worry about their looks because they can get a different job.

As I struggle to find words, her older sister, aged twelve, agrees:

Men are more powerful; they are firmer and stricter and people think that will be better for being a boss – because they'll put their foot down.

If we think we've cracked this equality thing – that we're bringing up our sons and daughters to believe they can be whatever they want to be – we really need to take a reality check.

▶ When I was a small child and thought about what I wanted to be when I grew up, I always thought, I want to be a man. It was just not possible in my mind to be a woman and a scientist or, a politician, or basically anything other than a pretty, silent girl on the hero's arm.

When I was asked to join the CBBC programme *Newsround* to film a segment on gender and children's career aspirations, the producer told me higher-ups were sceptical. They felt gender stereotypes were more of an adult problem, she explained, and were unconvinced we'd get any relevant material from the seven- and eight-year-olds. I said I thought she might be surprised. Within moments of the discussion starting (after comments about girls not being engineers because they can't do maths and men making better pilots because girls make too many mistakes), she was flabbergasted.

Despite women's gains in the job market, girls appear to be growing up with incredibly restrictive ideas about what career paths are open to them. Ironically, their visions of the future resemble the past far more closely than they do the present. My ten-year-old interviewee tells me:

Girls think of more feminine jobs, like fashion designer. I think most girls think if they want to do something in medicine that they can't be doctors – because mostly a doctor is a man and a nurse is a girl.

The truth is that these ideas are not just coming from TV and fairy-princess magazines. They are also shamefully reinforced, day after day, by the adults in the children's lives – from their teachers and neighbours to their own parents and families. We're forcing our girls into gendered straightjackets, and they're suffocating.

🐦 Got better marks at school than my 2 older brothers. Dad was livid about it and told me I'm not clever, I just try too hard.

🐦 A friend of mine was told by her dad that 'It's better to be dumb than to look un-pretty'.

🐦 As a young Indian woman, being told at age 12 that I should walk with my eyes down. Girls walking with their chin up gives the wrong impression.

From their first hobbies ('Pick something else: girls don't play drums') to early tentative academic and career ambitions, girls are taught again and again that only certain appropriate, preapproved paths are available to them.

🐦 Walked into my first GCSE Resistant Materials lesson and was told I 'must have got the wrong classroom'. I got an A grade.

🐦 I told teachers at school that I wanted to be an airline pilot. They told me I was suited to be a nursery nurse.

▶ I was told by my Chemistry Professor that I was 'too pretty to do science'.

The way that the obsessive focus on girls' looks plays into the dialogue around what they can and can't do is particularly poisonous. It inserts the self-consciousness of the watched, objectified woman into girls' internal narratives before they would ever have noticed it themselves. (One girl noted her bemusement at having her legs commented on, aged just ten: 'I'd never thought much about my legs before, they were just something I walked on.') And it teaches them lessons about their own value being measured by their bodies and faces – lessons that will stay with them for the rest of their lives.

> When I was about 9 years old, my dad started calling me 'thunder thighs'. I've never felt comfortable in shorts ever since.

> The T-shirt labeled 'Future Fox' when I was 6 [...] I could do anything when I grew up, as long as I was also pretty.

As girls hit the age of ten or eleven, this obsession with their appearance takes a distinctly sexualized turn. Suddenly they are defined not only by their looks but also, more specifically, by what boys and men think of them. And, in a culture that bombards us daily with overwhelming messages about the precise attributes that make a woman 'sexy', this often translates into a single, all-encompassing quest for thinness.

When interviewers ask me to point to a single project entry that has most moved me, it isn't a difficult question to answer. I point them to this one, the first that ever made me cry:

▶ I'm fifteen and feel like girls my age are under a lot of pressure that boys are not under. I know I am smart, I know I am kind and funny, and I know that everybody around me keeps telling me that I can be whatever I want to be. I know all this but I just don't feel that way. I always feel like if I don't look a certain way, if boys don't think I'm 'sexy' or 'hot' then I've failed and it doesn't even matter if I am a doctor or writer, I'll still feel like nothing. I hate that I feel like that because it makes me seem shallow, but I know all my friends feel like that, and even my little sister. I feel like successful women are only considered a success if they are successful AND hot, and I worry constantly that I won't be. What if my boobs don't grow, what if I don't have the perfect body, what if my hips don't widen and give me a little waist, if none of that happens I feel like what's the point of doing anything because I'll just be the 'fat ugly girl' regardless of whether I do become a doctor or not.

I wish people would think about what pressures they are putting on everyone, not just teenage girls, but even older people – I watch my mum tear herself apart every day because her boobs are sagging and her skin is wrinkling, she feels like she is ugly even though she is amazing, but then I feel like I can't judge because I do the same to myself. I wish the people who had real power and control the images and messages we get fed all day actually thought about what they did for once.

I know the girls on Page 3 are probably starving themselves. I know the girls in adverts are airbrushed. I know beauty is on the inside. But I still feel like I'm not good enough.

A 2012 report from the All-Party Parliamentary Group (APPG) on Body Image revealed that girls as young as five are worrying about their size and looks, and that one in four seven-year-old girls has tried to lose weight. The excellent Representation Project has revealed that by the age of ten that figure rushes up to 80 per cent among American girls, and also that the number-one 'magic wish' for young girls aged eleven to seventeen is to be thinner. It takes a while for that last figure to sink in. Just think of all the other things in the world that teenage girls could wish for...

In all my interviews, school visits and interactions, I have not managed to find a single girl who doesn't agree that this is a huge area of focus and worry.

Girls worry about being fat, because people judge them a lot.

My friend's sister was getting bullied and being told she'd be better off if she had an eating disorder so she could get thinner. She was 13.

One girl, aged fourteen, tells me girls worry about their weight 'all the time':

Guys look at Tumblr girls and Tumblr girls are meant to be perfect – that's the whole idea. The girls on the internet are perfect – amazing boobs, amazing figures, legs, everything and the girls know the guys talk about it and I guess they want to please the guys. They need that idea of perfection [...] if you don't have a thigh gap you NEED to get a thigh gap.

For those not in-the-know, a 'thigh gap' is achieved when a woman stands with her legs straight and together and a gap is present between her thighs. When I ask her how the girls go about this quest for 'perfection', she confidently explains:

Year 7 or 8, it's really common not eating, but when you get to fourteen to eighteen it's more diet pills and exercising all the time.

Another girl, a sixth former, meets me in a quiet North London café. Her voice barely louder than a whisper, she tells me:

I don't think I know any girls who don't have some sort of self-esteem or body-image issues. I have about six friends with eating disorders and so many friends who don't have eating disorders but they're disordered eaters – they'll only eat fruit for a day or something. And so many people who just feel anxious about it – they won't wear short-sleeved shirts because they're embarrassed about their arms. It's so common.

I ask her how far back the problem goes and her eyes glaze as she recalls a childhood of intense self-scrutiny:

I remember being embarrassed about my thighs aged six [...] I remember girls comparing their bodies in the toilet in Year 5. I would have been about nine.

She is passionately distressed by the *Daily Mail*'s decision, the day before we meet, to run an article by the infamous Samantha Brick, claiming that 'Any woman who wants to stay beautiful needs to diet every day of her life'. This piece seems quite obviously to be an attempt by the *Mail* to troll readers into online outrage, generating a storm of hits for the site. It strikes me that in this, as in so many other situations, it is young, vulnerable girls who suffer silent collateral damage.

She is utterly, unutterably beautiful, this seventeen-year-old girl who speaks with the eloquence and sadness of a much older woman as she tells me, 'I feel like people are watching me all the time [...] judging me [...] I never show skin or anything. I feel way too self-conscious to do that.'

I've sat in front of a screen full of threats and sexist jibes; I've watched stories of harassment pour in at a rate of one per minute; but I have never felt as angry or as frustrated as I did that afternoon, wishing there was anything in the world I could say to make this teenage girl realize how very much she had to be proud of, and knowing that nothing I could say would change the way the world had made her feel about herself.

My interviewee attributes her own slide into the grip of an eating disorder, aged fifteen, to the increasing levels of street harassment she was experiencing at the time:

There was a man who ran his hand up my leg on the tube – that was one of the first times I ever came to London to stay with my sister. I felt embarrassed and scared – mainly scared because I didn't know what he was doing and I was unsure. I didn't want to make a fuss [...] Losing weight seemed like the appropriate reaction to being looked at as a sexual being; it felt like the natural step [...] It's simultaneously fitting into this ideal of womanhood

and running away from it; losing your period while getting complimented about how thin and sexy you look. It's kind of reclaiming your body, but in a really negative way […] I remember feeling completely powerless.

This theme has come up again and again – with the girls I've spoken to in schools, the girls who've written in to the project, the girls I've met at events and speeches and interviewed for this book. Every one of them described sexual harassment and even assaults, such as unwanted touching and groping, as a regular part of life.

According to a 2010 survey by YouGov for the End Violence Against Women Coalition, nearly one in three sixteen- to eighteen-year-old girls said they had experienced unwanted sexual touching at school. A huge 71 per cent of that age group said they heard sexual name calling (such as 'slag' or 'slut') towards girls at least several times a week.

And yet – whether because the extent of the problem is so little-known, or because it is so normalized – it seems girls are being given neither the resources they desperately need to understand how to deal with it, nor the information to understand that they shouldn't have to face it in the first place.

When we were asked to create a video about the project for the Chime for Change initiative, we invited a group of young women to narrate their own first-hand experiences directly to the camera. Sitting quietly, her hands folded on her lap and speaking hesitantly, one girl explained how, at the age of thirteen, a man had followed her off one bus and onto the next, sitting down next to her each time. She had been taught to be polite, she said, so she answered his questions, even when he started asking her if she wanted to go with him to the park. And when he started running his hand up her legs, although there were other people on the bus, she said she didn't feel she ought to bother them.

When the director asked her how the incident had impacted on her behaviour, she whispered that she had learned you shouldn't wear shorts, even if it was summer. Sitting in the corner, behind a screen, I wiped away tears and bit my thumb so I wouldn't ruin the recording. When the case went to court, she told us, it was dismissed for lack of evidence. If she had spoken up, or made anybody else on the bus aware of what was happening, she said, it might have ended differently.

By the age of thirteen, this intelligent, thoughtful girl had been taught by society to be polite; taught not to offend a stranger, or to disturb other people on the bus. Because girls are socialized into submission, and into acceptance of others' behaviour – even when it invades their personal space. But nobody had ever taught her that she had the right not to be touched without her consent.

Similar stories repeatedly suggest that not wanting to cause a scene or upset anybody silences young women into feeling unable to protest.

▶ When I was a young, naive 15-year-old, I had to sit away from my mum and my younger sister on a flight. The business man next to me started chatting to me in French [...] I smiled and tried to look interested. I had always been taught to be polite.

After a while, he started to put his hand upon my leg. I felt really uncomfortable but didn't know what to say [...] I remember thinking that if I didn't make a fuss, he might stop [...]

I hadn't been given the knowledge and the confidence to react and stand up for myself when I started to feel uncomfortable with his advances. Having been always taught to be polite and not make a fuss, I was totally unprepared.

When people say women should simply 'stand up' to harassment, they're exhibiting a colossal lack of awareness of the sheer strength of this gendered socialization.

▶ If it wasn't for this site, I probably wouldn't know that I can say 'no' to unwanted sexual advances. Since the age of 12 I've been led to believe that if a man wants to have sex with me, it's my duty to let him, and that refusing someone who is pressuring me into doing something I don't want to do is just plain rude.

These girls are voiceless. Their harassment and assault is so normalized that they feel unable to object. Then they grow up into young women, and adults, who don't feel able to speak up either.
    Some are brilliant at fighting back:

🐦 Some random middle aged man was cat calling me (literally! 'Pss pss pss') and I told him: I'm not a cat. I'm only 15.

🐦 Boys, if you want my attention, please don't refer to me as 'Jugs'...

But they shouldn't have to be! Not everyone is equipped to. And not every situation is 'minor' enough to be dealt with alone.

▸ At 15 in class, a boy felt my leg and went to touch my genital area. When I yelled in surprise and pushed him away he called me frigid. My female 'friends' laughed at me and told me to lighten up. I felt even worse about it then.

I asked one sixth-form girl if she thought her friends understood that they don't have to put up with it – that somebody touching them in a sexual way without their consent is a form of sexual assault. She said: 'They'd never report being touched – it wouldn't be seen as something you could report to the police. It's just so common. Normalized. None of the girls I know would describe any of this as sexual harassment. It's just "boys being boys".'

And here's the worst part. As if all this wasn't enough, after they've been sexualized and hounded and harassed and bombarded from pretty much every angle with the notion that they are sexual objects, there to be sexualized and fantasized about and pursued then they get ripped to shreds for being too sexy.

Enormous pressure is on very young girls to be sexually active, to give in to boys' 'demands' and to acquiesce to various requests, from blowjobs to sending explicit photographs on mobile phones. But the moment they comply they face a stringent backlash of almost puritanical proportions.

One fourteen-year-old girl tells me: 'A lot of my friends have sexted and it's ruined their life; they've got so much hate for it.' She then breaks it down for me: 'If you're talking to a guy or you text with him he WILL ask for a picture.'

I ask her why girls feel they have to comply – particularly if they've witnessed others experiencing negative consequences.

You'd feel like you don't want to let him down – you think he likes you for who you are and he promises not to show it to anyone [...] then you send the picture and then he'll never speak to you again. The guy shows his friends and then the friend puts it up on the internet and then for the girls it's horrible – her friends will all turn against her and call her a slut and the guys at school will all come up and say they saw the picture and she'll lose all her friends.

As extreme as it sounds, this precise turn of events is relayed to me again and again, using near-identical language, by girls on their own, girls in groups, young girls, sixth-form girls, girls from private schools and girls from state schools. It seems to be, quite simply, the norm.

Sexting and sexual pressure is common. In my school when my friend was thirteen pictures of her were circulated. People teased her a lot [...] She was called a slut very often by boys in our class. If they were having an argument or banter, they'd just bring up the name of the guy she lost her virginity to. You could just see the colour flooding from her face when they mentioned his name [...] That's something they did with me as well. They'd bring up my ex-boyfriend's name and just mention it – as a way of putting me down – sort of embarrassing me. A boyfriend is something to shame you with later, but for him it's like a victory.

Yet another story, from another school, corroborates the routine:

When I was at secondary school, this girl took a personal picture of herself to send to her boyfriend. And when they broke up he

showed it to all his friends, so it got around, a lot of names were called towards her – he wasn't spoken to at all about the fact he broke her trust, but she was called everything under the sun.

Stories of 'slut-shaming' mingle and clash with extraordinary tales of sexual pressure, leaving young girls in a completely helpless situation. 'You just can't win', four of them separately tell me.

If the girl doesn't want to, he'll break up with her, go around and say she's frigid and the girl will get so much hate for being frigid; but if she does it she'll be called a slut, so you can't win – there's so much pressure on girls.

🐦 Branded a slut today by 2 random boys on Snapchat because I wouldn't send them nudes #logic

And, importantly, this potent mix of sexual pressure and sexual shaming, public humiliation and regular harassment is not only reported over and over again by students but is also corroborated by a large number of reports made by teachers to the Everyday Sexism Project…

▶ I am a secondary science teacher and a form tutor in Yorkshire. I witness on a daily basis the girls in my classes being called 'whore' 'bitch' 'slag' 'slut' as a matter of course, heckled if they dare to speak in class, their shirts being forcibly undone and their skirts being lifted and held by groups of boys, (I WANT TO EMPHASISE THAT THIS IS MORE OFTEN THAN NOT A DAILY EVENT, AND OFTEN BORDERS ON ASSAULT). On a daily basis

I am forced to confiscate mobile phones as boys are watching hardcore pornography videos in lessons and I have noticed sadly that as time has gone on the girls in my classes have become more and more reserved and reluctant to draw attention to themselves.

I am currently dealing with a situation whereby a girl in my form class sent a topless photograph of herself to her then boyfriend, said boyfriend then used this to blackmail the girl in to giving him oral sex which he filmed on his phone and then distributed both the photo and video amongst the boys in the year. This girl is now having to consider leaving the school and interrupting her GCSEs due to the abuse she is experiencing from her fellow pupils.

What I am seeing every day is incredibly worrying and distressing. It is getting worse and worse. I wanted to share this snapshot of my working life with others [...] The problem is that people are too willing to brush this issue under the carpet and dismiss it as just natural teenage deviance. However, being on the front line and dealing with this day after day I can tell you this is a completely different animal. There is an underlying violent and vicious attitude towards girls, a leaning towards seeing them as products to be used.

For many adults, even parents, the lives of children are a largely closed book, perceived through a grown-up lens that leans towards trivializing negative experiences as just 'boys being boys' or 'the way kids are'. It is so easy to turn a blind eye – to naively believe that nothing *too* serious could really be going on under that unturned stone. After all, we'd know, wouldn't we? The school would find out, or the children themselves would speak up. But, increasingly, girls are finding themselves trapped in a hostile environment, hobbled by the fear of being labelled 'uptight' or a 'tell-tale' and unlikely ever to mention what's going on. And so much of this is happening in a different world altogether, which for many adults is uncharted territory: the largely unpoliced Wild West of the internet. Here, for boys as much as girls, there are strong underlying messages about their place in the world and how their 'masculinity' or 'femininity' must manifest itself – aggressive and controlling or sexualized and submissive. The lines are stark and uncompromising. The instructions are clear.

What makes the cycle of pressure and judgement even more powerful is that, thanks to the advent of new technology and social media, there is no escape from it, even at home, away from school and peers. Not just from Facebook and instant-messenger applications but on countless other sites, too – like Snapchat, where users send images back and forth, or on anonymous 'question and answer' websites like Spring.me, formally Formspring, and Qooh. me. Websites with little risk of adult intervention or punishment. Young people create a profile, including a picture, but other users can send them questions without revealing who they are. It's a recipe for disaster, or more specifically, for extreme sexualized bullying. One mother of a thirteen-year-old girl asked her daughter's permission to let me view her profile page on Ask.fm.

The questions come thick and fast, aggressive, overtly sexual and from boys claiming to be from her school. 'Have you ever sucked a dick?' they ask her. 'Do you shave your pubes?' 'Bra size?' 'Have you done anal?' 'Can I bang you?' 'Is your c**t dry?'

They call her 'whore' and 'slut', make sexual demands ('Eat my penis'), arbitrarily threaten her ('I'd like to put a nail gun to your face') and even ask her to upload a video of 'you cutting yourself' (she refuses).

Her mother tells me: 'Even in Year 5 at a Catholic primary school the emails she used to receive from the lads in her year – about having a wank and watching porn – were obscene and disturbing.' And as she got older the sexual pressure only worsened. Eventually, her daughter was diagnosed with anorexia and depression, took an overdose and spent eleven weeks in a mental-health unit: 'Everything is appearance-based and sexualized. When she tried to be individual and had some facial piercings the messages read that they wanted to drag a magnet over her face, so she took them out.'

Acutely aware of the realities of a teenage girl's existence, she explains that she tries to educate her daughter about internet safety – explaining the importance of keeping her personal information private and blocking offensive accounts – rather than attempting to keep her altogether from the online world that is the lifeblood of her social being.

Of course, with this absolute internet focus comes instant, easily accessible porn. In a group interview one sixth-form girl tells me:

The view of women through porn creates assumptions – it means [boys] just expect women will take it, the man's in control, the women can just like it; and I don't think they can separate that the woman is acting and that isn't what relationships are really like.

Porn shouldn't be viewed as documentary – that's the problem: boys are looking at porn and they're told it's really real – it's 'amateur', it's real people – and they blur the line between entertainment and actual reality and that's the problem. Porn isn't the main problem. It's the fact that you're saying, 'This is what girls are like, this is real life, this is how they're going to react.' And also the age: most of the boys in your year will probably have been watching it since about fourteen – that's before you've ever seen your first girl naked – so that's how they learn about sex.

Another seventeen-year-old girl agrees:

I know that boys in my school were watching porn in Year 7 – possibly earlier. They started circulating pictures. And they were also making rape jokes – like saying, 'You're so hot I'd rape you.' Or just not seeing it as a very big deal. They have no proper understanding of what rape is. Some see it as a compliment. Some see it as just something they're entitled to. Or something women would enjoy anyway. 'It's not rape if you enjoy it' – that was something that was said a lot.

These girls are incredibly eloquent and insightful in conversation with me over lunch in a deserted classroom. And yet later, during a similar discussion with their whole year group, they clam up completely. They have so much to say about their very personal experiences – from painful tales of early street harassment to passionate distress at the impact porn has on their lives and relationships. But their silence in front of their male peers that afternoon is deafening, and confirms the impact of such treatment with depressing clarity.

Meanwhile the boys challenge me at every stage of the discussion, demanding justification of why a workman should get in trouble for shouting at women in the street (outrageous!) while the girls sit mute and tight-lipped. No wonder the messages we're sending our boys find such fertile breeding ground: they go unchallenged at every stage.

Meanwhile the misconceptions about rape to which the girls alluded abound in the reports we have received, both on the project website and in interviews. One parent even reported that at her child's primary school a part of the playground difficult to see by supervisors was known as 'the rape corner'. Other accounts included boys in Year 11 saying that 'rape is a compliment really' in a classroom discussion, and young boys thinking that a girl crying and saying no was 'part of foreplay'.

My stomach turned as I flicked through my emails one morning to see that a girl had contacted me in distress that her school's Year 11 prom was 'having a biggest rapist award'. Other awards included 'biggest slut'.

A sixteen-year-old wrote to tell us:

▶ My younger brother's 13. He had his friends round last weekend and I couldn't believe it when I heard them sitting in the front room discussing girls in their class in 3 categories 'frigid', 'sluts' and 'would like to rape'.

Another girl tweeted:

🐦 At age 11, a classmate on a school trip stated that 'no-one would rape me anyway because I'm too ugly'. Others only laughed at that.

And in a heartbreaking Everyday Sexism Project entry one schoolgirl wrote:

▶ I am thirteen and I am so scared to have sex it makes me cry nearly every day. We had sex education in Year 6 and I felt fine about it, but now some of the boys at school keep sending us these videos of sex which are much worse than what we learnt about and it looks so horrible and like it hurts and it keeps coming into my mind and at night I get really scared that one day I will have to do it. I don't want to speak to my mum or dad about it obviously and I feel like if I say to my friends that the videos and stuff scare me and upset me they will laugh at me and everyone will find out and pick on me for it. I try to think don't worry you won't have to do it for ages but everyone at school keeps acting like it's normal and we're meant to do it really soon like some of the boys keep asking me have I done it and can I do it with them and showing me the horrible pictures and things.

I know it sounds stupid but I just wanted to tell someone because I feel like it's unfair that girls have to have horrible things done to them but boys can just laugh and watch the videos and they don't realize how scary it is. Why did they talk about sex at school like it was okay but then the real life sex that we see is so scary and painful and the woman is crying and getting hurt?

Nothing has emerged more clearly from the Everyday Sexism Project than the urgent need for far more comprehensive mandatory sex-and-relationships education in schools, to include issues such as consent and respect, domestic violence and rape. It's not just girls who need it so desperately. For boys porn provides some very scary, dictatorial lessons about what it means to be a man and how they are apparently expected to exert their male dominance over women. It is as unrealistic to expect them, unaided, to instinctively work out the difference between online porn and real, caring intimacy, as it is to demand the same intuition of young women.

According to the data collected by YouGov for the End Violence Against Women Coalition, 40 per cent of sixteen- to eighteen-year-olds said they didn't receive lessons or information on sexual consent, or didn't know whether they did. And when we carried out an informal online poll, asking people whether their school sex-and-relationships education had covered issues such as sexual violence, domestic violence, assault or rape, more than 92 per cent of respondents said these issues were never raised at all.

🐦 When we asked about it at school last year we were told not to be inappropriate and that we might upset people.

🐦 No. I guess my school assumed that if they didn't talk about it, nothing would happen. They couldn't be more wrong.

🐦 I learned about it myself, the hard way.

These statistics were painfully borne out by numerous project entries from girls and young women feeling afraid, confused and anxious about sex and consent. Huge numbers of them simply had no idea they had the right to say no.

▸ Age 14: After splitting up with my first 'boyfriend', another boy hit on me when I'd been drinking whilst we were out. I said I didn't want to go but he pulled me into the woods and lay me down in a ditch. He started to put his hands down my knickers and I told him no. He pressed his finger to my lips and whispered me to 'shh', like I was a child. I was a child. I think I let him do that because I didn't really know what was right and wrong. I didn't know how to act, I didn't know if I was making a big deal, or being frigid. I never told anyone.

▸ Age 18: After going out with a close long term friend to a party, I stayed over at his. I slept on the floor and crashed out with exhaustion. I woke up with his fingers inside of me. I had no idea how to react. So I waited it out.

Both boys and girls are seeing mainstream porn that suggests a woman's role during sex is to be subjugated or humiliated, to please a man, and often even to be hurt or punished. And without receiving any counter-information to offset these norms, or mitigate them with ideas about consent, relationships, respect and boundaries, they are simply, inevitably, accepting these things as the 'reality' of sex.

It's futile to attempt to prevent young people from accessing porn on the internet. But that doesn't mean that we can't offset its impact with clear, targeted education to provide them, at least, with an alternative narrative and to prevent what they have seen from crystallizing into unquestioned, accepted assumptions. We might not be able to protect young women from the barrage of Photoshopped images and objectifying adverts regularly bombarding them, but we can at least arm them with the tools to analyse and rationalize the manipulation – and in so doing offset at least some part of the impact.

There is absolutely nothing to stop parents from supplementing and continuing discussions at home. But what about the 750,000 children who, according to the UK Government Department of Health, already witness domestic violence every year? Is it really sensible to assume that every child will learn what they need to know about healthy relationships outside school? What about those young people already experiencing sexual abuse, who may have been groomed to believe that it is a normal form of interaction?

Most of the teenagers I speak to tell me they don't think people their age really understand what rape is. One seventeen-year-old tells me it is surrounded by 'grey areas'...

If she said yes and then said no, is it still rape? If she's asleep is it still rape? If she's drunk is it still rape? Sometimes girls don't realize they can say no – they think it's their duty to have sex with men [...]

Her words are echoed by the sixth-form girls at another school:

The boys seem to expect because you're their girlfriend that they have the right to have sex with you [...] we need more education at a younger age.

One girl I contacted for an interview described a police talk given at her all-girls school in 2007:

The sort of advice they gave us to help prevent sexual assault or rape was: don't walk home alone; don't 'look drunk'; look like you know where you are going; and try to 'look ugly'. Looking ugly was surmised as: 'Pick your nose, pull your hair over your face'. The overall impression was that we were responsible for preventing rape [...] For years it coloured my view of rape. I've been sexually harassed a number of times and at the back of my mind for years was the voice of: 'This is probably my fault for dressing how I do. For drinking like I do.'

One girl who was raped twice as a teenager, by boys she knew, ended her account with the words:

▶ I always thought I was the problem. Since reading everyday sexism I've learnt it's not my fault. I felt guilty for all the events. And they should be taught things like that rape isn't only stalking a stranger down a dark alley, but taking advantage of a vulnerable girl, and how to recognise and understand when they are doing so.

Friendship groups, family, magazines, films, cartoon characters, porn, Facebook, boys: the wrong ideas come from so many places it's easy to see how they become accepted without question. And in every area – from the idea that they will be judged on their looks to the vital importance of weight loss; from the knowledge that only certain paths are available for them to the normalization of being groped and even raped – accepting these things without question means that girls aren't even aware of the possibility that things could be different.

As I finish my conversation with the two sisters, the eldest, twelve, says: 'But I think one day in the future people will see the day where there aren't just thin people that are on buses…' Then she pauses, and shakes her head.

'Actually, no, I don't think that. I think that will never happen.'

Chapter 4

Young Women Learning

'I don't know any girl at university who hasn't been touched or groped without her consent'

Answer on a student questionnaire

Vital Statistics

95 per cent of 16- to 21-year-old women would change
their bodies
Girlguiding UK, 2009

12.7 per cent of girls aged 16 to 19 have experienced
domestic abuse in the last year
British Crime Survey, 2010

Nearly a third of young men think that domestic violence
is acceptable if their partner has been nagging them
BBC domestic-violence Survey, ICM, 2003

One in seven female university students has experienced
a serious physical or sexual assault during their time as
a student
NUS, Hidden Marks Survey, 2010

Nearly 70 per cent of female university students have
experienced verbal or non-verbal harassment in or around
their institution
NUS, Hidden Marks Survey, 2010

Many young people view violence as a normal aspect of
intimate relationships
Wood, et al., 'Standing on my own two feet.' London: NSPC, 2011

🐦 Debate at Glasgow University, female student speaking, lad in gallery – 'nice knockers'.

🐦 Registrar at college wouldn't have recognized any female students' faces. Our chests? No problem.

🐦 On first day at Cambridge University, ancient don asked whether I had had to 'bend over' to get in.

🐦 Just got called a slag by two guys sitting outside the University of York library. A slag for books?

🐦 Told that being groped/touched/having a crotch rubbed against you unwantedly is 'a normal part of university nightlife'.

🐦 Quote for the day: Nice young women don't 'play with science' *choking on my tea* It's an fMRI scanner, not a Tonka truck.

It's March 2013. I'm standing in a lecture hall at Cardiff University and something is horribly wrong. In front of me is a sea of hands. I'm speaking to a group of about 100 students, most of them young women. I've just asked them who among them has been sexually assaulted. Almost every hand in the room is raised.

Only I didn't ask them like that. If I had, it wouldn't have looked this way. There'd have been a smattering of hands, doubtful eyes darting sideways at one another. But I didn't use those words. I talked about being grabbed or groped in a club; feeling a hand slide down to caress your bottom in a bar; having your breasts touched, tweaked, poked. I talked about somebody rubbing up behind you on a crowded tube, standing much closer than they need to; casually slipping a hand between your legs during a dance.

Sexual assault. It's something almost every female student in the room identifies with. But, when I talk to them more about it, almost none of them feel comfortable using the label.

Many of the students I've spoken to have been shocked to learn just what they have the right to be protected from. When I speak at universities and colleges, and describe the UK's legal definition of sexual assault, I'm often approached afterwards. 'This can't be sexual assault,' they tell me, 'because it's normal...' 'It can't be sexual assault, because it's just what happens when we go out with our friends...' 'It can't be sexual assault, because we wouldn't be taken seriously if we called it that – because we wouldn't feel able to report it...' 'It can't be sexual assault because that would mean that, for us, sexual assault is just a part of life.'

Already, by the time they hit their late teens and early twenties, young women are learning that the business of being groped and grabbed, having their bodies claimed and touched in public places without their consent, is just something they have to get on with. This isn't a culture that is confined to universities – similar experiences were reported with depressing regularity by young women in their late teens and early twenties outside higher education. Their project entries described instances of having 'my arse groped' as 'constant', 'always', 'common', 'regular'... The consensus was that 'During nights out, it is pretty much guaranteed'. And many of them related dispiriting tales of harassment and discrimination in their earliest experiences of employment.

🐦 Age 18 first job. Supervisor follows me into walk-in fridge and tries to kiss me EVERY DAY. Managers laugh.

In fact some young women outside the academic arena are facing even more severe abuse. According to a 2009 report, 'Dying to Belong', by the London-based Centre for Social Justice, young women in gang-impacted communities are 'often sexually exploited' and 'rape by gang members, as a form of reprisal or just because they can, is said to occur fairly frequently'. The report also states that young women 'are often passed around gang members [...] these roles have a devastating impact on girls and young women in gang-impacted communities, further reducing already very low self-esteem and worth'.

Isabel Chapman is assistant youth co-ordinator at Peabody, which provides young people's services, and has worked with several at-risk young women. According to her:

Not only are young women at risk of serious sexual violence from the entire gang they associate with, but also, increasingly, they are at risk of sexual violence and exploitation from rival gangs. Young women who may be involved in offending behaviour are conditioned to believe anything that happens to them within the gang is not reportable or insignificant because of their gang associations, therefore they become more socially excluded. This is an under-researched area and accessing the best ways to provide support to vulnerable at risk young women is a subject that needs more resources, funding and time allocated to it. If we are to address violence and sexual exploitation against young

women in Britain, there has to be a genuine change of culture. From the portrayal of young women in advertising and music videos, to the incredibly poor or non-existent sex education on our curriculum; because young women are constantly fed confusing messages about equality, sex and consent.

This problem remains under-examined in part because it's extremely difficult to access young women in these vulnerable circumstances, particularly without the risk of endangering them further. Their absence in this chapter simply reflects that obstacle of inaccessibility. I have chosen to look closely at the experiences of young women in higher education firstly because my visits to colleges and universities have brought me into such close contact with them; and secondly because the experiences of many young women not choosing the academic route are already reflected in the other chapters, from Women in Public Spaces to Women in the Workplace. In addition, I felt the topic merited closer attention because of the sheer multitude of project entries referencing it as a particularly hostile environment for women, with many pointing to 'lad culture' creating a breeding ground for misogyny specific to the student experience. It also bears closer examination as one of the key areas in which misogynistic attitudes may be forming and developing in the first place. But in no way should this be interpreted as an underestimation of the vast and complex problems faced by young women outside higher education, particularly those experiencing the heavy impact of gang culture. I hope this is an area into which I will be able to carry out further future research given the necessary resources.

At each visit to universities up and down the country to talk about the project, I distributed anonymous surveys to students. The idea was to get a sense of their experiences and gauge the status quo. I included questions about various forms of assault, from unwanted touching and groping to rape; and asked whether survey participants had been on the receiving end of sexism from fellow students or professors. In an empty train carriage rattling home in the dark after one of the first such visits, I spread the completed surveys out across the seats in front of me, read them and cried.

Of the forty female students who responded to the survey that day only two *hadn't* been groped or touched without their consent during their time at university. The bleak simplicity of the responses shook me. One student had circled 'YES' for the question 'During your time at university have you ever experienced sexism from university employees (e.g. Lecturers/Tutors etc.)' and had then written: 'Tutor groped me—' That extended dash felt like a kick in the stomach. It seemed to be a shrug of acceptance: what else was there to say?

Squeezed into the margin of one young woman's survey, and in response to no particular question, was the following:

I wish my society would stop making me feel guilty for being a woman, having a woman's body and the response I get for being alive and functioning, and no matter how I dress, for walking around in a woman's body and therefore getting what I deserve because having a figure means I get certain things from the world.

Several young women reported rape, with many communicating a sense of associated shame or embarrassment. One wrote:

A guy I was dating at the time forced himself on me without my consent. I don't like the word so I will underline it in the question. Unable to tell family – even to this day. Felt guilt for many years thinking I had led him on.

This sense of confusion about reporting and responsibility, not only concerning rape but also other forms of assault, was rife. On the topic of groping in nightclubs, survey respondents wrote:

[Abuse] happens so regularly and to so many people [...] there seems no outlet for reports/complaints.
It felt too trivial to report. Also I feared violence from drunk men if I reported [...] there and then in the nightclub.

So, even in situations in which somebody is groping them against their will, situations of sexual assault, situations in which they are so afraid of the perpetrator and feel so vulnerable that they fear violence, young women still respond from a position of defeat. Assault is considered 'trivial' – not worth reporting. Society has conditioned them to accept it simply as a part of life.

Where is it coming from, this idea of women as second-class citizens? Sadly there are many indicators in project entries and returned questionnaires that in addition to the plethora of external sources, such attitudes are also ingrained within our trusted educational institutions.

One of the biggest spikes in activity during the first year of the

Everyday Sexism Project came during Freshers' Week, when we were suddenly inundated with hundreds of entries from young women experiencing their first week at university. It started with a message from a student about to start studying physics at a highly respected London university. She forwarded me an email from the Physics Society, which had been sent to all first-year students:

Freshers' Lunch [...] This will be mainly a chance for you to scope out who's in your department and stake your claim early on the 1 in 5 girls.

Already studying a male-dominated subject – and as politicians and public figures around the country wrung their hands and muttered niceties about how to increase female participation in STEM subjects – here was a brand-new undergraduate being marked out as sexual prey; othered and set apart from her male peers during her very first week by an official university society.

And the othering of female students from official sources didn't end there. When several young women's entries mentioned their frustration at student nights expressly requiring them to dress as 'sluts' and 'slags', I started looking into the Freshers' Week events organized at universities across the country. Here are just a few of the ones I found:

Rappers and Slappers
Slag 'n' Drag
CEOs and Corporate Hoes
Golf Pros and Tennis Hoes

Tarts and Vicars
Pimps and Hoes
Geeks and Sluts

Over and over again, at events usually organized by university societies or student unions, young men and women are being sent the message that men are powerful, talented and successful while women are defined, every time, by their gender and sexual availability.

This is *not* about a prudish distaste of girls dressing as they choose. It's about the apparent *pressure* for them to do so – their lack of choice in the matter – which was highlighted by a huge number of the accounts we received. For boys, it seems, dressing up offers a fun chance to wear something kooky or tongue-in-cheek. For girls, it is about something else entirely.

One female student I interviewed told me:

We had an event as part of Freshers' Week where some of our friends went on stage. Loads of girls were lined up and they had to take all their clothes off – they were told to race to strip. Then there were competitions where you had to do various sex positions. They make it all out as a great thing but you get pushed into it and it's not a matter of choice.

It's very different for people who feel shy or more uncomfortable, because you don't have a choice – there were strict initiations and you had to do what everyone else did or you were just missed out.

Many of the Everyday Sexism Project entries echoed this combined sense of pressure and unease.

▸ One of the initiations into a social club within the first month of uni was to down a bottle of beer that a man was holding between his crotch. I didn't even realize what they were going to do as we were facing the other way when they shouted 'Down it bitch'. It was awful, but I felt like such a wet blanket with everyone cheering on [...]

For some the impact was even more extreme:

▸ One of the Freshers' events organized by our halls of residence was a 'girls and guys' pub crawl. We were split in to one group of 'girls' and one of 'guys' and each group went off on different pub crawl routes. All the girls were encouraged to wear pink and dress 'slutty'. We also had to come up with a 'slut name' which the older students encouraged us to write across our breasts. Upon arriving at each bar, one of the older students would shout out a word which was code for us to flash either our 'tits' or our 'arse' or dance in a seductive way in front of men in the pub. I didn't take part in this (or adopt a 'slut name') and was told that I was being too 'uptight' and not 'getting into the spirit of Freshers' Week'. The whole thing culminated in the 'girls and guys' meeting up in the student union, where we were informed that the older students had organized a competition with prizes. One prize was for the 'slut' who collected the most ties from the guys and one for the 'lad' who collected the most bras from the 'sluts'. I walked out on a scene of groups of drunk male students forcefully taking off the female students' bras.

On another occasion, I went out for the Freshers' night out

of one of the women's sports clubs. Our group bumped in to the men's rugby club in a bar. They were putting their freshers through their 'initiation ceremony'. All the rugby freshers had their trousers around their ankles and were standing in their boxers. They were encouraged to pick one of us to 'grind' with them (i.e. gyrate against them). One guy grabbed me and pulled me on to the dance floor and then told me I had to grind on him or else he'd have to do a forfeit. When I refused he told me I was frigid and grabbed a different fresher.

These two incidents made me feel extremely uncomfortable and alienated me from my fellow students [...] I couldn't believe I had come up against this kind of sexism in a university campus and it left me very disillusioned with higher education. These two 'fun events' ruined my Freshers' Week and left me feeling isolated and humiliated. I dropped out after two months.

This might seem like an extreme case, but it's by no means isolated – it was mirrored by thousands of similar accounts from young women realizing they were being left very few options during their first week of university. These young women were naturally keen to make friends and get along with everybody, but were thrust again and again into situations in which they were judged by their looks, their preparedness to dress 'slutty' and their willingness to perform highly sexualized 'initiation rituals'. And, while it's important to point out that there were a few young men who contacted us and described their discomfort at sexualized tasks (one, for example, was told to watch porn in his boxers while a female fresher sat on his lap to 'see if he got an erection'), the overwhelming majority of such demands were made of female freshers. Indeed, many of the men who wrote in to the project did so to express their own distress or frustration at seeing their female peers treated with so little respect.

Often this hyper-sexualization seemed to spill over from events and into a more general perception of female first years as sexual prey.

🐦 At my uni fresher's week, the 'crew' (designed to help new students) got points for scoring with freshers, especially virgins.

🐦 The boys who worked behind the Student Union bar used to play 'fuck a fresher' at freshers week. There was a points scoring system [...] bonus points if you brought the girl's knickers in, took her virginity [...]

It would seem the practice is so widely acknowledged that it has different nicknames around the country at different universities – from 'Fuck a Fresher' to 'Sharking' to 'Seal Clubbing'.

Going beyond the first week of university, experiences of sexism in higher education as a whole have formed one of the most commonly reported categories of the Everyday Sexism Project so far. In 2012 the Imperial College newspaper *Felix* published a 'joke' article that furnished male students with a pretend recipe for the date-rape drug Rohypnol, which was described as a 'fool-proof way' to make sure they'd have sex on Valentine's night 'for cheaper than the price of a hooker'. A 2013 article about 'slinging a bird' published in Liverpool's student newspaper the *Tab*, meanwhile, suggested that 'if you want to be a sly geez, slip your slice a little roofie and stick her in bed with one of your pals', 'wittily' adding: 'not that we condone the use of date rape drugs'. Good save, guys. For a second there, we almost thought you were misogynistic!

In 2011 an Exeter University society printed a 'shag mag' containing an article about how many calories men could burn in the course of stripping a woman naked without her consent. Elsewhere one student reported being given a printed set of 'rules' when he joined the university lacrosse team. It included the instruction: 'members don't date – that's what rape is for'.

During Freshers' Week 2013 a video was posted online showing eighty student leaders at St Mary's University in Canada chanting, 'Y is for "Your sister", O is for "Oh so tight", U is for "Underage", N is for "No consent", G is for "Grab that ass".' The story came just weeks after a poster advertising a freshers' event at Cardiff Metropolitan University prominently featured a picture of a T-shirt bearing the words: 'I was raping a woman last night and she cried'. Meanwhile a nightclub in Leeds promoted an event called Freshers Violation with an online video in which a presenter asked a male student: 'How are you going to violate a fresher tonight?' The student replied: 'She's going to get raped.'

To make matters worse, many university students have also reported direct experiences of sexism from their professors and tutors.

▶ I was in a lecture last week – IT systems. The lecturer put up a slide of 5 or so talking heads – people like Mark Zuckerburg and the founder of Google – and discussed their net worth. Then he pointed to the last picture – a blonde, attractive woman. He said: 'I put this one up especially for the girls. Anyone know who she is? [Silence] Well this is the late Steve Jobs' wife – worth X billion dollars by virtue of the man she married. So girls, stick to the IT guys – you never know, you might strike it rich.'

▶ I went to a talk at my University by an esteemed male professor who was giving advice on how to be a scientist. He said that if we want to succeed in academia as a scientist we needed 'male traits', those being competitiveness, confidence and impatience. Also mentioned that having children may be problematic career wise for women unless we had very understanding husbands. One female academic challenged him afterwards at question time and got dismissed. Left feeling very sad indeed.

This theme has cropped up again and again, reported by young women attending universities all over the world.

▶ In first-year physics class, the professor 'joked' to an audience of 150 students that a woman-physicist is like a guinea-pig (literal translation of guinea pig in Ukrainian = water pig): neither a pig, nor in the water (and hence, neither a woman, nor a physicist).

▶ I live in Mexico and a common phrase here is 'Calladita te ves mas bonita' (you look prettier when you shut up). I can't tell you how many times a professor at my university has said that to my classmates (all women, of course).

On many occasions such slurs are quite deliberate – like the engineering professor described in one project entry who unfailingly greeted the class with 'Good morning, gentlemen' while looking straight at the sole female student.

That Boris Johnson quip about women attending university to find someone to marry tapped into a much wider dismissal of women's academic aspirations. Luckily women around the world helped us enlighten the poor misinformed chap by kindly explaining on Twitter the reasons they had *actually* gone to university.

🐦 I went to university because I loved maths. Finding a husband never entered the equation.

🐦 I went to uni to study languages. No one actually told me they provided husbands too!

Some were clearly deeply concerned and pressed Boris for more of his invaluable insight...

🐦 I went to uni twice and still don't have a husband. Is it because I studied science? Advice appreciated.

🐦 As a lesbian, did I waste my time with that BA, MA and LLB? Should I cancel my PhD? Please advise.

🐦 Hello @MayorOfLondon. Which majors would attract husbands best? Should I find a kitchen at Uni and wait there? Please advise.

And men also joined the fray, lamenting:

🐦 Had to leave Uni as marriage-hungry women had forced me into forty weddings I couldn't pay for on a student loan.

🐦 Went to Uni to find a wife but couldn't find one amongst all the hard working, education driven women. Boris misled me!

These and more provided suitably clever ripostes to Johnson's sexism, but within an academic context it's not always so easy for a woman to fight back without jeopardizing her degree or even her potential career progress...

Project entries on this theme have poured in. After looking at her artwork, an external examiner told one student: 'I thought you were a man [...] but you should take that as a compliment.' Another was told by her lecturer that 'all the best female academics write like men'. One was repeatedly pestered for sex by a personal tutor with whom she had to meet weekly. Sometimes there was subtle, demoralizing gender bias; on other occasions the prejudice described was more overt.

▸ After approaching my tutor at university for help on an essay he had set (ironically) on 'Misogyny in Paradise Lost', he told me that I should be happy with a 2:1 because women couldn't get firsts as they weren't able to 'think outside of the box' like men. For every essay I wrote he gave me one mark off a first. He also told me 'not to go running to the department to complain' as 'girls' before me had. When I got a first for my degree I sent him a copy of my degree certificate.

Physical contact and unwanted sexual advances were also reported frequently.

▶ Senior lecturer and tutor wrapping his arm around my waist every time I went to speak to him and slapping the inside of my thigh to make a point.

▶ When I was a PhD student my supervisor had a bad reputation for being lecherous. He asked one of the women who worked in the office what her chest size was so he could buy her a jumper as a present. When I finished my thesis and had submitted he closed the door to his office and tried to kiss me when we were alone. I've also found out since he did this to a friend of mine as well. He shouldn't have a job in a reputable university.

As a society we are constantly questioning the issue with the 'pipeline' – asking how it is possible that girls achieve such fantastic grades at school and yet fall so far behind their male peers before they reach boardroom level. It's therefore vital that we look unflinchingly at how utterly different our young women's experiences of education are to those of their male peers, and how these differences are affecting them at this crucial period of academic and professional development.

▶ I have to wear high necklines or scarves to specific seminars in order to avoid a certain male lecturer staring down my top. As I feel uncomfortable being on my own with him, I do not ask him for help with work outside of lessons.

▸ At university my new lecturer asked me sexual questions and made a lot of sexual comments [...] it meant I didn't feel able to wait behind after class and ask him anything.

▸ Had an IT lecturer who would always sit very close on the bench to point out things you did wrong in your program (with 'casual' touches, etc.). I declined his invitation to an advanced programming group simply because I knew it was him leading that group. My friend joined it and was constantly groped but she suffered in silence because she wanted to excel at programming.

And there you have it writ large – succeed and learn at the cost of sexism, harassment, or at worst *sexual assault*. Or choose to avoid it, within a system that condones and allows it to continue, and suffer the detriment to your educational opportunities.

Another project entry revealed this very real risk:

▸ Last year, I was sexually harassed by one of my lecturers. He would routinely invade my personal space, tell me to rub my breasts against him, grab me, stare openly at my legs and breasts, and talk about sexually explicit topics in class instead of what was on the syllabus. One day after class, he asked me intrusive questions about my sex life to the point where he became visibly aroused. Finally, I told him to back off and he lost his temper with me.

I wound up filing a formal complaint after he started throwing away my work instead of returning it. I was told by members of staff that sexual harassment is something that happens to women in academia and that I simply needed to learn to put up with it. I was shunned by staff and students alike for being a troublemaker.

A year on, I'm still dealing with the fallout from the sexual harassment case. I am getting absolutely no support from the university – quite the opposite, in fact. It may sound naive, but I was shocked that, in 2012, female students at a world-class research university are still treated as second-class citizens and unwanted interlopers in a world created by and for men.

A similar bitter lesson was learned by Cambridge debater Rebecca Meredith when she took part in a prestigious student debating competition at Glasgow University in March 2013. She and her debating partner, Marelena Valles, were booed and shouted at throughout their speeches with sexual remarks and comments about their attractiveness – completely unrelated to the topic at hand. As Valles walked past at the end of the event, one young male competitor shouted, 'Get that woman out of my chamber!'

Perhaps most depressing of all was the taste Meredith got of the media treatment of women in politics when the story was reported in the national press, which she described to me as more upsetting even than the event itself.

Journalists were eager to claim that we were 'left in tears' by the proceedings (something which is factually false), and chose *not* to mention that we challenged the individuals involved and the organizers. Even within the media we were being portrayed as women who were deeply upset that men had shouted a few things at us. One newspaper completely changed the story – in their

version of events, we ran away crying because a boy called us ugly. [But] we weren't upset: we were furious!

Who could blame her if her political aspirations were, at best, seriously deflated and at worst abandoned? And what a blow for the political sphere, so desperate for fresh blood and a diverse intake, to lose at a single stroke these girls – and goodness knows how many more – who gave up, quite understandably, for other pursuits, when the abuse began to outweigh the benefit?

Outside the lecture hall or the debating chamber, an epidemic of sexist jokes, behaviours and harassment means that young women are learning these lessons daily in other contexts too.

The sexualized initiations and 'slut'-, 'slag'- or 'hoe'-themed events blend seamlessly into the backdrop of a youth culture increasingly saturated with sexism, normalized harassment and an ever-growing social acceptance of sexual assault and rape. This is a culture in which 'Spotted' and 'Confessions' pages on social networks have proliferated faster than you can count: pages where students are encouraged to write in and 'rate my shag'; pages with graphic and explicit descriptions of participants' peers and sexual experiences – often with names tagged, often including photographs taken or used without consent, almost always with female students the butt of the joke.

This is a culture that has seen websites like Uni Lad and the Lad Bible flourish. Here, across hundreds of articles almost exclusively about women, not a single female name appears. They are replaced with 'wench', 'slut', 'slag', 'hoe', 'tramp', 'slapper', 'bint', 'MILF', 'bird', 'gash', 'clunge', 'chick', 'pussy', 'bitch', 'whore', 'skank', 'cunt'... Here, 'lads' are encouraged to describe sexual conquests in the most aggressive way possible, reducing women to scores ('I was banging a solid 5/10') and ridiculing the 'wenches' afterwards. Here, women who don't want to sleep with a man are described as 'nobstacle courses', as if the idea of finding a way around their lack of consent is an entertaining game; here, users post comments about 'smashing virgins and having the bloodstains to prove it' and articles say '85 per cent of rape cases go unreported... that seems to be fairly good odds'. These sites, when challenged, tend to say (in the words of one, Holyland Lad Stories), 'Get a f*ckin grip. We'r havin a bit of harmless banter!'

One post on a 'lad' Facebook page boastfully and graphically describes a man knocking a woman 'clean out with one smack' and leaving 'her for dead on the side of the road'. A picture of Lady Gaga is captioned 'Smash or Dash?' One of the top-rated comments reads: 'Smash in the face with a brick.' Harmless banter indeed.

This word, 'banter', has become central to a culture that encourages young men to revel in the objectification, sexual pursuit and ridicule of their female peers – it is a cloak of humour and irony that is used to excuse mainstream sexism and the normalization and belittling of rape and intimate-partner violence. And it is incredibly effective, because – as we know – pretending that something is 'just a joke' is a powerful silencing tool, making those who stand up to it seem staid and isolated. But, as one young woman I interview explains:

140

I don't find it funny. These pages are not pages for jokes. There are no punch lines. They are not sexist jokes; they are just displays of sexism, displays of misogyny [...] I find it threatening, I find it terrifying [...] This is not banter.

What kind of 'banter' is it when young women regularly feel routinely humiliated and terrified for speaking out against their own objectification? These websites are symptomatic of a wider culture that is increasingly silencing young women, demeaning their ambitions and ideas and reducing them, again and again, to sex objects there to be used and judged and put in their place by their male peers.

And what of those male peers? It is important to say that, as with the wider point about the project not vilifying all males, misogyny is by no means a universal characteristic amongst university-age men. Many describe standing up to this 'lad culture', saying it sickens them as much as it does their female peers. But they are usually isolated in their intervention, and rarely report a successful outcome, suggesting that these often aggressive attitudes, though not universally shared, nonetheless dominate university discourse and experience.

▶ Couple weeks ago male friend says '9 out of 10 people enjoy gang-rape'. I call him out on sexism, calling him disgusting, he shrugs saying it was a 'joke'.

▶ A couple days ago a girl in the year below walked past. After she was about 20m away a guy in my year came up to me and asked,

'What do ya reckon is the arse on that?' I refused to comment saying it was wrong and that no woman wants their body judged in that way. His not-so-witty response is that, 'If they didn't want their arses to be judged they wouldn't have them in the first place!'

By this stage, what some young men are exhibiting is the potent culmination of exposure to a vast variety of misogynistic influences, from the tabloid press to lads' mags, online pornography to the Lad Bible, compounded by a glaring absence of education to offset the prejudicial attitudes formed as a result.

In a student culture promoting the increasingly militant silencing of girls' voices and objections, there is often little to challenge such attitudes as they flourish (and any objection is conveniently deflected by the stereotype of whining, moaning women). Meanwhile this cocktail of prejudice is mixed against the normalizing wider backdrop of yet more gender imbalance and casual sexism, as street harassment and similar displays of chauvinism are routinely witnessed. From seeing disparate pieces of women's bodies co-opted to advertise products, to hearing them referred to as mere numbers on a scale out of ten, these young men have been encouraged at every turn to dehumanize their female peers and classmates and to consider them merely as objects.

In just the same way that it is wrong to blame the victims of sexism, it is important too to acknowledge the extent to which these cultural factors combine to powerfully persuade young men that aggressive sexism is their expected role.

Of course, it would be inappropriately glib to suggest that these influences naturally translate into a direct impetus to assault female students, but it would be equally facetious not to consider their role in providing a backdrop against which such abuse is normalized and regularly condoned.

Discussing online 'lad' sites, National Union of Students women's officer Kelley Temple told me:

It's publicly normalizing a culture where people are gloating about committing crimes against women and that's being seen as something funny, seen as something to laugh about, to share.

Emma Carragher, Chair of the Cardiff University Women's Association, agrees:

Firstly, it encourages sexual assault – it becomes 'banter' – and secondly, it stops women from reporting it. Because sexual assault has become so normalized [...] Report rates are so low not because sexual assault isn't happening (ask any female student and she'll have a story of a friend or a friend of a friend's assault) but because women aren't reporting it.

Large numbers of project entries seem to confirm this impact, as a widespread sense of entitlement to female students' sexuality ensues:

▶ Another student at college outright told me I was having sex with him that night. I refused and told him that I'm still a virgin and want to find the right guy, and he was calling me a slag, a slut, a whore, for refusing to sleep with him and wanting to keep my virginity.

I thought that was the end of it until a few days later in a club, when he just appeared, straddled himself across my legs and started pinning me against the seat forcing kisses on me, and putting his hand down my underwear trying to finger me, and said, 'Now I've got you.' My friends came over when they saw and he quickly fled.

The impact is vast and wide. Again and again these sexist experiences – whether they involve events and initiations, lecturers and tutors or other students – seem to be having a very real impact on female students' experiences of university and college. They miss events altogether or attend and feel upset and anxious. They miss out on extra courses or opportunities for academic help. Their lecture attendance and use of the campus library is affected. This is not just 'banter'. This is not a 'harmless' trend.

A 2010 survey of 2000 female university students by the National Union of Students revealed that 1 in 7 respondents had 'experienced a serious physical or sexual assault during their time as a student'. Meanwhile 16 per cent had experienced 'unwanted kissing, touching or molesting', and 68 per cent had 'been a victim of one or more kinds of sexual harassment on campus during their time as a student'.

More worryingly still, the reporting rate was devastatingly low – just 4 per cent of female students who were seriously sexually assaulted reported it to their institution, and just 10 per cent to the police. Most pertinently of all, in this climate of normalized sexism and assault, of those who did not report serious sexual assault to the police, 50 per cent said it was because they felt 'ashamed or embarrassed, and 43 per cent 'because they thought they would be blamed for what had happened'.

Another project entry clearly displays the connection between this slut-shaming, rape-blurring culture and victims feeling unable to report:

▶ I was 19 and went on a school trip out of town. We all had some drinks and I accidentally locked myself out of my hotel room, and knocked on the trip leader's room to get help. I trusted him. He asked me in and, after I had thrown up everywhere, invited me to sleep in his bed with him. I passed out and woke up to him licking my vagina. I was confused and afraid. In the morning I realized he had raped me while I was unconscious; I was covered in bruises and my vagina and anus hurt.

I told the university and several members of staff blamed me for drinking. The rapist told my friends I was a slut and wanted it. No one believed me, and people thought I was trying to get attention.

That was three years ago and I still haven't reported it to the police.

Many entries described the normalization of discussions and jokes about raping girls. One young woman was in a car with four boys she knew when

▶ [...] one of the boys started joking about gang raping me and saying really vulgar and inappropriate things. All of the boys started laughing and I told him to stop and it wasn't funny. He continued to make the comments and kept talking about raping me. I felt very threatened [...] I told some friends afterwards but no one really seemed to care. I felt like I had overreacted but I had been really scared.

And, most hurtful of all, those young women who did suffer sexual assault or rape came up against the widespread belief that they must have deserved it, and were thus re-victimized by a confused incapacity to understand the idea of rape as a crime: the message, loud and clear, was that this must have been their own fault.

▶ I was raped in my second year of university. I had some great support from my family, and some great therapy. I thought this was the worst part, but when I felt safe enough to tell my friends, the questions started. 'Was I drunk?' 'Was I dressed sluttily?' 'Did I know him?' 'Had I led him on?' It broke my heart.

One second-year university student I speak to wearily describes the culture of sexism as 'subtle, difficult to really pinpoint and therefore almost impossible to tackle'. She notices a plethora of gendered insults – 'slut', 'whore', 'slag' – and says rape jokes are 'prolific'. When I ask her whether groping and unwanted sexual touching are common experiences, she replies:

It's not a common experience, it's an inevitable one. I don't know any girl at university who hasn't been touched or groped without their consent. I also don't know any girl at university who would consider it assault or report it.

Sadder still, though, is talking to this incredibly bright, intelligent young woman about the impact this culture has had on her personal ambitions and aspirations.

I'm actively political, involved in political societies at university and would consider myself relatively well informed. Sometimes I use Facebook or social media to share articles, or post things about political issues I feel passionately about – as do many of my male friends. They, however, do not receive comments like, 'I'm sure you know what you're talking about but please shut up', or indirect insults describing them as 'net-mum-aspiring bints' or 'ugly, angry feminists'.

It makes her think twice about engaging in the debate, she says. She has been involved in the Labour Party Society at university, of which she's been appointed vice president, but the culture of sexism surrounding her has made her reconsider her future plans. She points out – pragmatically, depressingly – that

The lads involved are intelligent, educated men who will go on to be leaders in industry, in politics, etc. If this behaviour and these attitudes go unchecked then they will pervade into all aspects of business and life in the future. Just as it seemed the 'boys' clubs' in industries were disappearing, 'lad culture' is forming new ones. Career-wise, I think it impacts women; and I've experienced this personally, when considering a career in the public eye. Looking at how women are treated in the media and how female politicians are discussed and insulted […] It makes it a lot harder to seriously consider a future in politics.

She isn't alone. Perhaps the greatest indicator of all that young women are suffering a barrage of inequalities threatening to impact on them in the very long term is their own appraisal of their future prospects across a wide range of different fields. This is starkly revealed by the student questionnaires I've collated.

I want to go into academia. Very white male dominated. Have experienced frequent sexism. Feels like a boys club.

As a science student, men are a lot more desirable to employers. I feel as a woman I would be taken less seriously than male applicants.

I think to go into the media, especially presenting, you have to be 'pretty' when men do not. Women presenters are also youthful, while men can work until an older age. You have to be a sort of 'sex symbol'.

I want to be an MP which is an incredibly male area.

I feel that men are deemed to be the 'professional' sex whereas stereotypes of 'weak', 'unintelligent' women definitely still remain.

Another describes how the media image of women has stunted her dreams before she has begun to pursue them:

I'm really passionate about being a war correspondent but I am scared about the expectations of the media. I am a size 10 yet

sadly I fear I may be too 'big' to be noticed for broadcasting, even if I stand in front of the camera with a bulletproof vest on.

Young women, it would seem, are being bombarded from every angle. In addition to facing normalized sexual harassment and assault, they are some of the biggest targets for the media portrayal of 'perfect', sexualized, sanitized, thin, white, blonde, large-breasted beauty. On top of everything else, they are juggling a raft of unrealistic expectations so vast it threatens to swamp them.

▸ It's almost every magazine and media outlet making me feel inferior and consumed with self-hatred because I do not fit some Photoshopped ideal. It's a culture that wants me to shut up and be pretty, that urges me to 'appear less intelligent' so I will attract more men, a culture that insists I must be miserable because I am single, that I'm not worth it on my own as I am. It's women's past being ignored and overlooked in the history books, it's our literature, art and music being a 'niche': it's our whole lives being seen as secondary, other, lesser – not equal.

It is devastating to hear them sum it all up – this perfect storm of media objectification, cultural dismissal and prevalent abuse. This is a young woman in our twenty-first-century society. This is her reality.

▸ I'm sick of walking home from Uni at 6pm and getting harassed every time; from people shouting things or making fellatio gestures out of their cars because they think they're 'funny' or that I should be 'flattered', or the people in the street who make kissing noises when I walk past, or shout 'slut' or 'get your tits out' at me. Flattering? How is that flattering? I'm on the verge of tears every time I get home.

When I go to a club, no matter if I wear something modest, or something that society deems 'slutty', I will get grabbed by someone, who thinks by doing so, I'll find them attractive, or I should take it as a compliment. I'm left feeling violated, and as if it's my fault. Why is it my fault? Because I'm a woman? Because I'm in a dress? Because I should be expecting it?

I'm tired of my voice being undermined because of my gender. I'm tired of having a man explain to me that I'm overreacting, when he has no idea what it's like. I'm tired of being told, when I'm angry, that I'm a pushy bitch, or that I must be menstruating. I'm tired of being called a slut, because I have sex, or because I don't have sex and reject the advances of some man in a club. I'm tired of having to watch my behaviour, watch what I wear, what I drink, where I go and be extra-careful to avoid harassment or worse, which is just going to happen no matter what I do. I'm tired of watching women be blamed for rape, that they should have seen it coming, shouldn't have drunk so much, shouldn't have worn that, could have prevented it, didn't shout loud enough, didn't fight back hard enough.

How can I believe the people that say women have equal rights? When the worst insult a man can be called is a woman, girly, a twat, a tit, a cunt, that he needs to 'man up' and the list goes on. My gender is not an insult. I'm tired of all this shit.

Chapter 5

Women in Public Spaces

'I committed the terrible crime of being female and out in public on my own'
Everyday Sexism Project entry

Vital Statistics

43 per cent of women in London aged 18 to 34 experienced
sexual harassment in public in the past year
YouGov, 2012

87 per cent of American women aged 18 to 64 have been
harassed by a male stranger
Penn Schoen Berland Associates, 2000

More than half of American women aged 18 to 64 have
experienced 'extreme harassment', including being grabbed,
touched, rubbed or followed
Penn Schoen Berland Associates, 2000

83 per cent of Egyptian women report experiencing sexual
harassment in the street
Egyptian Center for Women's Rights, 2008

95 per cent of women in Delhi feel unsafe in public spaces
International Center for Research on Women
and UN Women, 2013

More than 80 per cent of Canadian women have experienced
male stranger harassment in public
Macmillan, Nierobisz and Welsh, 2000

🐦 If you think whistling at me for my 'nice ass' is going to make me swoon, then by golly, mister, you sure know women.

🐦 Group of four men all slap my bum and laugh as I am forced to walk past them (on my own) to get off a late-night tube train.

🐦 Wouldn't flirt back to group of youths so they spat in my face.

🐦 When I was 14 I was walking down the street and a man grabbed one of my breasts. I was shocked and felt ashamed.

🐦 Guy simulated masturbating on my face on packed bus. Next month it happened for real, again no one said anything.

🐦 A man last night stopped me in the street and asked, 'Do you ride a bike?' I shook my head and he said, 'OK then, why don't you ride me.' Obviously I had sex with him instantly and we're getting married.

It's nearly 8.30 a.m. and I'm going to be late because I've stopped to change my clothes again. I'd wanted to wear a pencil skirt, because I'm going straight to a friend's birthday after work and would have liked to have been a bit dressed up, so I'd put that on at first. But then I remembered the group of men who'd been lined up along the wall outside my office eating their sandwiches yesterday, and the excruciating embarrassment of their detailed comments on my breasts and bottom. So the pencil skirt is now lying across the back of a chair, discarded. I don't *think* there's any way my second choice – office trousers with a blouse – could be interpreted as an invitation for sexual appraisal, but I'm not fully comfortable until I add the chunky jumper on top. Extra armour. Just in case. I grab my bike helmet and head for the door.

I'm cycling faster than usual to make up time but I still remember not to use the street where the traffic's particularly bad at this time in the morning. I'll avoid the worst of the beeping horns that way. I'm running through my notes for the morning meeting in my head, so I don't see the group of men in high-viz jackets standing by the side of the road until a sudden shout makes me jump out of my skin, swerving dangerously into the path of the car coming up behind me. I force my bike back onto an even keel, my heart pounding and my hands shaking.

'Look at those tits!' 'I would.' 'Nice view, love!' 'Alright, darling?'

It is not even 8.45 a.m. My face is only half visible, obscured by my helmet. This is the second day in a row that such harassment has ruined my journey to work. Everybody has a tipping point. With a sudden, impulsive rush of fury, I screech to a halt (almost causing another accident as the cyclist behind swerves to avoid me). Wrenching my bike up onto the pavement, I storm over to the now-apprehensive-looking group of men and ask them, pleadingly, idealistically, to imagine how it would feel if *they* had been unable simply to reach their workplace that morning without enduring the sharp embarrassment of having their physique, their sexual merit, publicly commented on and appraised for all to hear. How might it impact their day to continue to work feeling dirty and ashamed and scared?

The men look at each other and laugh. 'You want to calm down, love.'

Adrenalin is coursing through my body. The act of the confrontation is absolutely, exquisitely terrifying. There are four or five of them, and only one of me. With shaking hands I pull out my mobile phone and dial the company number displayed on the side of the lorry parked next to them. The men start to look concerned. One of them says: 'Now hang on...'

I hold the phone to my ear. My trembling fingers have misdialled the number. A tinny arpeggio sounds, then, repeatedly: 'We're sorry. The number you have dialled has not been recognized. Please check and try again.' The men are watching me closely.

'Yes, hello,' I say brusquely, drowning out the tone. 'I'd like to report a group of your workers sexually harassing me on the corner of ------- Road and ------- Street. They very nearly caused a road-traffic accident. Yes. Yes. Thank you.' The men have retreated into the cab of the van. They look utterly bewildered.

When I reach the office, I google the company name as the adrenalin slowly subsides, leaving a sick, weak feeling. The manager who answers my call says he is extremely grateful that I got in touch. 'I know exactly which team you are talking about,' he tells me. 'We know it happens, but unless people report it there's very little we can do. They'll be seriously reprimanded when they get back tonight.'

Until that day, in summer 2008, it had never occurred to me that the convoluted routes and extra precautions, the changed clothes and hastily swept-up hair were anything other than ordinary. Planning strategies to get through the day with the least possible exposure to unwanted attention and harassment was simply a part of being a woman that I accepted; as much of a necessary routine as carrying a spare tampon in my purse.

Of the tens of thousands of women's experiences collected by the Everyday Sexism Project, some 8,000 of them at the time of writing describe street harassment – experiences of sexism, sexual harassment and even assault in public spaces. In 2013, in a country where we'd like to believe women are as free as men to go where they like, when they like, the reality is that thousands of women are running a daily gauntlet of harassment that leaves some 'terrified to go out or walk home at night'.

When I started the #ShoutingBack hashtag on Twitter to invite people to share their experiences, thousands of stories flooded in within a matter of days, revealing the true extent of street harassment and the frequency with which it impinges on women's lives: 'Every day since I was 14', 'I've lost count of the number of times', 'Too many times to mention', 'At least once a week and often much more, regardless of what I wear, where I am, how I behave'… One woman said:

🐦 There isn't a day in Southeast London where I don't get shouted at, followed or stared down. It's like a disease.

In fact, street harassment is happening so frequently that many women report it simply becoming a part of their daily experience – and when something becomes part of your daily experience the danger is that you'll simply come to accept it as normal.

🐦 The sad fact is that now I just expect to be harassed or followed on my way home from a night out.

🐦 The women in my life tell me to ignore sexual harassment because 'they went through it too'.

🐦 My 14 [-year-old] gets cat called and whistled at so often walking to school she thinks it's just part of life.

There is a common misconception, particularly among those who do not personally experience it, that street harassment is restricted to gentle praise, or a cheeky comment here and there. 'Just learn to take a compliment' we often hear; 'a wolf whistle or two is just 'harmless fun'. One woman describes how after being 'followed home walking from school, I was told, "It's not as bad as getting raped so get over it".'

An instance of verbal harassment isn't a simple, single experience. It isn't even just about the person insulting or propositioning you. It's the shock of the initial approach, which often gets your attention with a visibly unpleasant jolt. It's the prickle of embarrassment when that makes your harassers laugh. It's the unease of suddenly re-evaluating your safety. It's the discomfort when they mention your breasts or your legs and you start panicking, mentally checking your clothing choices – despite the fact that you're in absolutely no way responsible for what's happening. It's the horrible burning shame of imagining that, since your legs or your breasts or your bum are being so loudly commented on, everybody within earshot is probably now staring at them. It's the guilt (as counterintuitive as that might sound) of wondering whether those people are now also judging you for being sexually evaluated in public. It's the fear, when the harassers you ignore start shouting that you're a bitch, a slut, a whore. It's the sense of dirty, overwhelming shame when nobody stops to help you and the message their silence sends is: 'You deserve this. This is not unjust enough to warrant my intervention. This is normal. This is what happens to women. Get used to it.' And it's the impact afterwards: as you begin to associate your own body parts with the unsolicited judgements that strangers have passed on them; as you reassess yourself and consider a change of style or clothing or – in the case of some women – even *body shape* to avoid going through the same thing again. (One project entry described a fifteen-year-old girl who was 'so depressed about constant harassment' that she 'begged' her mother for a breast reduction.)

Street harassment is *not* friendly flattery.

It begins with the shouting. The yelling, calling, summoning, whistling, evaluating and insulting. The boundaries between 'compliment' and curse are fluid and unpredictable; countless women have described cries of 'Hey sexy!' and 'Come here...' switching suddenly to 'Stupid slut' or even 'YOU WHORE, I'LL BEAT YOU SO HARD' when they declined to respond.

And from verbal harassment the sliding scale progresses. The sheer number of women who have described not just verbal but physical and sexual assault in public spaces is shocking. You can trace this escalation through the project entries: men 'touching me, rubbing against me' becomes 'took a photo up my skirt and ran off'; from 'Yeah, I'd fuck that' and 'Look at the tits on that' to 'sticks his hand between my legs and gropes me'; from 'being rubbed, dry humped or groped on a crowded train' to 'grabbed from behind by a man demanding my underwear'. The stories go on, and on, and on.

What the project entries make obvious is that every aspect of street harassment is interconnected. There is no 'harmless'. There is no invisible line beneath which it's just fine to sexually appraise and force unwanted verbal or physical attention on a woman but above which it crosses into abuse. Since I started the project, countless Twitter users, cyberspace trolls and even journalists have asked, again and again, 'Why make a fuss about something as minor as a wolf whistle or a catcall?' One *Daily Mail* journalist even spent nearly forty-five minutes circling back to the question, wheedling, trying to get me to admit that it was all just a bit of fun.

Why make such a fuss?

Because street harassment is perhaps the clearest manifestation of the spectrum of sexism, sexual harassment and sexual assault that exists within our society. Yes, it starts out small; but allowing those 'minor' transgressions gives licence to the more serious ones, and eventually to all-out abuse. We've heard the same words and phrases crossing over and echoing and repeating, from women who are shouted at in the street to women who are assaulted and women who are victims of domestic violence in their own homes. The language is the same. And if we say it's acceptable for men to assume power and ownership over women they don't know verbally in public, then, like it or not, we're also saying something much wider about gender relations – something that carries over into our personal relationships and our sexual exchanges. Because this is a line that doesn't need to be blurred. It should be clear and simple. Take it from the women whose experiences started out with just a little 'harmless' street harassment – a sexual 'compliment' or a wolf whistle, or a 'Hey baby' – but then turned nasty, became full-blown attacks. Ask them what the problem is with a harmless bit of fun.

🐦 Harassment started on the street, asking if I was married, ended with sexual assault on my doorstep at 3pm.

And, crucially, in fact, screaming a judgement about someone's fanny as you speed past in a fast car is *never* really a 'compliment'. People who shout at women in the street don't do it because they think there's a chance the woman will drop her shopping, willy-nilly, and leap into their arms! It *isn't* a compliment – and to call it that disparages the vast majority of lovely men who are perfectly able to pay a *real* compliment. It is an exertion of power, dominance and control.

And it's utterly horrifying that we've become so used to it that it's considered the norm.

▶ I was flashed twice on my route home, I was groped between my legs in a club, and had a man masturbate whilst telling me he wanted to suck on my tits in the street in broad daylight. I was walking home from a grief counselling session. Countless shouted comments about how un/attractive I am over the years [...] I consider myself lucky, relatively.

When we discussed street harassment on Twitter using the #ShoutingBack hashtag, some women said the saddest thing about the conversation was that they identified with almost every experience being shared. One woman wrote simply:

The only story I will share is that it started for me in sixth grade. Every day.

The problem isn't confined to only a small number of women – and certainly not only to 'hot' women, or women who dress or act in a certain way, or go to certain places at certain times of day. These myths are part of the victim-blaming culture that protects aggressors while placing guilt on their victims. A 2012 survey by YouGov for the End Violence Against Women Coalition revealed that a staggering 43 per cent of young women in London (aged between 18 and 34) had experienced sexual harassment in public spaces in the last year alone. Our reports concern a huge age range, from children as young as seven to women in their seventies and eighties. Many women have written to us in disbelief, finding it hard to cope with the fact that their daughters and granddaughters are now putting up with the same ordeals they faced themselves. They ask me, 'Is it really still going on?'

And often this weary normalization goes a step further, as women begin to internalize the perceived public attitudes towards them and their bodies.

🐦 The reason I hate my breasts is due to the unwanted attention they attract. I try to cover them up.

🐦 There are times I wish I wasn't female because I'm fed up of being scared of walking down the street on my own.

This sense of self-blame and the lengths to which women go to try to avoid street harassment was a recurring theme.

▶ Walk down the street with eyes on the ground, hood pulled up, and never leave the house dressed provocatively because I cannot stand the attention of cat-calls, honking horns.

🐦 I want to take up jogging but without a buddy too intimidated due to previous experience of heckling.

▶ I do things like put my hair up in a certain way that means it's hard to be grabbed at or if I'm really scared holding my keys between my fingers [...] I wear my headphones with the music turned up in town so I don't have to hear catcalls. I walk at a certain distance from groups of men in front of me. If they are behind me I take a different route. This is all just normal to me now. It's normal for a lot of women I know. It's everyday.

Women describe the emotional and psychological ways in which street harassment affects them to an extent that those who do not experience it might struggle to imagine.

🐦 Sexual remarks made to me when obviously pregnant made me feel like my unborn daughter was being molested.

🐦 Men 'just having fun' yelling abuse (often sexual) at me in the street has been known to trigger panic attacks.

🐦 The annoying part about street harassment is the feeling that I should then change myself. I victim blame me.

One woman's description of a single week's harassment in public spaces started like this:

▸ In the last week, I have had comments about my appearance at least every day. I have had three different men try to get me to go home with them, including one man who stated: 'I will fuck you and then you can fuck off home.' I was spanked by two different individuals, had my hair pulled and [was] pinned against a wall by another in a night club.

Yet, despite experiencing such aggressive abuse, her account ended with her taking the blame upon herself:

▸ It makes me feel so used up [...] I'm tired of it. I'm 26 now and sometimes I hate myself so much.

The ingrained public acceptability of street harassment is clear from the hundreds of stories we received of perpetrators becoming aggressive and violent when women tried to stand up to them or even simply ignored them. The phenomenon suggests that they are so accustomed to feeling entitled to harass women that they feel angry when such behaviour is denied.

🐦 A man in the street groped me then got angry and threw a brick at me when I protested. It missed me and hit my Mum.

🐦 Held against a wall because I refused to kiss a man much older than me when I was 16.

🐦 Propositioned by 3 older men [...] when I ignored them, one hit so hard across my upper thigh it bruised badly.

And another, and another, and another. These were not isolated incidents. There were countless reports – from women who'd rejected unwanted catcalls and had men hitting them, throwing objects, or trying to back their cars into them; and from others whose harassers physically pursued them, threatening violence and rape.

▸ Man leant from car window to ask directions, I said I was running for train (true) so he drove on pavement and pinned me against shop window, I had to clamber over bonnet to escape, him swearing at me.

Many women reported perpetrators expressing their sense of entitlement outright, reacting with apparent shock (and not a hint of self-awareness or irony) when their victim tried to deny them the 'right' to harass and touch them.

🐦 At a club, last year. Repeatedly groped. Told him to back off. He grabbed me roughly and said women can't talk to men like that.

🐦 Man put his hand up my skirt when walking down the road. Shouted at him that he had no right to touch me. He seemed shocked.

🐦 Walking home, guy stopped me, grabbed my breasts and tried to kiss me. I yelled at him, he looked shocked and annoyed.

It's really no wonder that our sense of tolerance becomes so entrenched: many entries we've received suggest that street harassment starts at a terrifyingly young age.

🐦 When I was 9 a man asked 'the girl with the dick sucking lips' to come here.

Another girl told us that she was aged just thirteen when a group of men in a van pulled over and asked her if she had a 'tight pussy'. She didn't even understand what they were talking about.

🐦 I started experiencing crude, cruel street harassment as soon as I started growing breasts at 12.

🐦 Stood on pavement with friend & van driver honks, it's been the usual since age 12 walking in school uniform.

So from an incredibly young age girls are being sent the message that it is normal – simply part of being female – to be sexually addressed, judged and commented on by strangers in the street. The impact this has on girls' developing sense of self and of their place in the world should not be underestimated. One project contributor clearly explained the effect such incidents had had on her ideas about the future:

▶ I am only just a teenager and it's horrifying, especially when it involves grown men honking at me in the street [...] I dress appropriately [...] In fact, even when I'm in my school uniform things like that happen. It's utterly embarrassing, and makes me fearful of things such as rape.

Not only is this girl, in her very early teens, already forming a causal link between women's choice of clothing and the harassment they receive, but she's also clearly connecting the entitlement strangers feel to her young body with a fear of sexual violence and assault. These are the formative experiences of young girls. These are the messages street harassment sends them. Men have the right to sexually appraise you in public. You are valued on the basis of what you look like and whether you provide men with sexual pleasure. If you dress in a particular way, you are bringing it on yourself and are at fault – but even if you don't, it is still something normal that will happen to you. You will experience shame. It is the precursor to the possibility of even more aggressive physical possession of your body in the future.

Just a harmless compliment.

And, of course, while the regularity and normalization of women's harassment in public spaces sends these formative messages to young girls, boys are learning from them too. Many of the accounts we have received detailed street harassment performed in front of young children, both accompanying the victim and the perpetrator. One woman told us of how, in the supermarket, one man commented to another:

🐦 'She obviously likes black c**k' [...] in front of my 8-year-old mixed-race son.

Another woman described a man who sexually harassed her from a van before he 'turned and laughed', 'winking' at the boy of five or six sitting next to him.

These inherently potent messages about gender-biased power and control surely help to shape the way our children see the world around them. We understand how it works: the everyday becomes the accepted norm, accommodated in the way we live; by making this allowance we reinforce the idea of acceptability and compound the sense of entitlement; that assumed prerogative is then exercised to an ever-increasing degree; and naturally we then find ourselves with even more of an everyday problem... To tackle street harassment, we have to break through that pernicious circle. We have to abandon the mistaken idea that street harassment is nothing more than a minor inconvenience, or a compliment taken the wrong way.

Encouragingly, there are definite indicators that speaking out about the problem – naming it and describing it, thrusting it, in all its forms, into the limelight – does have a positive impact.

For example, during our #ShoutingBack discussion, while women expressed their resignation and lack of surprise at the stories being shared, men were speaking up, voicing shock and outrage and, crucially, pledging to take action to tackle the problem.

🐦 I had no idea that these things happened to women walking the streets day or night. I am shocked after reading some tweets.

🐦 Makes me realize as a man who hates this crap, how much more there is to do. WE are the ones who can influence.

🐦 Definitely think the awareness is useful from a male point of view. Has definitely led to me thinking more about what I say and do.

Similar stories of realization and resolution are regularly posted to the project website.

▶ I've spent 15 or so very depressing minutes reading through the stories here being left shocked at the behaviour and attitude of some of the members of my own sex [...] Ordinarily I would be the first to suggest that surely such incidents of sexism are the exception rather than the norm but I feel less confident about that statement having read through these pages... It seems to me what is needed is that society (particularly the males who are not offenders) is to shout up or intervene when we hear and see instances of sexism. As only by all of us saying and demonstrating that this is not acceptable will we change things.

Opening our eyes is the first step. Once we understand the scale and severity of the problem, we then have to act – and to see success we need to act together. The project entries we've received overwhelmingly suggest that, as with other forms of abuse and bullying, perpetrators of street harassment are often able to get away with it because others simply turn a blind eye.

🐦 2pm on a main road a man groped me. When I screamed no one bothered to help, they all looked away as he casually walked on.

🐦 Standing on crowded London bus in summer, seated man puts his hand up my skirt. I shout for help. Not one person responds.

🐦 Sat on train, man sits puts hand up my skirt [and] tries to convince me to go with him. Loudly protest, no one helps.

🐦 Crowded bus stop, loudly invited by man to 'sit on his face' [...] No one reacted. I was 14.

To ignore what is happening is to be complicit, which perpetuates and exacerbates the problem by effectively telling harassers that they may act with impunity.

🐦 A guy leaned out of his car and shouted that the guy behind me was going to rape me. The guy behind me laughed.

Such inaction impacts long after the incident itself. Not just by offering sanction to harassers but also by suggesting to victims that the abuse they have received is somehow deserved and their problem to deal with. When I walk down the street and a man shouts sexually explicit comments about my breasts, or what he'd like to do to me – often referring to me as an object ('Look at the tits on *that!*') – it's not the comments that sting the longest, but the memory of the person on the other side of the road who kept walking, diligently scrutinizing their shoes.

As one woman described:

▶ [I was] cornered on a train in a two-person seat by a man who came on very strong and touched me, which I repeatedly, loudly objected to. When he refused to let me out for several minutes I tried to escape past him feeling incredibly scared – and he grabbed my behind with both hands. I screamed at him in shock and disgust and went to sit with a family further down the carriage, tears in my eyes. Everyone in the carriage had seen and heard what he'd done and how I protested. He continued to sit in the same seat and no-one reacted in any way. I went home feeling terrified, violated and dirty.

It's not always easy for passers-by to intervene, just as it's not always easy for women being harassed to stand up for themselves. The same complicating factors may apply: the location and nature of the attack, the possibility that the perpetrator might be armed or become violent and the danger of being outnumbered. But frequently another pedestrian or commuter *could* safely step in. And all too often they *don't* – perhaps simply because it's a bit embarrassing, or none of their business.

The simple act of sharing stories and raising awareness gives both women and men the strength and the impetus to make changes. Holly Kearl is founder of the Washington DC-based organization Stop Street Harassment. She says:

Street harassment is often an invisible problem or one that is portrayed as a joke, a compliment or the fault of the harassed person. In reality, it's a human-rights violation that restricts harassed persons' access to public spaces and the resources there. The best way to raise public awareness about the reality of street harassment is by sharing personal stories, and so initiatives like #ShoutingBack are extremely valuable because they give people an opportunity to share their story as an individual, but also as a group, to show how pervasive this problem is.

There are a lot of myths that exist about street harassment, including that it's a compliment and that women secretly love it. The thousands of stories shared on #ShoutingBack disprove those myths. I doubt that anyone who reads story after story about men groping, grabbing, flashing, stalking, or making sexually explicit comments at women can see it as anything other than gender violence and the human-rights violation that it is.

The sense of solidarity that also comes with sharing stories can make a huge difference, because women no longer feel they're standing up to street harassment alone. One woman wrote to tell us how she was introduced to the project page by a friend and read reams of women's stories...

▶ Then on the 4th of November while out running on a reasonably busy street in broad daylight, I was stopped and asked for directions [...] I obliged and as I showed him on the map on my phone he looked down my top, made a sleazy remark then grabbed my breast. On protesting he muttered [that] I'd 'a nice pair, what did [I] expect?'

The usual anger-but-not-quite-sure-what-to-do-about-it was replaced with something else [...] I'd read enough versions of same story just a few days previously.

I calmly took his registration and went straight to the police. I was surprised by how seriously they took it. They thanked me for coming in! They agreed with me – this guy was out of order and his behaviour was not ok! He's been charged and I'm realistic, it may or not make it to court. DNA tests are still pending. There were no other witnesses.

Regardless, thanks to this website and a couple of well-trained police officers, there is one guy who got the message, it's is not ok to see women as there solely for your sexual gratification.

The woman who sent in this entry was quite unusual in having reported the incident. Yet UK legislation on sexual assault is very clear:

A person (A) commits an offence if–
(a) he intentionally touches another person (B),
(b) the touching is sexual,
(c) B does not consent to the touching, and
(d) A does not reasonably believe that B consents

Under this definition, every one of the hundreds of women who have reported such experiences to our project was the victim of sexual assault – a crime that, under UK law, carries a maximum ten-year prison sentence.

Yet we are living in a society that not only downplays and accepts this crime but also deliberately normalizes it – telling women not to overreact, not to make a fuss out of nothing, or even to be glad of the attention. It is only when you really spell out the definition that the realization begins to dawn, even for many of the victims. Many women contacted the project after I wrote about the UK legal definition of sexual assault in the Huffington Post, their comments testifying to the great anomaly of our passivity to the crime.

Never thought about it before, but have now worked out that I've been sexually assaulted at least five times.

One of the blokes put his hand up my skirt and grabbed my crotch! Groping is too common on a night out! Never gets reported because it happens so often!

It seemed minor, scared the hell out of me though. I was crying by the time I got home.

We have created a social disconnect between the offence and its perception that is so strong even its own victims deny it. Which, of course, creates the ideal environment for such crimes to flourish.

But things are changing. The very fact of us sharing our

experiences of street harassment and protesting against them has begun to spark a movement to shout back. The British Transport Police has used thousands of the accounts collected by the Everyday Sexism Project to help them retrain 2,000 officers for Project Guardian, an initiative specifically designed to fight back against these crimes and their normalization. At the time of writing, 15 months after the launch of the campaign, reporting of sexual offences on public transport has increased by 39 per cent and the number of perpetrators brought to justice has increased by 40 per cent. Just a single week of action saw fifteen people arrested.

For every woman who manages to stand up and say *No*, there's another harasser who will think twice next time. For every bystander who intervenes, there's another crack in the culture of complicity. For every report made, either to an individual company or to the police, there's another perpetrator who will face consequences for their actions.

It's not always easy to stand up. The moment I confronted my aggressors is stamped on my memory so clearly because of the sheer, shaking terror I felt. It's not always safe to shout back, for a victim or a passer-by. But, across a variety of situations, there is a range of actions both victims and observers can take.

On Kearl's Stop Street Harassment website it is suggested that indirect interventions can be the safest and most effective. Bystanders don't have to confront the harasser himself – they can also check-in with the victim, simply stepping towards her and asking if she is OK. Sometimes, distracting the harasser with a simple request for directions, or the time, can signal in a calm and neutral way that somebody else is aware of and active in the situation, making the perpetrator feel less of a sense of impunity and sometimes giving the victim time to move away.

Many victims' accounts to the Everyday Sexism Project explained that their own silence often arose from a sense of shame or embarrassment. If you can find the strength to speak up, one way to win support from dithering bystanders is to clearly name what has happened and identify your aggressor – another clever tactic suggested by Stop Street Harassment. 'Man in the red T-shirt, please don't touch my legs' is a strong statement that draws attention and focus onto the perpetrator, instead of the victim, and clearly indicates what the situation is to those around you, who may then feel more empowered to step in.

It may be helpful to draw inspiration from the strength of other brilliant women who have stood up to their harassers in witty and wonderful ways – and there is no shortage of them reporting to the Everyday Sexism Project! Sometimes it's just the way they describe the incident...

🐦 Drive-by 'SLAAAAAG!' from white van man this morning. Speed of vehicle precluded discussion on gender politics.

🐦 I'm currently travelling round Europe & am amazed by the amount of men that are compelled to tell me I have large breasts. It's as if they think I need a reminder or something.

🐦 Was just told to 'cheer up' by two men. When I didn't, they yelled 'slag' and 'dirty little cunt'. This didn't cheer me up.

🐦 Young lad shouted 'milk my tits luv' at me from his bicycle earlier. He might need to pick up a biology book.

🐦 Every time I get cat-called and respond with a finger wave, the aggressors explode in anger. Feeling insulted? You don't say!

Then there are the brilliant comebacks...

🐦 Guy at bus stop 'I've a spare room, you can live with me.' 'Dude. Women are not Pokemon, roaming in the wild. I got a place.'

🐦 'Nothing more upsetting than when a girl with a rack like yours wears a sweater.' 'This conversation is a contender for more upsetting.'

🐦 Getting rated a '7.5' whilst in a queue because I have a 'great arse'. I rated him back as a -2 as he's a chauvinistic pig.

🐦 Once had a guy ask 'Would you mind telling me your bra-size?' I replied 'No, but tell me first how big your cock is.' Amazingly he was shocked and found MY comment highly inappropriate.

🐦 Thanks van-driver for kindly pointing out I have boobs. For years these odd protuberances have worried me. Thank you, kind sir!

Or, my personal all-time favourite, the woman who, when called 'big tits', looked down at her breasts and screamed as if she'd never seen them before!

▶ I was walking to college when a group of thirty-something men approached me. One of them asked me, 'Is it true you can get an orgasm from riding a bike?' (I wasn't even riding one) I replied, 'I'm more likely to get an orgasm from a bike than you.' His friends all laughed at him as I walked away.

In situations where it doesn't feel safe to act in the moment, it is often possible to report the harassment later – especially if it happens in a particular location or the perpetrator is clearly working for a specific company. The reports we've had of women reacting like this have been overwhelmingly positive, with almost all experiencing not just an attentive response, but, like I did, a sense of gratitude and willingness to solve the situation from the companies involved. I interviewed one woman who had reported a group of builders to the construction company after they shouted sexual abuse at her while she walked with an eight-year-old child. Two days later she was surprised by a knock on the door. It was the co-owner of the company, 'holding an enormous bouquet of flowers and a card', she told me.

[The owner had] had a heated discussion with the men involved [...] and told them it had to stop. She wanted me to go back with her so they could apologize in person. I declined, but I appreciated the sentiment, and how seriously my complaint had been taken. She told me that she had pleaded with them to think of their own wives and daughters before making 'comments' to, or about, women on the street. She was horrified.

Sometimes the simplest arguments are the strongest. As obvious as it might sound, just forcing people to stop and think about the reality of what they are doing and what it means can go a long way towards challenging received ideas about entitlement and anonymity in public spaces. One story we received illustrated this to perfection, and demonstrated the value of a simple, strong reaction to street harassment when it is possible.

▶ Walked past a group of men – one of them started shouting at me: 'Whoah! Come on darling!' and whistling, egged on by his friends. Crossed the street, went right up to him and said: 'Yes?' He looked really puzzled and the laughter stopped. I said: 'Well, you obviously wanted my attention. Here I am – what did you want to say to me?' He looked embarrassed then and sort of turned and shuffled away. I felt like the strongest person in the world.

Chapter 6

Women in the Media

'Teenager Elle Fanning shows off her womanly curves'
The Daily Mail reports on a fourteen-year-old child

Vital Statistics

Women write ⅓ of newspaper articles
Women in Journalism study, 2012

84 per cent of front-page articles are dominated by male
subjects or experts
Women in Journalism study, 2012

Only 28 per cent of speaking parts in the 100 most
successful films of 2012 were female
University of Southern California, 2013

1 in 5 solo presenters on UK radio is female (1 in 8 during
peak time)
Sound Women, 2013

Only 21 per cent of the 'notable deaths' reported in the
New York Times in 2012 were women
Mother Jones, 2013

Just 5 per cent of sports media coverage in the UK is
devoted to women's sport
Women's Sport and Fitness Foundation, 2011

Less than one in ten guests on comedy panel show *Mock the
Week* have been female
K7 Media, 2012

🐦 Life according to music videos, men wear suits & women gyrate topless & decorate them. I am no man's or woman's decoration.

🐦 There I was thinking it was fat, sugar and lack of exercise! Cosmo reveals 'your co-workers are making you fat'.

🐦 Working in a small restaurant staffed mainly by 16-year-old girls, the manager tells everyone to gather in the back room, he holds up page three and declares that this is our new uniform.

🐦 Within 2 hours of that woman egging Simon Cowell, the Daily Mail had found & published online a photo of her in a bikini.

🐦 I recently posted a comment on an online article on lads' mags in supermarkets in support of them being removed from the shelves. The response I got underneath? 'Are you a fat ugly lesbian then?'

🐦 Thank god, an all-male panel show. Finally, after all our waiting, TV totally owes us this.

Throughout history, everything that we do – everything that we believe about ourselves and other people, everything we plan for and work towards – has been shaped by stories. The stories we hear as children help us to imagine and dream what the future might hold. The stories we learn as we grow up help us to work out our place in the world. And the stories we tell when we are adults determine the legacy we leave behind.

So it is impossible to underestimate the impact of the fact that still, in 2014, women's stories are not being told. That women, in those stories we hear, are still portrayed as so incredibly limited, pigeonholed and stereotyped. And that so very few of those stories are told in a woman's voice.

As an alien coming to Earth for the first time and taking the media as your reference point for how the human race works, you could be forgiven for coming away with an incredibly distorted picture. The 28 per cent of speaking roles given to women in 2012's biggest films might give you the quite erroneous impression that the females of the species are significantly outnumbered by their male counterparts, though the sexualization of almost one in three of those roles would leave you in little doubt of their function.

The enormous age gap between the stars (disproportionately male, leading you perhaps to conclude that men are either higher functioning or simply more important) and their leading ladies would suggest a marital gulf of at least ten to twenty years. Meanwhile your understanding of the optimal age of females for reproduction would be deeply skewed by the idea that a woman like Angelina Jolie could have given birth at the age of one (to Colin Farrell, who plays her son in *Alexander*) while a woman like Francis Conroy (Peter Krause's mother in *Six Feet Under*) must have done so aged just twelve.

If nothing else, you'd come away with the certain understanding that there are *very* few circumstances in which it is acceptable to see an older woman on the silver screen.

You'd realize that women's looks are the crucial factor in

defining their value, that black women are to be sexualized and exoticized and disabled women pitied and portrayed as 'strivers', that lesbian and bisexual women's entire lives revolve obsessively around their sexuality, and that fat women are generally reserved to perform the function of providing the butt of a joke. You'd discover that women can be virgins or whores but rarely stray into the territory in between, that we despise one another's victories and find it impossible to resist bitching behind each other's backs, and that in order to achieve success we are either strident, masculine and mean or sexual and manipulative. You'd see that sexual violence is our greatest danger, but also a strangely erotic and titillating fate, and that the main function and purpose of our lives revolves entirely around finding an appropriate mate.

Though we consider it a single entity, the role played by the media in men's and women's lives is immeasurably different. For men, it largely reflects their reality, albeit a polished and aspirational version, and with the caveat that some groups are still underrepresented. We see men of all ages and sizes and shapes, in all different kinds of roles, usually at the centre of their own story. But for women the available roles are far narrower and less realistic. The media is both harshest critic and adoring fan – it reflects not our reality, but a constant and suffocating stream of unattainable ideals and derided failures, dehumanizing sexualization and crushing reminders of our own marginalization and inadequacy.

Small wonder, when (according to a study by the Center for the Study of Women in Television and Film) just 9 per cent of the top 250 US grossing films of 2012 were directed by women

– no improvement from the same paltry 9 per cent in 2008. The same report showed that women made up just 18 per cent of all directors, executive producers, producers, writers, cinematographers and editors on such films, translating to over four men for every woman working behind the camera.

And the impact of this misrepresentation starts young – when the Geena Davis Institute on Gender in Media looked at gender in family films released in the USA (that is, those specifically aimed at children) it found that male characters outnumbered females three to one, a ratio that has remained the same since 1946. And gender stereotypes are also rife in these early thought-shaping films – from 2006 to 2009, the research found that 'not one female character was depicted in G-rated family films in the field of medical science, as a business leader, in law, or politics'.

Remember the little girl who wrote about early aspirations?

🐦 We were asked what we wanted to be. I wanted to say a doctor but didn't because I thought girls couldn't be doctors. I was four years old.

Later, of course, these girls and their male peers grow up to become consumers of the music industry – to learn that women are, almost without exception, required to bare as much skin as possible when singing, despite the lack of correlation to their vocal performance, while male artists, remaining fully clothed themselves, will strew writhing, bikini-clad women around the sets of their videos like Christmas decorations.

They'll grow up with lyrics like those of The Wanted's 'Walks Like Rihanna', reminding them that their accomplishments are meaningless without an ability to shake their booty: she might not be able to sing or dance, the song tells us, 'But who cares – she walks like Rihanna!' They'll hear songs about sluts and songs about players; learn that low self-esteem is the sexiest thing about a girl; that dangerous and volatile relationships are the most desirable; and that girls should blame themselves if they're badly treated. And they will also learn, with pointed clarity, what is expected of them.

Some musicians, like Flo Rida, will at least be subtle enough to slightly mask their sexual demands with metaphors: 'Blow my whistle, baby'. Others, like Tyga, with 'Rack City', will be more explicit: 'Ten, ten, ten, twenties on yo titties bitch [...] Got cha grandma on my dick'.

And in everything from Justin Timberlake's 'Tunnel Vision' to Robin Thicke's 'Blurred Lines' they will see completely naked women surrounding the fully clothed men as they sing their sexual domination over them in no uncertain terms. 'I know you like it...' Timberlake croons a total of thirty-six times (sounds like he's trying to convince himself, if you ask me). 'I know you want it...' Thicke optimistically agrees. Some singers don't even bother *pretending* to consider the woman's consent – in the song 'U.O.E.N.O.' by American hip-hop artist Rocko, featuring Future and Rick Ross, Ross raps about putting 'molly' (a colloquial term for the drug MDMA) in a woman's champagne before 'I took her home and I enjoyed that / She ain't even know it'.

The titillating depiction of women in positions of vulnerability is also a worryingly frequent trope, from videos like 'Hold On, We're Going Home' by Drake (which sees a helpless, doll-like woman wearing only white underwear being violently kidnapped) to 'The Show Must Go On' by Famous Last Words (which shows an unconscious woman tied to a chair, the tension ramped up with close-up shots of her terrified face before she's throttled to death).

Both videos strikingly perpetuate the sort of gender stereotypes the project has found to be rife among young people. The former makes explicit that the woman has been kidnapped because she is considered to be property; she is being taken to wreak revenge on her male partner. Meanwhile the men storming to her rescue are hyper-masculinized, armed to the teeth and blowing things up during a violent gunfight. In sexy cutaway scenes she is a terrified, vulnerable victim; we see her trying to escape, her bottom wobbling above her suspenders, before being thrown to the floor by her captor – who then aggressively lies on top of her, suggesting a potential rape scenario. A clear link is drawn for boys between loving a woman, owning her and acting with extreme aggression to protect that right of ownership, while the woman's worth is clearly tied to her sexuality.

The Famous Last Words' video portrays the male singer with a split personality; we see him battling against an inner demon who goads him into attacking a woman. The video does at least imply that the violence is wrong, but still plays into damaging myths about masculine violence as aroused by women (suggesting this is inherent and difficult to control). And that violence is still presented in a melodramatic, sensational manner.

Such undertones are not niche- or genre-specific. 'Blurred Lines' hit Number 1 and got untold airplay, yet actually refers repeatedly to something resembling a rape scenario: 'I'll give you something big enough to tear your ass in two [...] Do it like it hurt [...]' We hear that the singer *thinks* he knows she 'wants it' but never that she has consented; he goes on to decide that he *is* going to 'take' her, and later must ominously check whether or not she can breathe...

Again and again, violence and intimacy are linked. 'Hit the Floor' by Bullet for My Valentine describes the singer approaching a woman from behind as she walks home; he shocks her by touching her unexpectedly, asks her not to scream and comes down on her 'like a ton of bricks' when she does. In 'Breezeblocks', meanwhile, Alt J cheerfully remind their listeners that any woman wishing to run away can be pinned down with breezeblocks. Problem solved!

I know I've said it before, but I could go on, and on, and on.

The significance of misogyny in music culture is twofold. Firstly it's extremely explicit – both lyrically and in the accompanying visual imagery, which is highly effective and easily absorbed; these videos, with their close-ups on the writhing, naked, available, sexualized female form, send a very clear message. Secondly, this particular form of culture is immediately accessible, making it a very direct line of communication with teenage boys in particular. The age restrictions applied to films containing similarly sexually explicit or violent content are absent from music videos, which are readily available on television and across the internet.

And then, of course, there's the time-honoured defence of the generation gap, whereby any criticism of or objection to contemporary music culture is belittled as 'prudish' or 'old-fashioned'.

Collectively, songs like those above – and the videos produced to sell them – with their casual stereotypes and sexualization and derogatory putdowns of women, form the background noise that seeps into our consciousness without us necessarily even realizing we're absorbing it. Just like *Nuts* and *Zoo* and *FHM* and all those publications that exist purely to send the message, loud and clear, that women are there as sexual objects to titillate and amuse and entertain and satisfy men. We rarely stop to think about how it must feel, as little girls, to grow up surrounded by this kind of wallpaper.

▸ In my 10-year-old daughter's class they are learning about news and newspapers. All children were asked to bring a newspaper in to school. More than half of them brought a copy of the Sun, and consequently spent the lesson gawping at page 3. What did they all learn about the role of women in society? At school. At the age of 10.

▸ I was in the supermarket with my 7-year-old daughter. She was looking for a comic and spotted the lads' mags – a woman in the front wearing a thong and sticking her bum into the camera. My daughter looked embarrassed and made a comment about why that lady isn't dressed. So we went along the shelf and turned all offending magazines over. It gave her the giggles.

And even when the lyrics refer explicitly to abusing women – even when a new study in December 2011 showed it was virtually impossible to differentiate between the copy printed in lads' mags and the words of convicted sex offenders – still there seems to be little dent in the plethora of this kind of content. We are drowning in it. And no: of course this isn't to say that lads' mags and song lyrics turn innocent men into rapists, or that a single image of a scantily clad woman directly causes immediate harm to the viewer; of course it's not that simple. But these are not a few one-offs. This is a culture steeped in misogyny and the objectification and subjugation of woman – and yes, it does have a real impact.

How do I know? I know because there's a lot of documented evidence to this effect – particularly in relation to printed media. According to The Representation Project, for example, three out of four teenaged girls feel depressed, guilty and shameful after spending three minutes leafing through a fashion magazine. Meanwhile the government's recent review into the sexualization of young people found 'a clear link between consumption of sexualized images, a tendency to view women as objects and the acceptance of aggressive attitudes and behaviour as the norm'. That report concluded: 'Both the images we consume and the way we consume them are lending credence to the idea that women are there to be used and that men are there to use them.' Then there's the recent UK-government report showing that 'between one third and half of young girls fear becoming fat and engage in dieting or binge eating' and 'over 60 percent of girls avoid certain activities because they feel bad about their looks'. It specifically cited media criticism of body weight combined with a lack of body diversity as a contributing factor.

Certainly both eating disorders and cosmetic surgery are ever on the rise. And, according to Dr Helen Sharpe, a London-based researcher working on eating disorders in secondary-school-age girls: 'Exposure to these magazines is robustly linked to body dissatisfaction. We also know that those people most unhappy and vulnerable to begin with are likely to be most affected by the images in a damaging way.'

Most of all, though, I know the impact is real because every week I receive project entries like this one:

▶ I look at images of women everywhere I go – in shop windows, on the sides of buses, in the tube, on the backs of newspapers, in magazines open in women's laps, on billboards, on videos, on TV, on the internet, popping up in my screen. They are all the same. They are taller than me, so much thinner than me, beautiful, flawless, perfectly made up. Many, many of them are revealing their long, toned legs right the way up to the tops, their flat, flawless stomachs in all their tiny, tiny glory, their ample cleavages looking perfect – not fat but perky. They are all that way – there aren't any that I can look at and think, she's a bit like me, that's OK. And they are everywhere. There is no escape. When I look in the mirror, I see myself and over the top I superimpose that image and all I see is the difference between us. When I meet new people I feel like they are looking through me to those differences too. She is everywhere and I can't escape her and I'm terrified my boyfriend compares her to me constantly and finds me constantly wanting. Know the funniest part? I'm a very normal size. I'm not obese or fat, I have a pretty good figure. But it's nothing compared to hers. And she's everywhere.

Meanwhile back in the cinema, a staggering number of films still fail to meet the incredibly low standards of the Bechdel Test, which merely requires them to include two named female characters who talk to each other about any subject other than a man. According to the Bechdel website, recent failures to meet their ludicrously simple criteria include mainstream Hollywood blockbusters like *The Internship*, *The Lone Ranger*, *The Avengers*, *Jack Reacher*, *Killer Joe*, *Men in Black III* and *Star Trek: Into Darkness* (which should get a bonus point for an underwear scene so blatantly gratuitous even the writer subsequently saw fit to make a public apology for it).

There is a feverish desperation to portray any young woman as a sexual object among a large swathe of the media that is so powerful as to transcend both relevance and respect. In the past year alone this rabid tunnel vision led to the portrayal of Amanda Thatcher (in mourning and speaking at her grandmother's funeral), Amanda Knox (on trial for murder) and Reeva Steenkamp (a victim of domestic violence and murder) as sexual objects for mass consumption. All – regardless of their very different reasons for being in the spotlight – were paraded in countless photographs for the delectation of the tabloid readers. Within minutes of her taking the lectern to speak in her grandmother's memory, nearly twenty high-definition images of the 'elegant Miss Thatcher' littered the *Daily Mail* website; slavering tabloids coined the moniker 'Foxy Knoxy'; and when Steenkamp was murdered the *Sun* ran a full-front-page photograph of her in a bikini alongside a lurid, titillating headline and a Blade Runner subhead that didn't even mention her name.

We're repeatedly given the same animalistic, one-dimensional view of women afforded by the same obsessive lens. It's this worn-out single setting that saw our finest athletes covering themselves in glory at the Olympic Games only to be depicted across the media as 'beauties', 'angels', 'radiant blondes' and 'babes', and being grilled about their pre-race beauty regimes with the same intensity that male athletes were asked about their technique. The same obsessive template that mysteriously sees only white, thin, long-haired blonde girls (who happen to show off their toned midriffs as they leap in the air with delight) gaining straight A*s at GCSE over and over. The same frame that focuses with morbid glee on the bright-blue eyes of Madeleine McCann year after year while scores of less-photogenic and non-white children quietly go missing and are quietly mourned or found.

In the relatively new world of online media, where outlets find themselves scrambling for fresh headlines every few hours instead of every day, there's been an explosion in the practice of creating 'news articles' out of the dress, behaviour and appearance of female celebrities. Here websites trample over one another to 'report' the appearance of an actress in a low-cut top or a reality-show star's barely noticeable weight gain: all in the name of easy 'filler' pieces to provide new links and headlines. Women's individual body parts are expounded with such detachment that they become almost entirely dehumanized – and occasionally even strut their newfound autonomy on the red carpet, if you believe this surreal *Mirror* headline from 2013: 'Rihanna's boobs go to fashion week in a lovely long red dress'… All the while, repeated and reinforced, is the message that a woman is valued and judged solely on her looks.

And it's not just the messages *about* women that are so damaging, but the messages the media sends *to* us as well. Never has a more apt photograph been sent *to* the Everyday Sexism Project than the one someone tweeted showing a clear disposal container full of discarded magazines with a sign saying 'shed your weight problem here'.

In the world of women's magazines, the flaws of women's natural bodies are headline stories, week in, week out. Hence such dazzling anatomical facts as 'She's got a belly,' once placed above a picture of Kelly Brook bending over momentarily on a beach, becomes front-page news.

'OMG! What has Madge done to her face?' shrieks a headline below a zoomed-in, unflattering picture of Madonna. Never mind that while it was taken she was speaking passionately to a concert audience about women's rights to education worldwide, and the life-and-death struggle of girls in Pakistan to go to school. Who cares? She's *clearly* had work done, right?

There's a sort of shorthand you pick up as you wade through women's magazines – a bit like the one you eventually realize is there to help you fathom cryptic-crossword clues ('confused' might indicate an anagram, for example, while 'goes back' signals a word spelled backwards, etc.). Gradually you come to understand that words like 'curvy' or 'confident' or 'full-figured' are code for 'fatty', 'fatty', or 'fatty'; that 'brave' means 'HA! Dumped!' and 'flaunted' means 'happened to wear while ten miles away from and completely oblivious to our long-lens paparazzo'.

So a headline like 'Brave Lauren steps out looking curvy as she puts split behind her' translates to: 'Try to restrain your glee

– Lauren piles on the pounds as she's dumped by her boyfriend!'
When of course what we're really looking at is more likely 'Lauren
happens to turn sideways slightly as she walks past camera
after popping out in varied company for the past few days; her
relationship's perfectly fine, thanks for asking'.

Weight is a major fixation. The tiniest fluctuations are picked
apart, scrutinized and swamped with intense and lascivious
commentary – whatever it takes to find enough text to run
alongside several close-up photographs. And there's a vindictive joy
in being able to draw criticism.

'Supermodel Kate eats pizza shocker' is a genuine headline
from one mag, while another actually captions a photograph of
Cara Delevingne wearing no make-up: 'There is a God!' An article
purportedly praising Sharon Stone's looks is betrayed by the
breathtakingly snarky headline: 'How to look amaze at 105'...

It's a scary business. The sentiment extends to a whole world
of *vital* breaking analysis of our female celebs, from those 'circle
of shame' pictures damning their shoddy unplucked eyebrows and
sweat stains (the horror!) to entire features lamenting their ill-
considered outfits and physical 'flaws'. All the important stuff.

'What a beautiful embroidered kaftan, Ashley' starts one such piece...
'Shame you're not anywhere near a beach – and next time wear a bra!'

There's also a nasty classist undertone sneering beneath these
features, like the one in the *Daily Mail* that smirks: 'Tulisa really is
a "chav in a tracksuit" as she heads to Tesco in sportswear.'

And then there's the dual Holy Grail of weight loss and
boyfriend, the importance of which is emphasized by the sheer
desperate urgency of the headlines:

NEW BODY PANICS!

Gemma's SOS to Josie: 'HELP ME GET THIN'

COLEEN'S BODY PANIC: Extreme yoga and juice diet to be size 8 in three weeks

'I'm terrified of getting fat again!'

KELLY'S SECOND THOUGHTS: I worry I shouldn't have let Thom go!

Frustrated Lauren: Why hasn't Jake proposed?

And the inevitable sensationalist conflations of the two:

KELLY COMFORT EATS AS DANNY FAILS TO COMMIT

'I've got my perfect body – now I can't wait to marry Jake!'

'Kieran won't fancy me if I keep bloating!'

Having absorbed the message that romantic success is directly proportional to weight loss, women are ready to be assaulted by a baffling barrage of commandments, directives and mandates: what to eat and what not to eat, what to wear and what to avoid wearing at all cost and – most crucial of all – how, EXACTLY, to give the perfect boyfriend-pleasing, man-snaring blowjob.

The most frustrating thing about all this is the unadulterated, blatant hypocrisy.

Women's magazines are masters at creating precisely those hysterical 'problems' they claim to teach their readers to 'fix' and thus profit from in the meantime. And, as time goes on, the list of fabricated defects of the female body becomes increasingly ludicrous as new problems are desperately conjured up in order that reams of copy can be spun teaching us how to diet, what to buy and how many sit-ups constitute sufficiently self-despising penance for the crime of being normal. (If you didn't think things could get any worse than the ridiculous invention of 'cankles' you clearly weren't prepared for the advent of the even more stupid 'kninkles'. No i'm not joking – google it.)

The hypocrisy only deepens. Some women's magazines and media outlets, particularly in the last decade, have begun to leap, posturing and preening, onto a bandwagon of faux concern about eating disorders and body-image problems while simultaneously continuing to peddle the quick-fix extreme diets, airbrushed underweight fashion shoots and obsessive calorie-counting features that perpetuate them. 'Curvy girls really do have more fun!!' they'll squeal, in an issue that criticizes a celebrity for daring to have white bread in their larder and extols the virtues of the all-kelp detox to 'fight the flab'. 'Curvy beauties hit the beach!' they'll proclaim, featuring Jessica Alba, or Katy Perry, or another celeb who happens to have worn a top in which their boobs are visible but who otherwise remains slimmer than the slimmest of the magazine's readers.

Perhaps the most flagrant example of this came in June 2012, when two editions of *Now* magazine hit newsstands at the same time. One was a regular issue, featuring a front-page image of model Abbey Clancy beside the melodramatic headline 'Oh no! Scary Skinnies' and a caption that warned: 'Girls starving to be like her'. Inside, an article claimed that Clancy had become so dangerously thin she was a role model for damaging pro-anorexia websites. The second issue, which appeared directly alongside it on the shelf at my local newsagent, was the *Now Celebrity Diet Special*. This too featured Clancy on the front cover, but beside the headline: 'Bikini body secrets... The stars' diet and fitness tricks REVEALED'. Yes. In the *same week* they claimed that emulating her look could make young women dangerously ill *and* used the promise of helping readers look like her to sell copies.

To be such a huge part of the problem is one thing; to pretend to be part of the solution while still pushing the same unattainable, unrealistic 'standards' is immeasurably worse.

It doesn't help that the narrative voice running through all this inequality – the newspaper inches reporting and reflecting it, the opinion pieces analysing it and the talk shows discussing it – are also (you guessed it) heavily dominated by men. A 2011 Women in Journalism study found that 74 per cent of national news journalists are men, while another study by the same organization in 2012 revealed that an enormous four out of five front-page stories were written by men, and 84 per cent of those stories dominated by a male subject or expert. When women did appear, it was most likely to be in the capacity of window dressing: Kate and Pippa Middleton were by far the most likely women to be photographed, while in contrast men like Jeremy Hunt would be pictured for (presumably) their job rather than their capacity to beautify the front page.

Naturally there follows a male-dominated influence on how stories are reported. This became gradually clearer and clearer in my own experiences with the media as the Everyday Sexism Project gained prominence. I've been told by newspaper photographers that their editors have sent them to take extra pictures because they reckon I'm a bit of alright and they'll put in more picture than words to keep the male readers happy. I said I'd really rather the words.

When the picture editor of one of the country's biggest newspapers confidently tells you (presumably *after* reading the article about your quest for gender equality, which his picture is to illustrate) that the key thing is to make you look 'as sexy as possible', you start to wonder about giving up the ghost.

The heavy male bias in newsroom staff and the sexist attitudes that often make their way onto our television screens and front pages also have a hampering effect on initiatives and news that should be considered positive progress towards equality. So, for example, instead of celebrating the achievement of Major Mariam al-Mansouri, the first female fighter pilot in the United Arab Emirates, when it emerged she had flown a successful mission in the campaign against the Islamic State, Fox News commentators instead used the opportunity to make sexist jokes. "The problem is, after she bombed it, she couldn't park it," said one, while another quipped: "Would that be considered boobs on the ground?" When Russian cosmonaut Yelena Serova hit the headlines in the same month, as she prepared to travel into space after years of expert training, journalists bombarded her with questions about how her parenting would suffer and how she would wash and style her hair in space. When Rona Fairhead CBE, Cambridge and Harvard graduate, British business ambassador, former chair and chief executive of the Financial Times Group and non-executive director at HSBC and PepsiCo, was announced as the preferred candidate to lead the BBC Trust in 2014, the *Telegraph* headline read: "Mother of three poised to lead the BBC." And when Nicola Sturgeon was primed to make history by becoming the first female First Minister of Scotland, two major national newspapers ran front pages about the appointment: one chose a headline about her "baby hopes", while another featured analysis of her fashion transformation from "death row hair and awful trouser suits" to being "sleek as an otter".

The impact of this kind of sexist reporting on high achieving women and their strides towards equality isn't only undermining, insulting and demeaning to the subjects themselves. It also has a major impact on the aspirations and perceptions of young women, learning from the media that they will be judged on their looks regardless of their achievements, and that even their most ground-breaking successes will still be acceptable fodder for sexist jokes. Multiple young women at university talks and events have told me they've reconsidered a career that might take them into the public eye for exactly this reason. We lose them before they even begin.

Part of the problem is that the men in high places just aren't getting it. On 19 June 2013, Caroline Lucas stood up in the House of Commons during Prime Minister's Questions to raise her concerns over media sexism. She pointed out that the government's own research showed a link between the portrayal of women as sex objects in the media and greater acceptance of sexual harassment and violence against women. She also asked David Cameron whether he would support a ban on the *Sun* newspaper being sold on the parliamentary estate until Page 3 was scrapped.

In response, Cameron and the men on his front bench laughed at her. George Osborne openly laughed as Cameron stood to address the question, and even Cameron – our prime minister – was unable to suppress a snigger as he finished his sentence. He refused to back Lucas's call for a ban, and completely ignored her question about sexual harassment and violence against women. The only conclusion watching voters could draw was that these Conservative front benchers (and their leader) thought not only that there wasn't a problem but also that the very idea of considering such issues was absurd.

(Remember the fifteen-year-old girl who wrote: 'I wish the people who had real power and control the images and messages we get fed all day actually thought about what they did for once.')

Exactly a week before, Lucas had faced more sniggering from a largely male panel as she outlined media sexism in a Westminster Hall debate on the same issue. She was also interrupted to be told by the Chair to cover up her No More Page 3 T-shirt if she wished to continue her speech. She did so, but with a deliciously wry smile she first held the *Sun* clearly aloft, open at page 3, declaring: 'It does strike me as an irony that this T-shirt is regarded as an inappropriate thing to be wearing in this house, whereas apparently it is appropriate for this kind of newspaper to be available to buy in eight different outlets on the Palace of Westminster estate.'

On that day – 12 June 2013 – the day Lucas was largely shrugged off, laughed at and ignored for suggesting that there was anything wrong with the gender balance of the UK media

– I bought *The Times*, the *Guardian*, the *Independent*, the *Daily Telegraph*, the *Daily Mirror*, the *Daily Mail*, the *Sun*, the *Daily Express* and the *Daily Star*. The main (almost full-length) photograph on the front page of the *Daily Telegraph* was of Lindsay Mills, described in the caption as the 'pole-dancing girlfriend' of US whistleblower Edward Snowden. She was pictured in a pouting pose, wearing only a tutu and a bra top. She bore (at best) peripheral relevance to the story about leaked US intelligence documents. The front page of the *Daily Star* carried a full-length picture of Tulisa Contostavlos in a bikini. The front page of the *Daily Express* had a glamorous picture of Cat Deeley with a facile, non-news headline describing her as 'the golden girl of Hollywood'. The front page of the *Sun* luridly screamed 'Teacher "fled with girl pupil after 4-month sex fling"'. That she was fifteen at the time of the event, and therefore under the age of consent, making it not sex, in fact, but statutory rape, seemed not to have troubled any of the paper's staff. The *Daily Mail* echoed the same sentiment, with the headline: 'On trial, teacher "who abducted besotted pupil"', keeping the focus clearly on the underage victim's motivations. The *Independent* front page included a seductive picture of the actress Kim Cattrall with the caption 'Sweet birds of stage age'. And the *Daily Mirror* joined the *Telegraph* and plastered Snowden's girlfriend across the front page, this time in little more than a pair of pants, under the headline 'The ballerina left behind'. For good measure, it also threw in a titillating description of the rape of an underage girl as 'Teacher's sex with girl of 15 while wife was out', making it sound more like a Carry On film than a clear-cut crime. *The Times* and the *Guardian*, just two out of these nine major news titles, had no content of sexist note – at least not on the front page. (By this stage, I was frankly too depressed to check inside.) The high number of stories featuring females might have made it a statistically anomalous day, bucking the trend of male front-page domination, but it was hardly a win for women.

Clearly nothing there to worry those men who laughed off Lucas's concerns. I'm not talking about heavy-handed press regulation, or stifling freedom of speech. I'm talking mostly about enforcing laws and codes that are already in place but are blatantly, baldly flouted when it comes to women. (And are meanwhile largely obeyed in many other areas, in line with other public norms and taboos.) The UK government, for example, is a signatory to the Convention on the Elimination of All Forms of Discrimination against Women, which dictates that states must 'take all appropriate measures to eliminate discrimination against women by any person, organization or enterprise'. What steps is the UK government taking to rectify the very blatant discrimination against women perpetuated by Page 3, or the utterly gratuitous 'up skirt' crotch shots that frequently grace the front page of the *Daily Sport* at child's-eye level?

Those front-bench men might say that a headline is harmless. They might scoff at the idea that what is printed in the newspaper, or played on the radio, or seen on the television or cinema screen can have any real, measurable impact on real women's lives and safety and self-image. Perhaps they think that way because it's difficult to realize, when the media reflects you and protects you and demonstrates your power and importance, how oppressive it can be when you're invisible. For a white middle-aged, middle-class man who sees his own face staring back out of every page, every news bulletin, every panel show, it must be difficult to imagine being one of many regular women looking through paper after paper, magazine after magazine, watching film after film and rarely catching a glimpse of yourself.

So to help them understand, I'd like them to hear about some of those women and how they told me their stories. I'd like them to know about the fifteen-year-old girl who wrote that the media portrayal of women has made her feel that she will always be worthless unless boys find her 'sexy', no matter what she achieves. I'd like them to hear from the gay women, and trans women and older women and fat women and black women and women with particular accents who all told me they looked at the media and never saw or heard themselves. This made them feel invisible – and convinced them that to be treated as invisible was inevitable, and natural, and excusable.

▶ We so rarely see a woman play the lead in good films or TV shows, we're always in a supporting role, as women are throughout life really. As we age we don't even get that it seems.

▶ I'm 43 and have two teenage daughters […] I was thinking back to the women who I watched on TV when I was young. Lucille Ball & Vivian Vance, both women in their 40s. Ms Cunningham on happy days. Jean Stapleton. The Golden Girls. Just a few examples. A person could write for a long time about the stereotypical roles they did or didn't play in their shows, but there is something physically striking about these women. They looked like normal everyday middle-aged women. So different from today's hyper-sexualized TV moms; Sofia Vergara, any of the Desperate Housewives, Mary Louise Parker. I'm at the point where I don't want to turn on the TV or go to the movies any more. I end up feeling terrible, insecure, inadequate, angry. It's not worth it.

I'd like them to know about a girl of just fourteen, who went to the same school as I did, who killed herself because of worries about the size and shape of her beautiful teenage body. They should hear that in his verdict the coroner declared the fashion industry 'directly responsible for what happened' and begged: 'particularly the magazines in the fashion industry, to stop publishing photographs of wafer-thin girls [...] because at the end of the day for their benefit, families like this must suffer [...] and until they control themselves it will continue.'

I'd like them to read all the entries from the women who wrote to describe how the *Sun*'s Page 3 had played a part in the abuse and harassment they've dealt with for years and years. The bank workers who were audibly compared by male colleagues to the women in a Page 3 calendar as they battled to be taken seriously in a predominantly male environment. The architecture student who was told, 'With tits like yours, you'd be more successful as a Page 3 model.' The woman who was just trying to take the tube when the man next to her flashed Page 3 at her, called her 'sweetheart' and spat on her. And the fourteen-year-old who was in her school uniform when a man on the bus showed her his copy and said, 'I shouldn't worry, with tits like yours they're not going to ask you to pose.'

Then I'd like them to hear from the women who wrote to Clare Short, when she campaigned against Page 3, to tell her it had been directly mentioned by their attackers as they were being raped. And even then – no – I wouldn't expect or want them to think that Page 3 and media sexism turned men into rapists – still no – but I'd like to dare to hope that perhaps they'd start listening.

And I'd really like them to hear this woman's story, most powerful because she told it in her own, brave words.

▶ I went to a nightclub in London last year for a friend's birthday celebrations. When we walked in I was really shocked to see the walls decorated with pornographic pictures pulled from lad's magazines and page 3. It was everywhere plastered all over the walls like wallpaper. It made me feel so uncomfortable but as it was a birthday party and nobody else was voicing any opinion on it I didn't say anything.

About an hour in I went to the toilet and didn't realize someone had followed me. He forced me in to a cubicle, hit my head against the wall, which was also still covered in pornography, and sexually assaulted me. I was shouting but the music was too loud. I was struggling but he was too strong. All I could do was stare at the pictures of naked women on the wall he was pressing my face into.

I reported it but after a year of toing and froing nothing has been done really. One of the officers I spoke to even commented about the nightclub I was in in front of me to his colleague saying something along the lines of 'oh isn't that the place with all the tits on the wall? Oh yeah, ha ha ha'.

It makes me feel sick now when I think of it. And when I see pornographic pictures on newsagent shelves and mainstream media, just accepted like it's normal and okay. I wondered and still think to this day whether the man who did this to me would have done it if he wasn't raised in a country where women are advertised as products to be used. That's what I felt like that night, like an object, like I was just one of the women on the wall and that's what he wanted so he took it.

I think the everyday sexism that happens in our media and mainstream press is the biggest and most important example in this country. I just think how can we fight the other forms of sexism if everyday the work is undone and undermined by the big booming message that screams from all of these 'WOMEN YOU ARE NOTHING, YOU ARE WORTHLESS, YOU ARE HERE FOR OUR ENTERTAINMENT AND WE WILL USE AND TREAT YOU HOW WE WANT'.

It's taking a lot of time and soul searching to try and make myself feel like a valid human being again, the law and legal systems have not helped me in doing that, I feel dismissed and ignored, yet again like a naked woman on the wall that's okay to use and abuse because I'm not a person. I really hope that one day I am really convinced that I am worth more than that, and that these voices from everywhere telling me I am not worthy of human status stop.

We live in a society where – like it or not – the media is written by men, for men. There's really no arguing about that. And this media – which perpetrates and perpetuates all manner of ill-advised ideals and norms – *does* affect women, and their lives, every day in every way. There's really no arguing about that either. And for the media to offer women more than a place as a commodity or a seat in the audience, something big is going to have to shift. From Page 3 to the Circle of Shame, lads' mags to sexist adverts, front-bench dismissal to the devaluation of women's voices in debate, the media, and those in power who turn a blind eye to it, have a lot to answer for. No, not in terms of direct cause and effect, but in terms of the creation and maintenance of a culture which fuels a continuum, from force-fed unattainable body image and mixed messages about 'real' solutions for imaginary 'problems' right the way through to teenage suicide and commonplace sexual assault. Perhaps we could finally have an open conversation about *influence* and *context*. And perhaps they would at least do us the courtesy of managing not to snigger anymore.

Chapter 7

Women in the Workplace

'I'm 21 and being asked at job interviews if I'm getting married, or pregnant'
Tweet sent to @EverydaySexism

Vital Statistics

Women working full time in the UK in 2012 earned 14.9
per cent less than men
Fawcett Society, 2013

In the City of London the pay gap rises to 33 per cent
Fawcett Society, 2013

In the finance sector the pay gap rises to 55 per cent
Fawcett Society, 2013

The average female executive earns £423,000 less over her
lifetime than a male worker with an identical career path
CMI, 2012

Women receive less than half the average bonus men receive
CMI, 2012

60 per cent of women in the UK have had a male colleague
behave 'inappropriately' towards them
Slater & Gordon, 2012

1 in 8 women have left a job because of sexual harassment
Slater & Gordon, 2013

🐦 When starting my first job as a welder 4 of the men went to the boss and told him he couldn't employ me because I was a girl.

🐦 Patient at work: 'I don't want to see some uneducated woman, I want to see a real doctor.'

🐦 A male boss said he'd 'love to bend me over' and more, I reported it to female supervisor who said I was being 'sensitive'.

🐦 Saw my hours cut every time I complained to a manager about the co-worker who sexually harassed me.

🐦 Male customer demanded to see manager even though I was manager on duty. I said: you mean you want to see a man? He shut up.

🐦 Chatting to a man on the bus home, was fine until I said I was a scientist. Apparently that's not a job for women. He really didn't like it when I said my qualifications disagreed with him.

When the Jimmy Savile scandal broke, bringing in its aftermath revelations about workplace harassment and misconduct, there was a general reaction of 'Yes – but that's just how things *were* back then'.

Nothing of the sort could *possibly* fly under the radar now, people said; it was 'another time'. Time and again the argument was made that it was the very specific, permissive culture of the seventies that silenced victims; it was that environment of normalized sexist behaviour and harassment in the workplace that meant they couldn't speak up.

The irony was that, even as they spoke about that far-away time when such attitudes were rife, thousands of women were recording their own stories on the Everyday Sexism Project. These stories covered everything from workplace inequality and harassment to regular sexual assault and these women were expressing near-identical feelings of being silenced by the same widespread acceptance or denial of the problem. Many even described their powerlessness to protest using the very same phrase: 'It's just the way things are'...

Perhaps to a greater extent than with any other form of sexism recorded by the project, reports on workplace sexism are often immediately and utterly denied. There are many quite understandable reasons for this. For a start, workplace legislation on sexual harassment is excellent, and, that being the case, many who would not dream of perpetrating find it very difficult to imagine others getting away with it. It often follows particularly covert and elusive patterns, too, frequently occurring in complete seclusion, in an empty corridor or a private office.

On the misguided basis that perpetrators must be overt, lecherous monsters, people often believe that nothing could possibly be going on in their own workplace. Frequently there are significant power dynamics at play: victims may feel unable to report the behaviour of a senior colleague, manager or boss; they may be afraid to risk losing their job or being branded a 'troublemaker' for speaking up. The inherent difficulty of proving a pattern of what can be very subtle behaviour, with little to evidence it, gets weighed against the cost of a tribunal and the potential resulting career suicide. Consequently only a tiny number of cases ever go to court or come to light.

In short, the vast majority of victims simply suffer in silence.

Besides the obvious, the trouble with this is that when workplace harassment does come to light it's often met with scepticism or a stubborn refusal to acknowledge the problem exists at all. This was perfectly exemplified in the case of the allegations of harassment and groping made in 2013 against Lord Rennard.

The intense subsequent media focus on the most 'minor' and 'grey area' incidents betrayed a total lack of public awareness of the true severity of the wider problem. Writing in the *Evening Standard*, under the title 'Let's not overreact to middle-aged boobies', Sarah Sands asked whether the case lacked 'a certain proportionality', playing down Rennard's alleged crimes by describing him as an 'unlikely Falstaff' and suggesting that, were the allegations correct, he would simply have 'made a fool of himself'. In the *Spectator*, Rod Liddle described the revelations as 'hilarious', and the women as 'bint[s]', and even bizarrely suggested that the victims' main anger stemmed from their realization that Rennard had allegedly propositioned so many others, making them jealous. Unless these columnists are living in a Benny Hill movie, it's difficult to understand such reluctance to concede that in fact *most* people would quite like to work in an environment free of unwanted sexual touching. It's hardly a radical perspective, wanting to go to work without being physically assaulted...

Meanwhile, on LBC Radio, presenter Julia Hartley-Brewer ran a segment on the Rennard complaints after Scotland Yard announced no prosecution would be brought. Referring to his alleged victims, she declared that 'Throughout this entire case I've been quite disgusted by how pathetic they've come across'; she later followed in the footsteps of Liddle's inspiring logic by making disparaging comments about Lord Rennard's appearance and astutely deducing that his looks were 'why the women complained [...] if he'd been young and gorgeous like George Clooney, we'd have been queuing up wouldn't we?' Gosh, yes! If only all harassers were *attractive* there'd be no crime to bang on about, would there! This theory would be flawless, were it not for that pesky first word in the phrase 'unwanted sexual contact'.

The irony of the simultaneous dismissal of supposedly hysterical, overdramatic victims and the complete inability to grasp the actual point is stupefying. As wryly summarized in this tweet to the project:

🐦 A guy sat me down to explain why feminism has no relevance in 2013 while stroking my leg the whole time.

The cavalier media response to the Rennard allegations (bumbling buffoon accidentally comes on too strong – what's all the fuss about?) would have it that 'so-called' workplace harassment merely constitutes clumsy, misplaced attempts at flirting between peers. The strong implication is that the poor perpetrator has every reason to expect his advances may be welcomed and thus – whoops! – *misguidedly* oversteps the line.

· This misleading idea of a man making a move in good faith (as if he really doesn't know it will be unwelcome) feeds into the narrative that has women somehow 'inadvertently' sending out confusing 'signals'. And who can blame a poor hapless businessman for grabbing your crotch if you have the audacity to attend a meeting in a pencil skirt with your hair in a sleek chignon, you brazen hussy? Never mind that you're expected to look smart and presentable, or that so many other women have reported being sacked or sidelined for *not* wearing enough make-up... Never mind the countless magazines sending you the message that a businesswoman who doesn't dress in catwalk chic, day-to-night, power-lipstick glory is an unsuccessful one. Never mind how mind-blowingly offensive it is to the average male to suggest he's too stupid to tell the difference between a well-pitched business plan and a come-hither seduction play...

It's the same school of thought that starts squawking about 'political correctness gone mad' every time there's an allegation of sexual harassment or inappropriate workplace behaviour. How will anyone ever create a fun, cooperative workplace atmosphere, they ask frantically, if nobody can take a joke anymore? For God's sake, women, when will you give up this ridiculous insistence on bodily autonomy and START LEARNING TO TAKE A COMPLIMENT!

But the argument just doesn't stand up. It's laughable really to think that people have such a difficult time understanding the definition of *unwanted* sexual advances. Or the difference between consensual, two-way banter and uninvited, sleazy, sexual comments, or wandering hands. And for me – having worked in a brilliant office that happened to be all straight and all female yet somehow still mysteriously managed to remain full of laughter and camaraderie – it's really difficult to understand the argument that a lack of, ya know, *illegal* sexual harassment will somehow put the kibosh on All. Levity. And. Repartee. EVER.

But, worse still, this 'misunderstanding' narrative utterly fails to recognize two vital factors: the severity of the majority of the incidents and the inequality of power frequently reported between victim and perpetrator.

Believe me, across all the thousands of women who've told us their experiences of sexism in the workplace, not a single one of them could possibly have been a simple case of 'misunderstanding'. We aren't talking about a gentle 'You look nice today' being met with outrage and a full-on banshee attack by an outraged, uncompromising female. We're talking about professional women being told to strip at office Christmas parties, told to sit on their bosses' laps if they want their annual bonus, seriously sexually assaulted by senior male colleagues, groped, grabbed, touched, licked, fondled against their will and subjected to regular, vitriolic and offensive misogyny. We're talking about sixteen- and seventeen-year-old girls, in their first jobs, being accosted, groped, intimidated and harassed on a regular basis by much older bosses, managers and overseers. We're talking about regular and serious harassment, prejudice and assault.

▶ Male colleague after putting the phone down to a client, 'I Wish I could stick my c**k in her ear and f**k some sense into her'. I am not over exaggerating, this kind of thing is an everyday occurrence in my office, along with comments about the size of my breasts.

▶ My manager bullied and sexually harassed me over a period of a year. In December last year he grabbed my face with both his hands and licked around my lips as if he was kissing me. I pulled my lips tightly together to stop his tongue in my mouth. When he released my face I put my face in my hands and said go away. He then said 'mop the wet patch up from under your chair woman'.

▶ My first male boss repeatedly made passes at me on a work night out. Literally grabbing me and pushing his drunk, sweaty face at mine, trying to kiss me, hands all over me. I told him he was married, too old for me and I worked for him. He told me he didn't care, didn't care, and didn't care.

My desk was right outside his office door and I was uncomfortable and embarrassed for months. It should have been him who felt uncomfortable, but I don't think he was.

Many of the workplace experiences women relayed to the project were serious enough to constitute sexual assault. And yet, again and again, women also reported feeling unable to speak up, for a variety of complex reasons. There is often the fact of a power dynamic to consider, for a start. Innumerable entries recount stories of harassment perpetrated by senior male colleagues whose authority amplified the victims' feelings of fear and hopelessness and ultimately constituted a firm obstacle to formal complaint.

🐦 A guy at my work told me he'd get me fired if I didn't have sex with him. His brother was the boss.

It frequently being the case that there's no physical evidence of the crime, a victim may have to rely on their word being taken at face value. At best, an employer will take an allegation of harassment seriously, investigate fully and ensure that the victim's job and career are not negatively impacted by the experience. At worst, victims have reported losing their jobs and even being blacklisted within their industry. And in between is a murky gamut of risks, from being labelled a 'troublemaker' to losing clients or opportunities and being marginalized and unable to properly further an existing career. Little wonder, then, that so many of the women who told us their stories felt unable to register complaint through official channels.

When I was 23 my arse was regularly pinched at work. I was too afraid of losing my job to report it.

I work in a male-dominated business environment, every off-site meeting one of the male team members try to get off with me, last time the Director tried to sleep with me, dragging me to his hotel room and leaving finger shaped bruises on my upper arm for over a week.

I didn't and won't report it to HR as I want to get on in my career and don't want to be sacked.

Two senior male colleagues made jokes about my knickers [...] I had no idea why they were speculating about my knickers. I felt utterly humiliated and belittled. Handling the ensuing meeting was difficult. I felt ashamed, but they should have felt ashamed.

▶ I worked in a shoe store when I was 16. The manager walked past me one day and slapped my arse. It completely freaked me out, but I felt I would be ridiculed if I complained, so I didn't say anything.

And, so often unreported, the problem runs rampant. The project entries on workplace harassment testify to its complexity and the many different ways it can be manifest.

It starts at recruitment stages: from interview questions about pregnancy and family plans to inappropriate sexual demands. Before they even land the great pleasure of working in a job where they might face rampant sexism and harassment, women often must first navigate a downright biased selection process.

▶ I worked at a top law firm in recruitment and have heard partners assessing female candidates according to their attractiveness.

▶ Male professor at a uni I used to work at doesn't hire 'attractive women' to work in the laboratory as it would 'distract the men from their work'.

One of the most commonly reported problems in the recruitment process is phrased in various ways across the entries but remains essentially identical:

🐦 I'm 21 and being asked at job interviews if I'm getting married, or pregnant. Pretty sure this is illegal.

For the record: it's not illegal to ask this question, but it is illegal to choose not to hire somebody because of the answer – so it's difficult to justify asking it in the first place, since it should bear no more relevance to the interview than a question about the colour of a candidate's front door.

Sometimes there is no subtlety at all: one woman was simply asked outright for oral sex during an interview.

Once employed, many women notice quietly pervasive sexist norms within the working culture around them that serve to indirectly belittle and dismiss their value.

▶ International visitors from company's head office came for a meeting at which I, the only female in management, had to report. I walked in with my report and they asked for coffee, white with two sugars.

Others described their ideas being disregarded without consideration only to have male colleagues repeat them verbatim moments later to praise and reward.

▶ A female friend of mine in an office meeting proposed a logical, simple solution to a recurring issue. Blank stares from the group and a 'We've never done it that way' from the senior (female) manager. A male colleague then makes the exact same suggestion and the room nods enthusiastically and congratulates him on the idea.

Many reports to the project suggested that the simple fact of *being* a woman is frequently sufficient to warrant derision. We've heard some charming stories on this theme. One woman described a male colleague whose answer to any disagreement from his female peers was a loud announcement that they must be 'on their period' because they were 'all hormonal'. (Cue one of the wittiest of all comebacks reported to the project: 'If I had to bleed to find you annoying, i'd be anaemic.') Another referred to a boss who'd told her: 'I don't know what you are saying, I don't do woman speak.' But thank God sexism doesn't exist in the workplace anymore!

Reports also suggest that this commonplace nonsensical assumption of *female* inferiority often translates into a similarly casual assumption of women's *professional* inferiority: whereby women are naturally perceived to be junior to their male colleagues. In fact we received the following entry on the day we launched the Everyday Sexism Project:

▶ Me, 'I'm an architect'
Man, 'An architectural assistant?'
Me, 'No... an architect'
Man, 'Oh... gosh... well done.'

And since then similar stories have just kept coming...

▶ Told a guy where I work and he replied 'Oh are you a receptionist?' 'No actually, I'm a DNA scientist'. *awkward silence*

One barrister described a conversation with a law student on work experience:

▸ […] the student turns to me and asks: 'So, are you Steve's secretary?' Seeing the look on my face he realizes his mistake and splutters: 'Oh sorry, I mean his PA?'

Leading on from this general atmosphere of ignorance is the steady drip, drip, drip of verbal harassment – and by that I mean everything from inappropriate sexual questions to misogynistic comments to rape jokes.

▸ I am a computer scientist and work at one half of Oxbridge. I'm in my 30s, have a doctorate, a good number of independent publications and several years' experience. My male head of department refers to me as a 'clever girl'.

▸ In an office that I used to work in, I have been told I am a prude by a male colleague for not wanting to discuss my sex life or for being unhappy with listening to his sexual comments. Another colleague suggested that I should get a boob job as a joke and reacted badly when I told him I did not want to overhear his commentary on the appearance of all of the women in our office. One further male colleague told me that I obviously just didn't have a good body and this was the reason why I disagree with strip clubs.

When just a single instance of this kind of socially accepted dialogue is noted it's perhaps difficult to appreciate the potential cumulative impact on a woman's working environment. But actually the scope for injury is huge because such discourse, given licence, will generally only deteriorate over the course of time.

▸ Every day I am subjected to verbal humiliation from my male colleagues. They think that it is one big joke but it is extremely upsetting to be the victim of their jokes. If I am to wear a piece of new clothing, I get shouted at [...] This doesn't happen to any of the men in the office. Once they have finished shouting and silence falls, there is always one man that will shout 'show us where you piss from'. They proceed to break out in hysterical laughter. This is incredibly embarrassing.

And then of course there's physical contact, groping and assault. Many such incidents fall into the category of the unseen and vigorously doubted – almost (like the actions of Roald Dahl's atrocious Miss Trunchbull) simply too outrageous to bear believing. But much of this physical touching is also played down or disguised as harmless, friendly fun. A bit of opportunistic fumbling around the office water-cooler of a morning is, apparently, both flattering and hilarious. The odd office-party-breast-grope-tongue-down-the-throat-bottom-squeeze is a jolly good hoot! But let's face it: 'friendly molestation', in the workplace or otherwise, is something of an oxymoron.

🐦 I used to get my bottom slapped by the male managers at work, once with a fly swot by the deputy manager – all a joke, you know.

▸ A colleague in my previous job used to grab me inappropriately. For example, grabbing me by the waist to pull me towards him, touching my bum. He was very explicit about how he fancied me and even though he knew I was in a relationship he continued to make inappropriate comments and behaviour. I complained to my line manager who instead of supporting me, gave me excuses.

▶ On a night out, stood in a crowd of male colleagues who were considerably older than me (I was 19) when one of them interrupted me by leaning through the circle and touching my boob while the rest laughed. Not one of them said anything or even seemed to think it was wrong.

Like the normalization of street harassment and the multilayered media culture that so desensitizes us to the use of women's bodies as currency, the frequency of many of these occurrences in a single workplace can lead to a wider acceptance of such sentiments – whether in company policy or around the boardroom table. The more such incidents crop up – from a 'little' sexist joke here to a 'cheeky' pat on the bum there, a 'tongue-in-cheek' comment about the hassle of maternity leave to a 'joke' about a colleague's sex life – the more they lubricate the wheels of a system that comfortably maintains the male-dominated status quo. And, just like any hierarchical status quo, the more it repeats itself, the more comfortable it becomes for its beneficiaries to maintain it, whether as perpetrators or passive bystanders or ostriches with their heads in the sand. And the harder it becomes for its victims to speak out, as they stand on ever shakier ground.

So, far from being the rare or non-existent problem so many people would have it, workplace harassment not only manifests itself in nasty, diverse variations but also often exists in horrifying combinations that pile up to create an utterly unbearable atmosphere for victims. Each different incident adds greater cumulative weight to the next, while every indication of employers' and colleagues' acceptance of the prejudice presses down even harder on top.

▶ When I was 16 and in my first job, a sales rep visited the company and grabbed my breasts when I was in an office on my own. A few years later I overheard a couple of senior managers talking about me with some of my peers in the corridor - they described me as the small, skinny bird with big tits. One replied that he would like to bend me over the desk and give me one - several others jeered their appreciation of this comment.

The obvious key factor in harassment and abuse that happens in the workplace is the potential for career damage it carries. No other scenario yields quite the same implications. One can't help but wonder, judging by the number of women who report workplace prejudice, whether the ramifications of such a persistent bias might be far greater than the sum of their parts.

▶ A senior adviser to me, while working late during our busiest period of the year: 'What are you still doing here? Isn't your boyfriend getting hungry? He must be lonely.'
    Same guy a couple of days later as I'm preparing to take some work home with me: 'You know, a married woman should never take work home with her. I mean, it's natural for a married man,

but a married woman shouldn't be distracted at home.'

This guy affects the projects I get to work on, so I mentioned the comments to my boss. He said they were inappropriate but 'what can I do, it's just how he is.' Didn't push it further because I didn't want to be labelled as 'difficult'.

As the owner and Director of a company, I would sometimes attend bank meetings alone. Nine times out of ten, the manager would greet me and then ask 'when will your husband/the owner be here?'

It was fundamentally satisfying when I bought them up short on it, but ultimately, I'm pretty sure it affected the business. The perception was I couldn't quite be the boss, there had to be some murky male owner lurking in the background, or back in London, whereas the truth was I owned the entire company.

It seems possible that gender bias impacts on women's overall representation in the workforce. A recent study by scientists at Yale University, reported in the *Proceedings of the National Academy of Sciences*, seemed to indicate that such inherent assumptions about gender, made without employers even realizing it, could be having an enormous effect on women's professional prospects. The randomized double-blind study saw applications for science-based jobs sent to research-intensive universities. The CVs were identical, but some carried male names and some female. The study revealed that recruiters (both male and female) rated the 'male' applicants as 'significantly more competent and hireable' than the identical 'female' applicants. What's more, they also offered the 'male' applicants a higher starting salary *and* were more likely to offer them career mentoring. Mediation analyses concluded that 'the female student was less likely to be hired because she was seen as less competent'.

Pause for thought indeed.

Many of the project entries support the idea of unconscious bias and illustrate where the intricacies of the problem make it very difficult to challenge the status quo.

▶ When I was in my early 20s I was kept on clerical grades whilst male colleagues advanced to management level. When one of the male managers left and I was given the job, it was down-graded to a clerical grade. I was told the previous incumbent had been overpaid. When I left, the job was upgraded to management again!

You might think (this being the twenty-first century and procreation generally being considered in the best interests of society as a whole) that women's rights in terms of pregnancy and motherhood would be pretty watertight. But project entries from working women on this subject have regularly indicated that some time-honoured sexist attitudes prevail here too.

Women who chose to have children described how their competency and dedication were later brought into question. One woman was told by her boss not to return to work with 'leaky boobs', and a common swipe seems to be the idea of 'baby brain'; many women were automatically thought to be no longer 'up to the job' even when they returned to work with full dedication.

One PR executive was banned from pitching to new clients after she became pregnant, because bosses said her 'future commitment to the account' would 'clearly be in doubt'. A waitress described her boss's quite scandalous instruction to 'have an abortion or resign as my colleague was pregnant first & 2 pregnant workers was unfair'.

Certainly it very often seems to be the case that when a woman's career suffers negative impact subsequent to having children it's because external forces have conspired to cap her potential. Her own intentions or decisions apparently have little to do with it.

▶ A female colleague recently announced she is pregnant. Everyone in the office assumes she will quit work and are already talking about replacing her even though she is discussing maternity leave, not resignation from the company.

▶ As soon as I announced my pregnancy, they started ignoring my work, assuming I'd never come back from maternity leave.

▶ I am in my early 40s, a professional, with a PhD and 15 years of experience. I recently came back from maternity leave to my overseas posting, to meet the new boss for the first time. In our first meeting, he explained that I would no longer be in charge of the unit I had been setting up for a year due to my 'special circumstances', and because he wanted to make sure that he respected the rights of my baby to have his mother around. He also stated that while I was nursing it will be difficult for me to focus on my job, so he was being generous by giving me less responsibility, and downgrading my position.

That this is truly, appallingly discriminatory is even more starkly evident when you realize that UK employment law carefully provides for the protection of women in pregnancy and motherhood. There are optional 'keeping in touch' days designed to avoid any surprise changes to the woman's job during her leave, the right to be made aware of and take advantage of any pay rises and promotions during her pregnancy, and the same rights regarding redundancy as any other employee. It is absolutely, categorically illegal to select a woman for redundancy because of pregnancy, yet in 2005 the Equal Opportunities Commission revealed that around 30,000 women *every year* lose their jobs as a result of pregnancy discrimination. Campaigners have suggested that this number is likely to have risen dramatically since, as a result of the recession.

Perhaps the greatest injustice of all is that the same handicap is by default served even to those women who have no intention of having children. We've had countless reports from women who say their careers have been disadvantaged regardless simply because as their age and gender put them in the 'baby risk' category.

🐦 Myself and my female business partner were turned down for a contract last week as we're too much of a 'pregnancy risk'.

For one woman who already knew she was biologically unable to have children, missing out on a job because she was considered a 'baby risk' was a bitter blow.

So, if women are facing sexism, harassment, discrimination and even sexual assault in the workplace, why aren't more people aware of the problem and why isn't more action being taken? According to the Equality Act 2010, the provisions to protect women in the workplace are extensive. They are protected both from direct and indirect discrimination on the grounds of sex. They are protected from harassment – perpetrated by not only their employer but also third parties, from whom their employer has a responsibility to take reasonable steps to protect them once they've been made aware of the issue. Harassment includes unwanted conduct of a sexual nature; or unwanted conduct related to a person's sex, which either violates their dignity or creates an 'intimidating, hostile, degrading, humiliating or offensive environment' for the victim.

It is difficult to see how a single one of the experiences quoted in this chapter – or, indeed, of the thousands of workplace-related entries submitted to the project – do not fall firmly under at least one of these categories. And yet the problem persists. The complex and interwoven difficulties making it near-impossible for victims to speak out are exacerbated by flagrant flouting and circumnavigation of the law.

Many women who do find the courage to speak out – via their company's HR department, perhaps, or a manager – are met with rebuttal. Reports to the project suggest that there's an alarming propensity for denial and disregard, even from those whose job it is to combat such problems and ensure fair treatment of employees.

🐦 Went to HR about sexist and flirty CEO. Told to put up with it as I'm 'young and pretty and they're men, what do you expect?'

▸ I have taken my case to HR but they simply ignore me due to the sensitivity this case could bring to the press.

▸ My boss, who was in his 40s, tried to kiss me after the Christmas Party. I was 22. I went to the woman who coordinated the graduates and told her what had happened. I was told that this was to be expected in an office and if I ask to move it would affect my future career. So I continued in my position but felt so uncomfortable I would make myself throw up before I met with him.

▸ HR manager told me on our first day 'If you are going to report sexual harassment, first think about what you were wearing that day.'

Sometimes the options are laid starkly bare:

▸ I'm 18 years old and work as a receptionist in a car showroom. As the only female member of staff I'm forced to endure sexually charged comments on a daily basis from men old enough to be my father. I've complained to my boss about this (also male) who dismissed it as what passed as banter in all male workplace. The message I got from the meeting was if I couldn't handle the situations other workers put me in, then leave.

Sadly this pattern of dismissive response is evident even in those women's stories concerning allegations of serious harassment and sexual assault.

One woman was sexually assaulted by a male colleague at a conference and reported the incident to the event organizer. Her complaint was met with a conspiratorial wink and a whispered, 'I hear he recently got divorced.'

A young female engineer who was physically assaulted at work reported the crime to her boss only to be told to 'sweep it under the carpet'.

One woman was raped by a colleague on a work night out. 'Guess who lost their job?' she wrote grimly. 'Not him.'

The impact of such reactions on the victims, both emotionally and in terms of their career, cannot be underestimated. The young engineer told us:

▶ Because there were no witnesses or evidence of assault nothing could be done. I left the company shortly after that and now have a good career, although for a long time after I blamed myself, lost a lot of confidence, and went through a period of deep depression. Nine years later I still experience the odd sexual comment which makes me question as to why I remain in the industry. At the end of the day however, I've put a lot of hard work into getting to where I am and am passionate about what I do so why should I give it all up? Sadly though, I feel that if I were to give advice to a young female looking to follow a similar career path I would be very weary indeed.

When we talk about workplace harassment people tend to automatically think of women in offices putting up with the odd sexist joke. The common and simplified response is the question: 'Why didn't she just complain about it?' But of course in many cases women do not have direct recourse for such action. For thousands of people working freelance or in jobs like bar tending, there is no access to an HR department at all. Sometimes the option to report through official channels simply isn't there. And if the Everyday Sexism Project entries have demonstrated anything it's that harassment and sexism occur across the whole gamut of job types and descriptions.

A female vicar in the Church of England was repeatedly asked if there was a man available to perform the wedding or funeral service ('Nothing personal!'). A young DJ described how constant harassment and groping had brought her to dread the job she'd once loved. A midwife and a marketing consultant suffered near-indistinguishable experiences of sexual assault by senior male colleagues. A secondary-school teacher was heckled with sexual comments and jibes from young male pupils. A woman working in the office of a world leader was filing documents when she was told, 'That's where I like to see a woman: on her knees.' A City worker was told to sit on her boss's lap if she wanted to get her Christmas bonus. A junior hospital registrar received the same demand from a senior consultant when she asked him to help her interpret an X-ray. The captain of a wind-farm support boat had male recruits turn away because they didn't want to work for a female skipper. A racehorse owner wouldn't trust a female vet to touch the prized animal. A female pilot was scorned by passengers and colleagues.

Again and again, it amounts to women having to make an uncomfortable choice. Deal with the harassment or discrimination and get on in your career, or report it and risk losing everything. Be open about your plans for motherhood and risk being sidelined, or keep quiet only to be affected anyway by ingrained stereotyping and assumptions about your life choices and biological urges. It isn't the way it should be. It isn't even legal. But right now it certainly seems to be the way it is.

One woman's story completely summed up this status quo:

▶ An arm round my shoulders with the hand resting on my breast [...] I had a senior manager who frequently used to try and do this to all the female staff necessitating a side-step movement to get away. A complaint was made but nothing changed.

Quite wrongly, the onus is currently on women in the workplace to develop coping mechanisms and contingency plans rather than on perpetrators to stop offending or on companies to deal with the problem. 'Advised against pursuing an investigation in my sexual harassment case,' one woman told us: 'because it would "harm my career" as a woman in science.' That's a conclusion about as ironic and misguided as the one drawn by some media outlets about the women who spoke up about being groped by a senior politician being responsible for putting women off going into politics.

It's extraordinarily unhelpful when people suggest that it is *women* who must take responsibility for workplace gender imbalance, and *women* who hold the key to fixing it. The notion that women must simply be stronger, or somehow learn to 'deal with' these incidents, is ridiculous. To imply, as people frequently do, that women are simply too shy and retiring and do not push themselves forward professionally is plain daft. And all of these things serve as an enormous kick in the teeth to the thousands of hardworking, talented and committed women out there who are stepping up, who are putting themselves forward – who are, in fact, fighting tooth and nail for a seat at the table – and yet finding the door closed in their face regardless.

The woman who wrote this project entry sure as hell knew how to stand up for herself...

▶ Guy at work used to think it was OK to only ever address me as big boobs. 'Morning big boobs' etc. I started addressing him as 'small penis' – he soon realized that maybe saying 'morning Kate' would be a better way to address me.

But the brilliance of her witty comeback doesn't mean that she was suddenly free from the realities of working in a structurally biased professional world intrinsically stacked against her at every turn. Nor does it mean that the sexist assumptions made about her (and their potential knock-on impact on her professional interactions and career) were necessarily resolved. The overt harassment was silenced but its root remained.

The issues holding women back in the workplace are immeasurably larger than any individual. And, yes, while a single individual may well be able to take certain measures to advance her career within the existing framework, it is the framework itself – and the wider cultural attitudes surrounding it and influenced by it – that have the greatest impact. *These* must be tackled in order to see meaningful, widespread change.

You need only glance at the relevant statistics to realize how much greater the problem is than any individual woman's attitude. A stubborn pay gap of between 10 and 20 per cent (depending which figures you look at) persists, despite equality legislation and apparently equal opportunities. (It's been forty-five years since those women at Dagenham fought for parity of pay and set the foundations for legislation on our behalf; you'd think this wouldn't still be a problem.) The Fawcett Society reported in 2012 that comparing all work, women earned 18.6 per cent less per hour than men, with the figure standing at 14.9 per cent for those working full time. They pointed out that the pay gap varies across locations and sectors, rising to 33 per cent in the City of London and soaring to 55 per cent in the finance sector. According to a 2013 Citizens Advice Bureau publication, '*Well, actually...*', the unemployment rate for men in March 2012 stood almost exactly where it did at the end of the recession in 2009 (1.54 million, representing an increase of only 0.32 per cent), whereas female unemployment had increased by almost 20 per cent to 1.13 million – the highest figure for twenty-five years.

The gap in pay is mirrored by a gap in attainment at the highest professional levels – according to 2014 statistics from the Judiciary of England and Wales, only 7 out of 38 Lord Justices of Appeal and just 19 out of 106 High Court Judges are female. According to the *Times Higher Education* only 1 in 5 UK university professors is female, while they make up just 15.6 per cent of the teaching staff at Cambridge. Only around 10 per cent of UK engineers is female (less than half the proportion of many other European countries). As of October 2013, just 6.1 per cent of UK FTSE 100 companies had female executive directors (the figure stands at 5.4 per cent for FTSE 250 companies) and women made up just 23.8 per cent of FTSE 100 non-executive directors.

The reasons for these inequalities are many and complex, but the glib argument that women make 'different choices' and choose to 'sacrifice career for family' falls short on two counts. First, even if this argument is accepted at face value, it fails to entirely explain the pay gap. A report released by the Higher Education Careers Services Unit in 2013 showed that, even at the point directly following university – long before many people even begin to consider families – female graduates are already earning thousands of pounds less than their male peers. The longitudinal study of 17,000 graduates showed that 1 in 5 men earned more than £30,000 after their degree, while just 8 per cent of women commanded the same salaries. The problem persisted across almost every career path, and remained even between graduates who studied the same subject and attended the same university. In law, for example, female graduates' starting salaries typically stood at £20,000 – a staggering £8,000 less than their male peers.

But the second problem with the idea of women 'making sacrifices' for family is the very notion that having children will necessarily impact on a woman's career but not on a man's. This reality, compounded by inflexible working hours and a lack of shared parental leave, is often quoted as if it were an immutable fact that women must simply accept, rather than a long-existing prejudice that could and should be altered.

Rarely does anybody stop to peek a layer further and ask why is it that women have those different 'priorities'? *Why* is it that making the decision to have a family is something that we talk about as a reasonable cause for a setback in a woman's career, but never consider in relation to a man's? *Why* is it women who have to make these choices at all, while men are seemingly able to waltz serenely into the sunset with top-flight career, 2.4 children and company car – the whole shebang?

Why do we continue to insist, even in the twenty-first century, on asking the archaic question: 'Can women really have it all?' instead of unpicking the deep societal bias that allows such rhetoric to persist in the first place? Why don't we stop to question the sexist paradigm in which women are the primary carers of children and the elderly and the part-time work they frequently must take on in order to maintain these responsibilities is paid less by the hour than full-time jobs and has few prospects for career advancement? Why do we keep asking why girls aren't as 'interested' in business and engineering or as 'driven' and 'ambitious' as boys, instead of stopping to consider the impact of the repeated background nonsense that tells them science isn't feminine, strong women are 'shrill' or 'bossy' and that their natural role – as the thousands of dollies and playhouses and cookers in the girls' section at the toy store will confirm – is to care and clean and cook and keep house?

From childhood onwards, both implicitly and explicitly, women are discouraged from certain careers or from having a career at all. They are subject to subconscious and overt bias at every stage of employment, starting with applications and interviews; they suffer verbal harassment and physical assault in the workplace then face being silenced or sacked when they complain about it; and they are written off and marginalized merely for approaching biological fertility. Isn't it time to set aside the questions about what *women* should bring to the equation and focus on some of these things instead?

Chapter 8

Motherhood

'When I told my marketing-director boss I was pregnant for the first time she said, "Well, this isn't a part-time job"'

Everyday Sexism Project Entry

Vital Statistics

30,000 women lose their jobs each year as a result of pregnancy discrimination (almost 8 per cent of all pregnant women at work)
Equal Opportunities Commission, 2005

Only 3 per cent of women who face pregnancy discrimination seek legal advice
OnePoll, 2013

A woman with a child aged under 11 is 45 per cent less likely to be employed than a man
UK Equalities Review, 2007

More than 70 per cent of recruitment agencies have been asked by clients to avoid hiring pregnant women or those of childbearing age
UK Equalities Review, 2007

30 per cent of domestic violence starts or worsens during pregnancy
Lewis and Drife, 2001; McWilliams and Mckenna, 1993

1 in 6 pregnant women suffers domestic violence in the UK
Research from Hull Royal Infirmary, published in the
British Journal of Obstetrics and Gynaecology, 2003

🐦 I'm so tired of people on the street calling me sexy. I'm 6 months pregnant, bro. You literally just need to leave me alone.

🐦 Friend of mine works in a law firm, recently got pregnant. They're hiring for her replacement. She won't have a job after.

🐦 I am constantly expected to justify my reasons for not wanting or having babies and put up with people telling me that I will change my mind.

🐦 Met a man who said he'd never employ a woman of childbearing age as they could 'ruin' his company if they got pregnant.

🐦 "All single mothers are sluts who get pregnant to get benefits and housing."

🐦 I was 8 months pregnant, walking through the pub I worked at. A regular says: 'I heard pregnant women need a good seeing to, want help?'

From contraception to abortion and baby weight to childlessness, the common misconception that women's bodies are public property is never stronger than when the subject is reproduction.

Once more, it starts minor. So minor, in fact, that you'd be chided for making a fuss. Newlyweds being repeatedly asked when they're going to start popping out tiny humans as if it's suddenly their urgent, public duty. Intelligent women, quite in command of their faculties, stating their intent to remain childless and being condescendingly assured: 'You'll change your mind, just you wait and see.' The inexplicable erosion of boundaries that turns a pregnant belly into an electromagnet for the outstretched, groping hands of passing strangers. To object to such 'well-meant' intrusions would be considered churlish – an overreaction. But the idea that we should listen to anyone and everyone's advice and opinions about what we should do with our own uteri stems, ultimately, from the notion that women's reproductive systems (and, by extension, women themselves) exist for one purpose, and one purpose alone. Somehow, this seems to translate into a merry free-for-all that mysteriously doesn't seem to extend to penises despite their equal role in the initiation of the whole process.

That sense in which everybody has a say amounts to nothing less than a public invasion of pregnancy. Albeit that it's supposedly joyful and friendly, it's easy to understand why women might resent being swamped by unsolicited advice and having strangers touch their bodies willy-nilly. As one man tweeted to the project:

🐦 My pregnant wife's bump was apparently an invitation for strangers (men and women) to cop a stroke.

This is a common theme, stemming, I think, from the fact that when a woman conceives, that single fact takes over her whole identity in society's eyes, as if her individual features somehow melt away and she morphs into a cookie cutter 'pregnant lady'. But in reality there are numerous reasons why a pregnant woman might dislike someone touching her body without permission. (For a woman who has previously experienced abuse it could be terrifying.) It is ironic, given the alienating isolation women often face in the workplace when they fall pregnant, that in the public sphere they battle the opposite problem – the idea that everybody in society at large seems to think they have a stake in the process. Likewise women may feel very exposed and vulnerable when they're at the receiving end of a barrage of 'well-meaning' advice. For some, this uninvited commentary can feel very disempowering and invasive, particularly if they are already experiencing anxiety about the pregnancy for myriad possible reasons. For others, it's simply annoying. At best it's really quite rude. Male-pattern baldness affects around half of all men in the UK by the age of fifty, but we don't see strangers approaching them in the street and commenting on the sparseness of their follicles, or copping a confident feel of their scalp, as if the biological process, by dint of its visibility, was somehow a public matter.

▶ I was out for dinner and a musical event at a local venue [...] As I was paying for our bill the (male) owner of the venue asked how my pregnancy was going and said, much to my shock, 'It is so good that you've kept your weight down, that is so important.'

These invasions say much about attitudes towards women generally. The indignity of public ownership is something that crosses the boundaries of just about every aspect of sexism in our society. Clumsy overenthusiasm about our reproductive state might come from an inherently well-meaning place but the fact is that it also denotes the idea of women as passive objects of utility.

If the reports we have received are anything to go by, many, many mothers find themselves subject to harassment not *aside* from their maternal status but *because* of it.

▶ I was walking my 5-month-old son in his buggy, down Oxford Street. Middle of the day, wearing a knee-length black dress. A man stopped me, told me I was a 'fucking MILF' and then proceeded on his way with a grin. This isn't the only time this sort of thing has happened – in fact it's more vulgar when I'm with my son. I believe it's because women appear more vulnerable when they're with small children – usually I'd challenge that sort of behaviour, but I wouldn't put my son at risk so keep quiet.

As for the idea of reproduction as the primary purpose and function of women, well... What could be more limiting to our collective identity? Entirely preposterous it may be, but it nonetheless forms a background disquiet that helps mould the way women feel about themselves and their sense of validation.

For some women, the underlying message that childbearing is the single most exalted experience of every human female causes huge distress.

▶ Maternal, no children, mid-forties. Have been made to feel very much a lesser being and a complete failure for not having children. There are TV programmes I can't bring myself to watch, adverts I can't bear to see. Images of the wonders of birth and motherhood bombard me. I don't/can't resent it and I'll still get excited and a surge of joy at the prospect of a friend/relative's pregnancy, but, I am grieving (and it is real, heartstopping grief) for the children I haven't produced. So, having not found the man to make the baby with, I guess I'm not ruling the world as I've failed myself and all womankind.

One woman told her own family that she didn't intend to have children and was asked, 'What's the point of you then?' Another told us:

▶ Telling people that I haven't the health or energy to parent a child never stopped the comments. Telling them I'm gay didn't stop them. Telling them my primary illness is genetic and likely to be inherited by any child didn't. Telling them pregnancy could leave me paraplegic didn't.

We received the following entry from a woman describing herself as 'childfree by choice' but also citing a medical condition that leaves her unable to have children:

▶ I get insulted frequently for this. Told I'm unnatural, heartless, and most commonly selfish. I often get treated like a pariah among friends and family with children, or even strangers [...] I get treated like a child-hater, which I'm not [...] I get threatened, insulted, derided and told I'm not a real woman, or that I'll inevitably change my mind when I'm older/more mature. (I'm nearly 30, apparently old enough to do everything apart from decide I don't want a baby.)

A definition of womanhood based on a presumed ability and desperation to procreate is incredibly heteronormative, and gender essentialist too. Naturally there are many who don't subscribe to it for that very reason...

▶ My boss asks if I would want a family one day, so I say, 'Possibly, but not for a long while yet. I'll probably adopt.' He laughs and says, 'No, I don't think you will. You just need to find the right man to change your mind. All women want a man to give them their own children, I don't think adopting would suit you.' So, I reply, 'Actually, it probably would. I'm infertile. Also, I'm a lesbian.'

One woman wrote to the Everyday Sexism Project after seeing an article in the national press arguing that women of childbearing age (all women, not just those who are pregnant) should be denied anti-depressants because they could be harmful to a hypothetical foetus. Her entry laid bare the very suggestion of reproduction above and beyond anything else as wholly counterintuitive.

▶ One of the things my body can do is carry a pregnancy and give birth to the baby. If I am going to use it for that, it is up to me. But I may (and do) also want to use it for a zillion other things, many of which require me to be in a fit state of mental health. I am a person living inside this body and I am more important than a theoretical future being that could exist or the abstract principle of what some other person thinks my body should be used for. It is MINE and it is going to be used by ME for whatever I want.

For many women, both in the UK and further afield, such assertion of autonomy is simply not an option, though, so strongly are cultural beliefs entwined into legislation. Worldwide, one of the most basic forms of sustained gender prejudice is the denial of women's control over their own bodies and reproductive systems. In 2011 *alone*, the Guttmacher Institute for sexual and reproductive health and rights reported that legislators in American states introduced more than 1,100 provisions relating to reproductive health and rights. Of those that were enacted, 68 per cent restricted access to abortion services.

In 2012 Savita Halappanavar, a thirty-one-year-old in Galway, Ireland, was denied the right to a life-saving operation under legislation that prioritizes motherhood over autonomy. Following her death, her husband said that hospital staff citing Irish anti-abortion policy had refused to allow her the abortion she needed – despite her pregnancy being non-viable. A jury found that she died as a result of 'medical misadventure'. What a euphemism.

Around the world, women are dying because of men's ideas about what they should and shouldn't be allowed to do with their own bodies. Childbearing carries enormous physiological implications and risks, even in healthy full-term pregnancies. The decision to carry and give birth to a child simply isn't one that should be made by anybody other than the woman whose body is involved. And yet here, once more, we see puritanical, archaic objections to female autonomy that aren't applied to other comparable situations. The fact that birth control and abortion weren't available many years ago doesn't mean that every child – even those conceived by rape or incest – is a 'gift from God' that a mother has no choice but to bear. We *do* have a choice now; and, just as scientific advancement has given us far greater control over other 'natural processes', such as disease, it has also allowed women far greater self-governance over their own bodies. Our judgements and decisions should be made within the existing framework, taking those advancements into account.

Moralistic panic over birth control and abortions can have devastating consequences. Providing for safe, legal abortions does not lead to a significant increase in uptake – women have abortions all over the world, regardless of legality. But women who are forced to seek unsafe illegal abortions may pay with their lives.

Worldwide, 47,000 women every year die and millions more are injured as a direct result of complications from unsafe abortion. And other basic health needs can also be compromised – 58% of US birth control users cite other reasons for using it apart from contraception. But in 2011, members in the US House of Representatives voted to ban all federal funding for Planned Parenthood health centres, which, if not stopped by the Senate, would have prevented millions of women from getting not only birth control but critical health screenings, according to 'This is Personal'.

Whilst arguing about viability and the date at which a foetus becomes a 'person', we often utterly fail to take into account the absolutely definite, not at all hypothetical life of the mother. (See, for example, the untold psychological impact on a woman visiting an abortion clinic of being picketed and bombarded with abuse by protestors holding bloody signs or screaming curses). It is most striking of all that in a debate that revolves almost entirely around the concept of 'humanity' there is so very little humane thought given to women at all. The shadowy idea that abortion is a shameful and immoral act allows those who, largely, have little experience of it or of the need for it, to frame the debate, while the voices likely to give us the most useful and relevant perspective of all are entirely silenced. And of course this only skews the debate even further.

▸ While in Year 10 my science teacher felt it appropriate to share his views on how he believed abortion was too flexible and should not be allowed up to 24 weeks. After telling him that I believed that it should be allowed up to 24 weeks he looked at me in disgust and told me that 'those' women should not be allowed to have children at all.

▸ A male colleague told me men should decide about abortion law and time limits because women are too emotional and have a personal bias which is why we have 24 weeks which he says is 'really late' and puts too much focus on 'what the woman herself wants'.

▸ I was watching one of those round table political discussion shows this morning and the topic of abortion came up. There was one woman on the show, and she was trying to speak up on several occasions. The three men next to her were in an intense discussion on pro-life (no exceptions) versus pro-life (exceptions like rape and health risk) and kept cutting her off and telling her to hold on. I could hear a woman off-set laughing because she obviously could not believe what was happening. The woman at the table had this smile plastered on her face as she tried several more times to get a word in edge wise. She even started sentences like 'Well since this is a women's issue…' but the man next to her said 'Hold on one second let me finish' and continued talking to the other men. It was painful and sickening to watch. On the topic of abortion the only woman at the table did not get to speak even once before they went to commercial and dropped the subject entirely.

▶ My husband just said that a woman should be able to decide to take her top off for men if she wants to that she should have control over her own body but that a woman should not be able to have an abortion because that is murder.

In among the censorious, pseudo-religious, moralistic panic that forms the mainstay of most political debates about abortion, stories from real women are notably lacking. It must be so very simple to pronounce judgement and dust off your hands and walk away very secure in the knowledge that you will never have to really think about, really feel, in your own body, the reality of what you have just said. It is real women's stories that are missing – the stories that might reveal to these black-and-white thinkers the true depth and complexity of what they are really discussing. But then, of course, that would make things much more awkward to discuss in such handy, clear-cut terms. The comfortable myth of abortion users as selfish, irresponsible creatures rather than human beings like you and me would be all too quickly shattered. The reality is very different.

▶ I had an abortion, and I can't tell anyone besides my partner because I am so afraid. I chose not to ask for support from my family because they are very 'traditional'. I am a highly educated, bread-winning mother in a 15-year relationship [...] I am a successful human being, and I have a right to direct the course of my life and protect my own family. Although I am successful, we are not rich nor do we have infinite time. I want the best life possible for myself, my partner, and especially for my daughter. This was the best (not easiest) possible decision for all of us, and yet I still feel ashamed and silenced.

Our society has such a knee-jerk tendency to vilify and dehumanize women that in discussions of pregnancy and abortion the role of men is almost never mentioned. Still the euphemistic and somehow judgemental description of a woman 'falling' pregnant is used, as if reproduction is something she carelessly does all by herself, comparable to forgetting to buy milk, say, or getting an ill-advised tattoo. And in this relentless focus on women's responsibility, men lose out on crucial support and help, too. Precious little counselling or care is made available to those whose partners lose or abort a child, for example, because such things are portrayed so unremittingly as 'women's issues'.

For women experiencing some of the common mental-health symptoms frequently associated with pregnancy, sexist assumptions and stereotypes about women and motherhood can be deeply damaging. As one interviewee explained:

Honestly, until I became a mother I thought sexism had all but died out. I was largely unaware of it and had always achieved

what I wanted regardless of my sex. Then I got pregnant and all of that changed.

After twenty years of happy infertility (I never wanted to be a mum) I accidentally got pregnant in 2007. I decided to go ahead with it (I kept being told it was a miracle conception) but the enormous shock of a baby I didn't want was devastating. From the moment I discovered I was pregnant the sexist pressure was on. I saw my GP the day after I took the test to discuss my options but she instantly assigned me a midwife for the pregnancy. It didn't occur to her that I may not want a child. I recall clearly that it was at that moment that I felt I was 'wrong' for not being overjoyed at my situation and all because, as a woman, I was supposed to be overjoyed.

I developed post-traumatic stress disorder and post-natal depression with suicidal tendencies after the pregnancy and this became a full breakdown in 2010 from which I am still recovering. My daughter – who I now adore – is five. The sexism came into it when seeking help. I was a woman with a new baby so it was assumed that I was delighted and fulfilled. My gender seemed to mean more to people than my individuality.

Everyone around me, apart from my very closest family and friends, thought that as an infertile woman all my dreams had been fulfilled. They were incapable of understanding why I had such a problem with this shock change in my circumstances. Even the mental-health professionals I've been in contact with have all struggled to understand why a woman would not want to be a mum. It was only the understanding of those closest to me – those who knew that I was never going to glow with maternal instinct – that saved my life.

There were so many times when I felt I was screaming but no one could hear me and during all of this time I became increasingly mentally unstable, isolated and desperate and I also attempted suicide. I wanted to be heard as an individual but all anyone heard was what they thought a woman 'should' be. I feel as if I have spent the last five years fighting not just my illness but the inherent sexism that comes with being a mother.

Sadly, this exalted status of 'mother' as almost another category altogether, quite separate from personhood and individuality within our culture, can have lasting and deeply felt effects.

It's now been five years since the birth of my daughter and the sexism is as strong and pervasive as ever. Not a day passes without me having to battle the assumptions and expectations demanded of me because I am a woman and a mother. It's in adverts, on packaging, in magazines, on TV, in newspapers, in the comments of strangers, in the schoolyard and in children's books.

An average day will start with news reports about how the actions of mothers (not fathers) impact on their child's health. I take my child to school to be referred to by the teachers as 'Mum' rather than my name. I go to the supermarket where the baby aisles are strewn with pics of glowing women, rather than men, and where the clothes aisles are nothing but pink for little girls. When I use the internet, parenting websites are loaded towards women as the nurturers and carers (Mumsnet, Britmums, etc.). When I meet extended family on weekends I get asked when I am 'having another one'. (Never, by the way.) When I play with my

daughter we are assaulted with images of princesses, puppies and pretend kitchens, which I fight with every atom of my body. It's endless and it's exhausting.

The whole area of maternity is fraught with a multiplicity of contradictions and hypocrisy – teen motherhood is sneeringly condemned, while 'career women' who 'leave it too late' are caught in a crossfire of pity and accusations of cold, hard, selfishness. Women are constantly reminded that reproduction is their pressing raison d'être, yet bombarded with headlines like these (of course from the *Daily Mail*) suggesting that selfish women spewing out babies are ruining the very fabric of our society:

Now three in five doctors aged under 30 are women: fears for care standards as junior doctors fall pregnant

What kind of woman gets pregnant just to take a year off work?

As one woman wryly retorted on Twitter:

🐦 How dare we go and have babies. The poor patriarchy.

Meanwhile women are closely watched and pressured to stay fit and do everything right while pregnant, but too much exercise (or whatever other innocent activity the tabloids have deemed potentially harmful that day) may provoke a cascade of indignant outrage.

'Pregnant women should avoid the sun'… 'Pregnant women

hit by rickets because they're not getting enough sun'... 'Pregnant women who drink "lightly" could have brighter babies'... 'Pregnant women are told: Don't drink at all' ... 'How can pregnant women ensure their babies will be healthy? By eating fry-ups'... 'Pregnant women who eat chips increase risk of having underweight babies' ... 'How healthy eating could STOP you getting pregnant'... 'A fish-rich diet gives mothers silent nights' ... 'Pregnant women warned over tuna'...

And my personal favourite: 'Pregnant women are confused about their diets'.

The list goes on and on (and these are from the *Daily Mail* alone – that fine publication boasts an impressive stable of 215 articles for the search term 'pregnant women should'). There's certainly plenty to sustain a serious state of guilt-induced anxiety throughout your entire pregnancy ('Pregnant women should avoid anxiety at all costs'...).

It's enough to make the mind boggle at the miraculous survival of all those healthy pre-women's magazine babies.

And, don't forget, when you have a moment's break from the brain-bending exhaustion of working out what you ABSOLUTELY MUST and DEFINITIVELY MUST NOT eat and drink you're also obliged to take the time to pick a tribe – be a sexy MILF, a hockey mom, an earth mother, a full-time mum, a yummy mummy, a slummy mummy, a scummy mummy... Because here, as with every other aspect of 'womanhood', there is a rigid categorization with little room for alternatives or grey areas.

The problem with pregnancy is that in a society hellbent on judging you first and foremost as a woman (rather than as an individual person) in any given situation, your condition becomes the immediate focus of the lens through which your every move, outfit and mouthful is analysed.

Suddenly the decision to leave the house becomes, according to the tabloids, an extrovert ploy to 'put her bump on display'; the choice to carry a particular handbag, meanwhile, is a coy attempt to 'keep her bump covered'... (See the recent *Daily Mail* headline: 'Kate Winslet continues her pregnancy parade as she shows off baby bump at Toronto Film Festival'. What the *Mail* has done there is to accidentally confuse 'doing her job' with 'parading' and 'showing off'.)

Then there's the media's complete inability to distinguish between the natural changing of a woman's figure during pregnancy and its usual hyper-driven disgust at an inch of female fat, leading to disturbing coverage that conflates the two. As scream a couple of recent magazine headlines:

Jessica Simpson's fat days are numbered... she just popped out baby number two

Pregnant Kim's Nightmare 65lb Weight Gain!

The obsession with baby weight and the not-always-so-subtle suggestion that these lazy women have basically let themselves go and become disgusting fatties are reinforced by myriad articles interpreting everything a pregnant woman wears as a desperate attempt to 'cover up' or 'disguise' or 'hide' her baby bump...

Keeping Mum: Drew Barrymore hides her baby bump under slimming horizontal stripes

Black to cover up the baby bump: Petra Ecclestone hides her heavily pregnant shape in dark outfit

Perfect and pregnant: Molly Sims hides her baby bump in a super chic dress and heels combination

All of this combines to promote the unhelpful dual fallacies that (first) gaining weight while pregnant is somehow 'shameful' and akin to getting fat, and that (second) women are in control of the shapes of their bodies throughout pregnancy and immediately afterwards. Both concepts are fuelled by stories artificially pitting pregnant celebrities against one another and the relentless scrutiny of any woman's post-partum figure.

The parallel pregnancies of Kim Kardashian and the Duchess of Cambridge provided the perfect example of this media obsession with competitive gestation, as well as the arbitrariness with which it is possible to mould perfectly natural and uncontrollable bodily processes into cause for either enormous praise and admiration or denigrating disapproval.

As Kardashian's bump grew, the world went into a feeding frenzy over her weight and diet, with online memes springing up comparing her to a killer whale after she wore a black-and-white dress, and magazines fabricating stories about her apparent 'despair' at her own burgeoning size. A London newspaper plastered her photograph on their front page because she happened to eat a portion of chips. Under the headline 'Pregnant Kim Kardashian Succumbs to Cravings and Gorges on Burger and Chips' there followed a non-story astutely inventing details about how eagerly she 'tucked into the calorific meal'.

Elsewhere headlines focused unendingly on her swollen ankles and the size and shape of her bottom. In one particularly awful example from *Now* magazine's website ('Is it just me, or is Kim Kardashian giving birth out of her bum?') the incredible inanity of the accompanying article was evidence of a desperate scramble for some text – any text – to justify the gratuitous, cruel headline and a guffawing 'look how big her bum is' moment:

'Ever since her rapper boyfriend Kanye West got her up the duff, her bum is growing at a faster rate than her baby bump!' (It wasn't.) 'So it totally begs the question: Is Kim Kardashian going to give birth out of her bum?' (It didn't, and, needless to say, she wasn't.)

And, just to lay to rest any remaining doubts we could possibly have about the intended spirit in which the piece was to be taken, it ended with the snide reminder: 'Rest easy girls, no matter how many Easter eggs we eat this week, we will never have the biggest bum in the world. Great, isn't it?' (No, it isn't.)

Now compare this hyperbolic and gleeful mudslinging to the equally cringe-inducing sycophancy-fest that surrounded the Duchess of Cambridge during her pregnancy, with constant references to her 'svelte' and 'streamlined' figure implying some kind of virtuous, intentional suppression of her bump. The fallacy of control was most nauseatingly expressed by *Vanity Fair.* Voting her top of their 'best-dressed bump' list (evidence in itself of the idea that women are expected to use their nine months of pregnancy as some sort of fashion-plate opportunity, much like dressing for the races or a beach holiday), the mag raved about her 'bare minimum of a bump'.

Meanwhile the *Daily Mail* went a step further in making it quite clear that they considered the difference in the women's appearance to be a matter of class, with a crass 'bump off' article that compared a series of photographs of Kate in long, covering coats with images of Kim in tight dresses, nauseatingly describing the duchess as the 'picture of maternal modesty' while Kim was branded 'brash', 'trashy', 'mumsy and clumsy'. The 'mumsy' jibe (an ironic insult in an article *about* pregnancy) and the praise for Kate's 'barely visible royal bump' once again reiterated the idea that, while women are expected and demanded to fulfil their biological function, the ideal scenario is for them to magically not *look* as if they are doing so at all. Lest we forget that the media is driven by men, for men …

But it's the setting up of celebrities against one another that's the cruellest public spin on motherhood – the transformation of what is already a difficult, emotional and physically demanding experience into some kind of endurance-challenge spectator sport, with all the added pressure and insecurity that will inevitably cause. Spare a thought for any pregnant mother reading the *TMZ* article headlined 'Not All Famous Preggo Chicks Have to Be HUGE', which shamelessly clawed into Jessica Simpson and Kim Kardashian by lining them up next to the duchess and crudely concluding 'well, one of these things is not like the other' while helpfully observing of Kate's physique that you could 'BARELY tell she was with fetus [*sic*]'.

Add to all this the absolute slew of articles about losing baby weight, 'showing off' svelte 'post-baby' figures (always with a 'celebrity steps out just x months after giving birth!' headline for comparison purposes) and a total dearth of media coverage of real women's post-baby bodies. The result is a toxic combination of shame, guilt and self-flagellation for new mothers at one of the most vulnerable and draining points of their lives, complete with all the (let's face it) much more important things they could really do with focusing on.

It's a strange quirk of our media that, while certain aspects of women's bodies (what they look like at eighteen, say, or after breast implants, or slathered in baby oil and airbrushed) are so overexposed that we come to automatically and quite inaccurately consider them the norm, some *actual* norms are so resolutely kept from our view that we're utterly unprepared for them. This is especially pertinent in the case of pregnancy – and never has it been more astoundingly exposed than on the Duchess of Cambridge's exit from the maternity wing of London's St Mary's Hospital just hours after giving birth, her post-partum baby bump clearly visible.

The media, both traditional and online, exploded. What was wrong with her? People *demanded* to know. Had she really had the baby? Was there another one in there? Had she got fat during her pregnancy? A quick-thinking Sky News reporter asked a midwife in an on-air interview why Kate still had a baby bump. Twitter exploded as stumped users searched for answers: 'Why's Kate Middleton still fat with a bump? She's already had the baby', asked one flummoxed user. 'Why does Kate's belly still look fat when they're outside holding the baby?' wondered another, concisely expressing the depth of their consternation with an added 'wtf'. Myriad commenters stuck to the plain facts: 'Kate looks fat. Lol.' Others flavoured their observations of the new mother with extra objectification and misogyny: 'I'd fuck Kate with or without her afterbirth bump.'

The stunned reaction revealed the seeping of the media correlation between pregnancy and 'fatness' into the public consciousness and gave an ugly glimpse of the extent to which, for some people, any woman, at any time, will always be seen as a sex object. But most importantly it revealed an enormously widespread lack of any kind of public awareness or education about the real impact of pregnancy on women's bodies – the changes they go through and the reality of how they will look different at different times.

When the BBC capitalized on the inevitable ensuing slew of 'Kate bump' Google searches with a story showing photographs of women's post-birth stomachs, there was an outpouring of emotion from women and a shocked realization that here, incredibly, was an angle on the female body that many of us had simply never seen before. As one woman commented on the BBC article: 'After I gave birth I was shocked. And horrified. I had never seen an after-pregnancy belly with stretch marks and sags exposed. At all. I hadn't heard about it. I didn't even know that it existed.'

And it's not only expectant mothers who are apparently fair game for public commentary, criticism and condemnation, but any mother at any time, according to a range of recurring, trite headlines about whether women can 'have it all', what 'Mums' are feeding their children, how 'Mums' are letting their kids watch too much television, whether 'Mums' should be making different choices – with never a father in sight or mind. A recent episode of TV talk show *The Wright Stuff* gave a prime example in its debate: 'Should Mums Only Work for the Money? Is it selfish to leave your kids in nursery or with child-minders just because you fancy getting out of the house a few hours or days each week?' Because, after all, what other reason could women have for a career than getting out of the house? We all know it's only men who derive fulfilment from academic and professional endeavour! The study that led to this mum-centric debacle referred to children left in the care of others, so could have applied to mums *or* dads, but was (like so many 'scientific' findings) interpreted as a potential slur against only women. (As in the *Metro* story of August 2013 that took a scientific study about both spouses' ability to tune out their partner's voices and turned it into the refreshingly original story: 'NAGGING NOISES: Good news husbands: it's easy to ignore your wife'.)

Such headlines expose and compound the inherent societal assumption that ultimately it is a woman's duty to produce children, a woman's responsibility to ensure their wellbeing at every stage, and a woman's fault if anything goes wrong. As the thousands of entries we have received from women in the workplace testify, workplace equality laws and initiatives have yet to truly make a dent in the stony conviction that it is a woman's career that should really take the hit for the price of parenthood. And after all, people still ask, what 'real' woman wouldn't care more, deep down, about her child than her career? Quite natural for men, of course, who have worked so hard and put so much into their prized jobs, to want to maintain a balance and not allow new fatherhood to derail a promotion or an ascending career path. But for a woman to voice the same priorities? Cold. Hard. Selfish.

One woman who recorded her story on the project website was excited to return to work after the birth of her first baby, but:

▶ As I walked into the office [...] the first question asked by a more senior male colleague that I would be working for was: 'Hi, so who is looking after your baby?'

That afternoon another senior colleague – friends with the first one – thought it was acceptable to ask straight whether I would be properly involved in the new project, as 'women are not as committed to work after they have a baby'. He has 3 children but apparently the commitment only affects women [...]

Other women had not even *had* their babies when they started to impact negatively on their careers. One was dismissed by her manager in front of colleagues with an airy 'Well she's just a ball of raging hormones'. Another described how her boss insisted on waiting until after the birth before filling in the paperwork for her return from maternity leave, 'in case I'm besotted with the baby'. Another wrote:

While pregnant, I was told by ex-boss I should resign. He said he couldn't plan around me having another baby in the future. And when I took it to HR, I was told he was 'probably just thinking out loud'.

These entries are corroborated by recent data analysed by the House of Commons Library, which found that fully 14 per cent of women who take maternity leave (adding up to around 50,000 women every year) are discriminated against when they try to return to work. Some are forced into positions with less responsibility, according to the data, while others effectively face constructive dismissal.

I interviewed a HR manager, who told me:

Women going on maternity leave are regularly seen as an issue by male managers. They immediately feel it's a problem, despite example after example of that not being the case. The presumptions are that the woman will somehow become a problem simply because she is pregnant. In my experience it is very rare for a woman to behave any differently at work because she is pregnant; unless there is a physical issue of course. From what I have seen, almost all managers want to avoid having someone working part time in their team – female managers are equally as culpable as male in this. It's far too easy to engineer a refusal to accept a flexible-working request. Businesses should go in with the attitude of 'How do we make this work' rather than 'Let's prove it can't work'.

Sleepless nights and close attachment to their new baby are commonly cited reasons levelled at post-partum mums to underpin the idea of their potential workplace incapacity. Ironically, of course, new fathers suffer many of the same sleepless nights and feel the same close attachment to their new baby, yet somehow this seems to lead to far less 'well intentioned' concern about the potential impact of parenthood on their careers.

The strange habit of seeing mothers and fathers through completely different lenses holds strong in other situations too. Witness, for example, the level of public vitriol reserved for teenage mothers, from reality-style shows to media debates such as BBC Kent's recent phone-in on the question: 'Do teenage girls get pregnant just to get a council house?' To listen to such headlines you might honestly be forgiven for assuming that teenage girls were indulging in some sort of trendy new craze for self-insemination, so clear is the implication that this is something *they* do, a decision *they* make, a responsibility *they* must shoulder and, as is often suggested, a burden *they* are foisting on the poor overstretched state.

So acute is our hysteria about teenage motherhood that a 2013 poll conducted by Ipsos MORI showed that the average member of the general public believes that 15 per cent of girls under sixteen get pregnant every year. (The actual figure is around 0.6 per cent.) And penises, once again, get a free pass. In fact this obsession with the idea that pregnancy is somehow a selfish choice made by mothers comes across again and again – whether it's in stupendously ignorant arguments about maternity leave being a 'burden' that women selfishly foist onto employers, or in public attitudes towards pregnant women more generally:

▶ I'm heavily pregnant at the moment and was travelling into the city, by bus. When I got on, I walked towards the seats which are reserved for elderly/disabled/pregnant individuals. A man was already sitting here and looked at me, knowing I wanted 'his' seat. He asked me did I want special attention due to being in my condition. I replied that I would appreciate the seat. His response was that I 'should have thought about that when doing the business'.

▶ While I was pregnant with my oldest, I worked in a post-press mailroom […] On my way to the bathroom, I crossed paths with a co-worker, a man in his mid-40s. He looked me up and down, glared at me, and said, 'Oh, THAT'S exactly what I want to see on my lunch break. A pregnant woman going to the bathroom!'

It strikes me that the vast majority of these inequalities come back to the same bizarrely stubborn insistence on considering pregnancy and reproduction something that women do, by and for themselves. The idea that women are 'selfish' for taking maternity leave, or that their jobs shouldn't be safeguarded if they 'choose' to 'go off and have children' is quite ridiculous when you consider the fact that society depends on reproduction in order to physically continue. These women aren't flouncing selfishly off to a spa for nine months with no regard for their professional duty. A lot of them are just as cheesed off about the potential damage to their career as their employers are! But, given that reproduction is something *people* do together – and, frankly, is something we can't carry on without – it doesn't seem outrageously demanding to ask that we all chip in to deal with the costs. And that means paying a lot more attention and respect to the role of fathers in this whole process too.

One new mother described how:

▸ I will be going back to work later this year while my husband
stays at home to look after our baby […] At a recent baby fair,
various reps for part-time stay-at-home money-making schemes
converged on me and ignored my husband completely. Because
obviously, if anyone's going to stay at home it must be the woman.

All our local parent-and-child sessions are geared towards
mothers and babies – except, of course, for the Saturday session,
which is specifically for 'dads and granddads'.

Even among those who accept my going back to work as perfectly
reasonable and normal, there is always surprise when I tell them
my husband will be doing the majority of the childcare. As though
it's inconceivable that a man might prefer to look after his own
child rather than hand the baby over to a (presumably female)
child minder.

Countless other situations have been reported to the project by
men who have been variously ostracized, stigmatized or praised
for performing parental duties that would have been considered
perfectly normal for mums. Like the man who was standing right
next to his child when a stranger loudly alerted everybody in the
vicinity to the presence of an abandoned baby. 'Yes,' he said, 'the
baby one foot to my left is without its mother. She's my daughter.'

It's not just in the phase of babyhood that this discrimination
applies, but throughout the child's upbringing – where the closer
involvement of fathers and greater respect for the role they play
can only be beneficial for everybody, children and parents alike.
Whether it's the media reporting on every study about parents as a
revelation for 'mums', the world of advertising showcasing weary

mothers parenting away while dads prance mischievously in the pub like overgrown schoolboys, or businesses refusing to provide adequate provision for paternity leave, dads come up against barriers and disapproval at every stage of the child-rearing process. This leads to a vicious circle of social assumptions about their inability to parent properly, which are passed on loud and clear to young boys and feed straight back into narratives about female domestic responsibility and expected gender roles.

Many men even reported being 'congratulated' for 'babysitting' their own children as if it were some special achievement, or a sign of overcoming a natural incapacity. One woman told us:

> ▸ My husband and I had our first child last year; I go to work and he stays at home with the baby. I often get asked, 'How is he doing with all that babysitting? Has it been hard to teach him how to take care of a baby?' He's her father. He doesn't babysit, he PARENTS. And since he's with her for forty hours a week that I'm not, he's frankly quite a bit better at taking care of her than I am.

Some women understandably express their frustration when dads are praised like dancing monkeys for managing to complete a few hours of childcare, but really this attitude is equally sad for dads themselves.

One man reported shocked disapproval from the GP when he, instead of his wife, arrived with their baby daughter for one of her early check-ups.

Many men struggled to care for their children in public places where baby-changing facilities were restricted to the women's toilets. One man reported a baffled and stony-faced staff member asking,

'Can't you just do it on the floor?' And so, inevitably, tackling such prejudice – whether it relates to workplace inequality or stereotypical public assumptions about parenthood – is essential and will be beneficial to everybody, men and women alike. And, as with so many other forms of sexism, we not only need legislative change (in this case to ensure things like flexible working hours and equal parental leave) but also a cultural shift (a move away from the stubborn belief that providing a vessel for a foetus is the pinnacle of female purpose and achievement). And no, this really isn't an exaggeration: women actually are faced with this archaic idea on a regular basis – the ridiculousness of which is laid bare by these women's dry comments in a recent conversation on our Twitter feed...

🐦 I've been told: 'single childless women over the age of 28 have no right to live'.

🐦 Damn it, I have less than three months to live. I didn't realize these things mattered!

🐦 Bugger. I'd like lots of astronomy at my funeral, please . . .

🐦 I should have been dead 12 years ago.

🐦 I'm over 28, married & childless. Does that mean I just need to lose a limb or summat?

🐦 Apparently I've been dead for two years. I actually quite recommend it.

Chapter 9

Double Discrimination

'I've had men say that I'm "attractive for an Indian" & "one of the good ones"'
Tweet sent to the Everyday Sexism Project

Vital Statistics

Women whose partners are unemployed or in 'unclassified' jobs are nearly 6 times more likely to die from maternal causes than those with partners in employment
Centre for Maternal and Child Enquiries, 2011

Half of LGBT people in the European Union avoid public places because of harassment
European Union Agency for Fundamental Rights, 2013

50 per cent of disabled women have experienced domestic abuse compared with 25 per cent of non-disabled women
Women's Aid, 2007

Almost 1 in 5 black, Pakistani and Bangladeshi women in the UK is unemployed, compared to 1 in 14 white women
APPG on Race and Community, 2012

More than half of women sex workers have been raped or sexually assaulted and 75 per cent have been physically assaulted
Home Office, 2004

Only 18 per cent of television presenters over the age of 50 are women
Labour Party study, 2013

🐦 'You're gay, not a woman.' My sister's reasoning for the non-invite to a family hen night.

🐦 I get 'ni hao', 'konnichiwa,' 'herro' and 'love you long time'... silly me to think standard catcalls would suffice...

🐦 Because I was a prostitute, he felt it was OK to force himself upon me. When you are a prostitute, people stop seeing you as a person.

🐦 Sitting in my wheelchair, waiting for a friend to pick me up, men shouting from a car 'you could at least get your tits out'.

🐦 Last night walking home, a car full of men yelled 'I bet you'd be grateful if I raped your whale sized pussy, fat bitch'.

🐦 I suffered a tirade of verbal abuse about my trans status, in which terms such as 'hermaphrodite', 'lab rat' and 'mutated multi genitalia' were used.

One of the problems that makes sexism so difficult to tackle, or even to talk about, is that we all view each instance of it from a very individual perspective based on our own experience.

Take, say, a man who, every six months, witnesses just one instance of catcalling, after which he goes about his business without giving the matter a second thought. And then take a woman who on a daily basis experiences several such instances of harassment and has also on more than one occasion ignored the catcalls only to have the situation escalate into something more aggressive. Those two people would, understandably, react very differently to a hypothetical description of an isolated instance of harassment. The man would probably consider it minor, insignificant and even harmless, while the woman would likely view it as more serious and potentially damaging. This is partly why it's so hard to discuss the problem of sexism – and why, when we do, the narrative (often led by those in the first category) turns so frequently to whether or not the problem really exists at all, or whether it's simply exaggerated. Our limited ability to view things through the lens of another's experience is even more pertinent when considering the intersection of sexism and other forms of prejudice. Unless we've experienced something similar ourselves, it's virtually impossible to imagine how it feels to experience multiple forms of oppression at the same time.

The concept of 'double discrimination' isn't conjecture – these are real, concrete problems reflected in alarming statistics. Many LGBTQIA (lesbian, gay, bisexual, transgender, queer, intersex or asexual) people experience harassment and violence on a regular basis. According to the NHS, trans people are at a 'greater risk of depression, self-harm and suicide than the general population. A 2007 survey of 872 trans people found that 34 per cent of respondents had considered suicide. According to the UK government, 88 per cent of transgender employees experience discrimination or harassment in the workplace. A Royal College of Obstetricians and Gynaecologists (RCOG) enquiry in 2004 showed that in the UK 'women from ethnic groups other than white were, on average, three times more likely to die' in childbirth than white women, and that the maternal-mortality rate for black African women was seven times higher than for white women. Unemployment figures for non-white women are consistently far higher than for white women. According to Women's Aid, disabled women are twice as likely to be victims of domestic violence as non-disabled women.

Since the Everyday Sexism Project started, many of the stories we have catalogued have described not just sexism but sexism intermingled with other forms of prejudice – racism, homophobia, transphobia, classism, ageism, disableism, stigma around mental-health problems, and more. Again and again, we've heard from women in same-sex relationships being fetishized and asked for threesomes when they're just trying to walk down the street, trans women mocked and belittled and hounded from public spaces, Asian women being labelled as 'easy' or 'obedient', sex workers accused of being complicit in their own assaults, disabled women infantilized and patronized and countless similar stories.

I chose to include this chapter in order to put a spotlight on these issues of 'double discrimination' (or, indeed, triple or quadruple) because it has proved to be a major recurring theme within the project and is a crucial focus for modern feminism. The severity and frequency of the problem merits closer examination. However, it should be noted that, though this section is designed to give these intersections between different forms of prejudice the attention they deserve, they also run throughout the other sections of this book, just as they should be present in all feminist discourse and activism. The inclusion of this chapter does not conveniently distance and compartmentalize its subject matter as one clean-cut area of sexism, and nor is it intended to 'other' those subjected to such double discrimination.

Intersectionality means being aware of and acting on the fact that different forms of prejudice are connected, because they all stem from the same root of being 'other', 'different' or somehow 'secondary' to the 'normal', 'ideal' status quo. So, just as women suffer from sexism because our society is set up to favour and automatically take men as the 'norm' from which women deviate, so the same is true for people who are 'different' from other dominant norms – such as being heterosexual, white, cisgendered, and non-disabled. (A person who is cisgendered identifies with the sex they were assigned at birth – in other words, they are not transgender.) People also often face prejudice as a result of other characteristics, such as age, class and religious belief. The principle of intersectionality is actually pretty simple: if all these different kinds of prejudice stem from the same root, then it is arbitrary and ineffective to attempt to eradicate one of them without acknowledging its intersection with others and trying to work together to tackle all forms of inequality. Or, from a feminist perspective, if we are to tackle the fact that women have been historically oppressed because of characteristics that are seen to be 'different' from the male norm, how can we protest such treatment while simultaneously excluding from our own movement the needs and agendas of those with other stigmatized characteristics? (This is particularly true in the case of our trans sisters, who some feminists believe should be excluded from some areas of the movement by virtue of not fulfilling required 'characteristics' of womanhood – a deep irony for a group fighting for equality regardless of sex.)

And on a concrete, practical level, the importance of intersectionality when fighting sexism is reinforced by the huge numbers of project entries we have received that clearly demonstrate the double discrimination of two or more kinds of prejudice combined.

Many women of colour, for example, have described suffering not only from both racism and sexism but also from a particular brand of racist sexism that conflates and exacerbates the two.

▶ I am Japanese. Frequently told by white men that Japanese, Chinese, Filipina, Asian women are 'better' than the 'feminazis', 'femic*nts' in the west and 'know how to treat men'; we will cook and clean.

🐦 Told I look like a Russian-Mongolian rape baby... Then he pulled the skin around his eyes...

▶ I was walking on my university campus with my boyfriend, when we walked past a group of guys, one of whom shouted out 'What did you pay for her then? Is she a mail order?' (My boyfriend is Chinese and I'm half Indian.)

🐦 Male strangers grinning at me and loudly inquiring 'CHINA OR JAPAN?! The worst thing is, I'm neither.

When I interviewed the writer Reni Eddo-Lodge she explained:

Not all women experience incidents like street harassment in the same way. In particular it's helpful to consider how racism and exotification impacts into a black experience of sexual harassment. Often I've noticed a racialized dimension to the street harassment I've received – particularly since I cut off my relaxed hair, went natural and have a little afro. Calls in the street of 'African queen', 'ebony princess' and the like refer directly to my race as well as my gender. I think this is an issue when navigating the first stages of any relationship as well (particularly if it's a mixed-race relationship); you find a considerable amount of your time being eaten up by wondering whether you're being taken seriously as a human being or being viewed as a novelty, or an exotic entity. The very idea of this makes me feel uneasy.

I think the exotification of black women can be traced back to the days of empire and colonialism, particularly the Hottentot Venus Saartjie Baartman. There's particular fascination with African women's bodies and because of the likes of hip-hop videos – the production of which is controlled by black men in a heavily male-dominated industry – our bodies are rarely equated with innocence and piety and instead are deemed as permanently sexually available. An added dimension of this is that these African body features are celebrated and considered mainstream beautiful in lighter-skinned women such as Jennifer Lopez, but seen as tacky and trashy in darker-skinned women like Nicki Minaj.

In fact, I can't tell you about the amount of times I've opted not to wear a miniskirt or short shorts on a hot day because 1) I know how my hips and thighs will look in them and 2) I know what conclusions people will draw about me because of this.

This idea of black women as 'exotic', hyper-sexualized creatures can be seen again and again in cultural stereotypes. Try typing 'pretty' into Google image search and you are greeted with pages and pages and pages of white women's faces (the fashion industry is notoriously white; of the seventy-five British *Vogue* covers since the beginning of 2008, black women have featured on just three while Kate Moss *alone* has graced nine); but type in 'sexy' and suddenly far more women of colour appear – though they do remain far less represented than white women. Many project entries described the impact of this stereotype on real women's lives:

🐦 People attach this hyper-sexualized image to me because of my skin colour and talk about how spicy and exotic I am.

But often this racialized aspect is overlooked because the sexism is more obvious, and in-your-face. This case is strongly argued by Ikamara Larasi of the black-feminist organization Imkaan, who gives the example of the music video for the Major Lazer song 'Bubble Butt'. This starts with three white women dancing listlessly in their bedroom, before a giant black woman flies through the sky (implying exoticization to the extent that she isn't even from the same planet) wearing a costume that leaves her bottom completely exposed. She lands and snakelike pipes come writhing out of her mouth (as a Medusa-like mythological creature, othered to an extreme degree). The pipes slither through the bedroom window, 'plug' into the white women's bottoms and pump them up to huge, caricatured balloons. The rest of the video consists almost entirely of 'twerking' – a dance move that involves energetic shaking and wobbling of the buttocks and is associated with black culture. But (because of the exposed bottoms of the women in the video, and lyrics like 'Damn, bitch, talk much[...]I'm trying to get into you') the inherent racism is often largely overlooked by those protesting the sexism of the song.

In fact, twerking itself is a perfect recent example of the hyper-sexualization of black women, having been famously and deliberately adopted, alongside other aspects of black culture, by former Disney pop princess Miley Cyrus, in her bid to shed her pure, good-girl image for something more 'risky' and 'sexy'. But by consciously employing a dance move associated with black women (and indeed by using black women as literal objects and props, as she did during her notorious VMA performance), Cyrus has simply contributed to the idea of the appropriation of black culture, by a woman, as an immediate means to appear raunchy, oversexed and vulgar. This is a tool that Cyrus, as a white woman, may pick up and put down again should she ever wish to lay her 'risqué' persona to rest. The same cannot be said of the black women whose image she's helped to caricature and over-sexualize.

🐦 I'm a barmaid – the white women behind the bar get standard sex/head jokes, I get asked to twerk.

But, as with the Major Lazer video, the mainstream outrage about Cyrus's transformation has focused near exclusively on the nudity and sexualization it embraces, while its problematic racist implications have been completely ignored.

We know that sexism is not just a frustration, or a discomfort, but can actually impact hugely on women's lives, careers and success. When prejudices intersect the same is doubly true. From education...

▶ Known to be a lesbian by my boarding-school administration, I was forcibly set up on a prom date my last year at school. The guy would not keep his hands off me, and told me the faculty had said he had to kiss me to make it a 'real date'. (I am guessing they thought corrective kissing wasn't as serious, but just as effective, as corrective rape.) After I tried to end the 'date' by returning to my single-sex dorm, he followed me across the campus. I eventually shoved him into the duckpond (still in his rented polyester tuxedo). I was not allowed to graduate; he was.

To employment...

▶ When I sat down to be interviewed, all he spoke about was his strong desire for dark-skinned Black women. How he loves our skin. How his first wife or lover was Black. He kept looking me over and nodding his head in approval of my looks and whatever other fantasies he was playing out in his head. He hardly spoke about the job.

To personal safety...

▶ Told by a male acquaintance that he likes Chinese women as they 'don't make a drama' over rape, and view date rape as just the guy being pushy. When I called him a disgusting prick the guy told me I don't count as Chinese because I was born in the UK.

And, as similarly demonstrated by accounts of other forms of sexism, these combined prejudices become evident at a tragically young age:

▶ I reported a boy at school who had been making racial and sexual remarks to me and other girls of ethnic minorities for about a year. Because, even though teachers and other students could hear the disgusting comments he was making about me being a 'black whore who he wanted to put in a cage', a Pakistani girl being a 'bomber' and stating the only attractive females were white, it was dismissed and nobody said a word.

As Joy Goh-Mah succinctly explained on the Media Diversity UK blog, when men approach her with phrases like 'I love Asian women!' or 'Asian women are so hot!' or 'Japan, Korea, China?'… 'They aren't speaking to me, they're speaking to their idea of an Asian woman, their fantasy made flesh. They're speaking to every Asian woman they've ever seen in the media, every Asian porn actress they've ever leered at on their computer screens. My personality is rendered invisible, obscured by the lenses of racial stereotype.'

The great effect of media stereotypes on the treatment of particular groups of people – especially those suffering various forms of 'double discrimination' – is a vital part of the problem. The incredibly narrow media presentation of women as beautiful, sexualized objects is clearly detrimental and of great concern to feminism. Of equally great concern should be the overwhelming likelihood that the majority of women made visible to us in everyday media will be young, heterosexual, cisgendered, middle or upper class and non-disabled.

According to new figures released in May 2013, just 18 per cent of television presenters over the age of fifty are women. The percentage for disabled women, LGBTQIA women, and women of colour is likely to be even lower.

The problem is exacerbated and inflamed by two key factors. First, such women are so rarely portrayed on screen as to be considered strange and unusual. Second, when they *are* present they have generally been moulded into hackneyed caricatures that play to every stereotype in the book and exist solely to satisfy a specific storyline – *about* disability, or lesbianism, for example. Which of course encourages the notion that certain characteristics are somehow all-consuming and utterly defining.

▶ I am a gay female and I often feel as though the media only seems to have one specific idea of what a female is/wants/desires. I often feel alienated and unseen/un-acknowledged. I would like to see the media become more complex and diverse including WOMEN in their audience, not just ONE specific TYPE of woman. I am made to feel like because I don't fit into a specific stereotype I am not worthy of being seen and I am ignored.

▶ The dearth of any women in the media anywhere near my size (I'm a UK 18) who isn't a) a pathetic lonely loser, or b) the 'before' shot on a weight-loss show.

▸ Can we talk about the lack of representation of WOC [women of colour] in the media? When we are portrayed, it's usually as being 'oppressed' and in need of saving.

▸ I very, very rarely see a woman on TV, fictional or real, who's my age *without children* and not depicted as either lonely and bitter, or a hard-driven career woman. Because reproduction has to be something we either tragically miss out on, or only choose to forego for huge financial gain.

▸ As a physically disabled woman, I feel invisible, both in the media and in real life, as it were. No one seems to think that I have a sexuality or even sensuality. There seem to be very few characters in films and TV shows who are incidentally disabled and/or queer. I'm going back a fair few years now but Dr Kerry Weaver from ER is the only one who springs to mind. A lot of the time, it seems as if disability or non-heterosexual sexuality is part of the plot rather than a character just so happening to be disabled/queer with no big deal made of their identity.

▸ The ideal woman lauded by the media is thin, conventionally attractive, perfectly groomed and shaved, an ideal that is hard to reach for many women, but impossible and out of question for women of colour since beauty is linked to being white. You may try to be 'pretty' when you're white, but you'll never be when you're not white.

▸ Next to no programs portray lesbians as just one of the

characters, without being a story feature and portrayed to meet (hetero male?) viewer expectations. I'd note that we are a diverse bunch and don't have a 'look' so much! As for the portrayal of lesbian families, except for high profile Australian people like Penny Wong, there are none that I know of. If that's demoralising for us, I can't imagine it's good for our kids either...

▶ I'm fat. I've been heavy since my thyroid stopped working at 8. I've only very rarely seen positive images of women like me in the media. People my size are portrayed as stupid, weak willed, mean, annoying or worthless, despite the fact that most of the recent research into obesity contradicts the assumption that being fat is primarily a matter of will rather than genetics. Fat people can be brilliant, creative, strong, loyal, loving, and beautiful, but we're almost never shown that way.

▶ The media's complete failure to be able to cover trans folk in any way that considers them as people first and trans second – instead it is always made to be their entire identity, whether in the rare television shows when a trans person features (either as part of an episode specifically focusing on being trans, or as the butt of every joke, with the frequent suggestion on shows like 'How I Met Your Mother' that accidentally kissing a 'chick with a dick' is the worst, most embarrassing thing that could ever happen to anyone) or in the papers, where they insist on referring to people like Chelsea Manning as 'Bradley' and 'he' irrespective of her own wishes.

▶ Working-class women are rarely portrayed in a good light in the media, and equality of opportunity rather than focussing on women at the top is something feminism needs more of.

▶ As a 40-year-old woman, I find myself, often subconsciously, questioning whether what I am wearing is 'appropriate' for my age – but why should I? Why should my age dictate my wardrobe? The media shaming of women who are 'mutton-dressed-as-lamb' has instilled in me a terrible fear of looking 'ridiculous'. Most of the time I actively resist it and wear what I like, but sometimes I get scared and buckle.

▶ I'm bisexual. That in and of itself has so many negative stereotypes attached to it in terms of media representation [...] Bi men are often typecast as being effeminate and weak. Their bisexuality is just a cover for coming out as gay later on. And for bisexual women – well, my sexuality is for the entertainment of men only [...] We are portrayed snogging other women to get men to buy us a drink, or, of course, in pornography. I can't discuss bisexuality without some guy thinking I'll be up for a threesome. Like my sexuality is the only thing about me, instead of just another aspect of a human being. If I have a male partner, then people think it was just a phase, and if I have a female partner then I'm 'experimenting'. There is no legitimate representation of bisexuality in the media at all – so forget about older bisexual men and women!

And it is easy to see how such media stereotypes leak into the general public's perceptions and consequently their behaviour:

▶ Another bi woman here, sick of all the misconceptions. For me, people seem to not be able to believe that I can even be bisexual because I haven't had sexual experience with another person at all. Well, straight people can say they're straight with no experience and no one is sceptical of that!

And of course the battle can feel endless – because it is a far more complex issue than just achieving representation in itself. It's also about the *way* in which people are represented. It's about the fact that, even when they are finally acknowledged and included, women facing complex discrimination are so frequently used as tokenistic representatives of a particular group rather than being viewed as a voice or an expert in their own right. It's about their voices being silenced in mainstream debates. Because when, say, one disabled woman sits on a panel of experts discussing a wide and varied topic, such as local politics, she might easily find every question about minority or women's issues directed to her while the general political questions go to the non-disabled men sitting in every other chair. It's about the co-opting of their achievements: as when Jeanne Socrates completed a nine-month round-the-world sailing trip and headlines omitted her name altogether; instead defining her by her age and childbearing status – 'Grandma becomes oldest woman to sail around the world non-stop'.

And always the ongoing othering makes every battle harder to fight – because shouldn't women simply be grateful just to be included? How uppity and churlish it would be to complain about such a thing, when one has 'made it' into the hallowed inner ring in the first place. Similarly, when these women are fighting for their inclusion in the feminist movement – fighting just to establish what needs to be on the table – they have that much less breath and energy and momentum left when the real battles finally begin.

Before trans people can even begin to fight for equality, for instance, they first have to overcome enormous ignorance and lack of understanding about their experience:

▶ A close friend of mine is a trans man and has been told many times by people who knew him before his transition (which began towards the end of his time at high school) or have seen pictures of him as a child that 'it's a shame such a pretty girl wants to look like a guy,' implying that his gender identity is a choice and deliberately neglecting the duty of anyone born with female organs to look 'feminine'.

Before a disabled person can even start working towards equal rights, they first have to contend with a society within which most people still subscribe to the medical model of disability, which holds that a person is disabled by their impairment (i.e. a mental-health issue prevents them from getting a job, or a physical impairment restricts their ability to access certain venues) rather than the social model, which suggests that it is not the impairment in itself but the lack of accessibility created by our disablist society that makes a person disabled (i.e. our stigma around mental-health issues prevents that person from getting a job, or a lack of adequate measures to make a venue fully accessible prevents certain people being able to enter).

And women like Tulisa Contostavlos, despite huge achievements and enormous creative success, still find themselves having to overcome prejudice, again and again, on the basis of their perceived class, as if it is an insult or embarrassing slur they can never escape. It is kept in reserve to shame them and immediately put them down in any situation.

One of the reasons why it is so important to let members of oppressed groups tell their own stories in their own ways is that it's so easy to think you're getting it when you're not. In much the same way as many of the men writing to the project said they thought they knew about sexism when they imagined a catcall or a wolf whistle but had no concept of how it actually impacted on women's lives, living it every day, influencing every choice and thought. Because it isn't just about the individual incidents; it's about the collective impact on everything else – the way you think about yourself, the way you approach public spaces and human interaction, the limits you place on your own aspirations and the things you stop yourself from doing before you even try because of bitter learned experience. As the writer John Scalzi brilliantly and simply put it on his blog, Whatever: 'In the role playing game known as The Real World, "Straight White Male" is the lowest difficulty setting there is.' It is not a collection of individual moments, but a constant setting that influences everything. Of course, this doesn't preclude individual circumstances from impacting negatively on people's lives – it's not to discount the difficulties faced by, for example, heterosexual white men from disadvantaged socioeconomic backgrounds – but it's a ballpark starting point that helps us get the general idea.

For many of these women, the prejudice they experience has an absolutely enormous constant impact on their whole lives that is far greater than the sum of the individual incidents they experience, and is increased by living in a world that sends them constant messages about how they should expect to be treated.

Jasmine, a trans woman, told me:

I remember my dad saying those fateful words, 'Don't ever come home and tell me you're gay'; how then would he react to the news that I wasn't actually his son, but his daughter?

Fear kept me in the closet for a very long time; fear of violence, of being rejected by my family and friends, and of losing my job (I've met several trans-women who lost their jobs when they came out, or were disowned by their parents, spouses, or children).

She was forced to endure seven years' waiting before she could transition, because of a prolonged period of training during which 'it would only have needed one of my instructors taking exception to me to make life extremely hard'. For those who haven't experienced it, spending seven years unhappy – hiding your true identity because of a very real fear that the world would reject you so violently that your entire career might be jeopardized – is difficult even to begin to imagine.

She perfectly captures the extent of the stigma and lack of acceptance experienced by people who are othered in our society when she explains:

Many people have told me that I'm brave for undergoing all the surgery I have (five surgeries so far – one lasting eleven hours

– with more to come), but in fact the hardest and most terrifying thing by far was telling everyone. Not only did I risk estrangement from family and friends, but my employers are the only company in the whole of the UK to provide the service that I'm trained for. If they or my co-workers reacted badly, I could [have lost] a very high-paying job, which I enjoyed very much, and which I'd spent seven years training for.

For many women who face double discrimination, even carrying out the simplest everyday activities that many people would not think twice about can be fraught and painful. As Dee Emm Elms, a trans woman and brilliant writer, explains on her blog, Four-Color Princesses:

I notice that a lot of trans women don't put pictures of themselves on the internet. I've asked a lot of them why, and I get a variety of reasons. Unsurprisingly, a lot of it has to do with danger. I've been told that it's fear, but it's not the same kind of fear for everyone who feels it. For some, it's the fear of stigmatization. For others, it's the fear of recognition. For many, it's the fear of becoming the victim of the very real threat of physical violence and/or sexual assault. Since starting this blog, I've gotten death threats. I've gotten rape threats. I've gotten threats about everything in-between. I've been told I'm not really a woman. I've been told I'm not really a man. I've been told I'm not worth the air I 'waste' by breathing. I've been told I'm the root cause of hurricanes and tornados. I've been told I'm fat. I've been told I'm ugly. I've been told I'm going to Hell.

And this sense of instantly being judged and condemned purely as a result of others' preconceptions also comes across painfully clearly in the entries we have received from disabled women.

🐦 Strangers saying: 'You're hot ... for a girl in a wheelchair.'

▶ I have a long term illness that causes chronic exhaustion and means I need quite a lot of help from my family. I've been told I'm selfish for not having children.

▶ I'm physically disabled, and live in chronic pain. There is no cure for my condition and it will only worsen with time. On days when I feel up to walking rather than using a wheelchair, I frequently have to stop and rest and am frequently grimacing with pain when walking. Every single time, without fail, I am told by men to 'smile, it might never happen' or 'cheer up, it'll get better'.

▶ I was once assaulted by an older man twice my size getting onto a bus because he thought I looked too young to be using a walking stick so I had to be a 'scrounging lazy little bitch'.

▶ Seriously: I DO need my mobility aids, I AM genuinely disabled, yes, at my age (27), and NO, if I want your help I will ASK you. STOP touching me!

And every now and then through the thousands of stories we have collected comes a recurring word or description that echoes through the pages, used by woman after woman after woman to describe her lived experience. In the case of older women, that word is 'invisible'.

▶ You really do become invisible when you hit middle age. Look around at all the middle aged women you see wearing red coats or bright colours. It's so that people don't bump into us in the street because we're physically invisible.

▶ I'm now 51 and I definitely am beginning to feel invisible.

▶ I'm 43 and disappearing…

▶ As a grandmother of 3 and in my mid-50s, I find I am invisible everywhere!

▶ Not so long ago, my mum and I were talking, and she said something which is going to stick with me forever: 'When you're a woman over forty, you disappear.'

▶ I just turned 60. Have had trouble getting jobs for ages due to being invisible. But, hey, the upside is I don't get sexually harassed anymore either.

▶ I am 60 years old on Thursday but have been invisible for at least 10 years. Older people, women especially, just live on the sidelines of society, that's how it feels anyway. We are under-represented in every area.

▶ Society seems to expect women to disappear. And certainly we become a joke as far as being thought attractive is concerned. I have achieved much of value in my life and much to be proud of. It is insulting I am only considered worth noticing during my supposed childbearing years and after that am not worth anything.

I am sick of being invisible – in the media, the supermarket queue, and most definitely the power tool shop. Turn 50 and become invisible to the world.

As men approach the late-middle age at which their experience and knowledge, their skill and talent are most respected and in demand, the same characteristic is used utterly to dismiss their female peers from consideration – whether as professionals, members of society, or sexual beings.

For some women what becomes oppressive in itself is, ironically, the invisibility of the characteristic that sets them apart. As one woman with a chronic illness explains:

▶ Being unable to work, date, have a social life, looking 'odd' because I'm ill and exhausted – those things make me feel invisible. There are a lot of illnesses which have no visible symptoms, and a lot of illnesses that men (and, sadly, some women) don't want to discuss publicly. Anything related to bladder / bowels / reproductive system isn't 'polite' to talk about, I'm learning. I've encountered people who'd like me to be invisible AND silent.

For some women, the issue is complicated and exacerbated by further factors, such as receiving different kinds of discrimination from different angles. Nimko Ali is of Somali heritage; she's the director of Daughters of Eve, a not-for-profit organization that works with young people affected by or at risk of FGM (Female Genital Mutilation), with a UK focus. She told me:

Because I live in two different worlds I kind of walk this tightrope between living in the UK and being from a certain community or heritage. I kind of get it two-fold, so it's basically being objectified by men in the West because of the way I dress and then being told, in another way, I shouldn't be dressing like that – again being objectified by men from the same community with the heritage that I have [...]

I was 13 years old, I was coming back from the dentist with my mother and the local cleric was talking at my mother about me about the skirt that I was wearing – because the grammar school that I went to had a specific length skirt which was too short in his eyes, and I remember being really, really angry that this man talked to my mother like that just because she was a woman and talked about me as if I didn't exist [...] that was the first time I stood up and said, 'This is unacceptable. And just because I am a woman, I won't be spoken to like that.'

Growing up I was very athletic as a teenager, so there were stereotypes of what girls should look like and me not looking like that – and then in another kind of population where I was from, because I didn't wear a headscarf again I never truly belonged, because it was this whole thing of everybody had a view of what

women should be and that wasn't me. For me it was like being the black sheep of two different worlds.

I don't accept that there should be a cut out picture of how women should look like – whatever culture or colour or heritage they're from.

Other women described similar experiences of suffering prejudice both from within their own communities and from outside:

🐦 I have been called an 'uppity slag' & 'coconut' by hardline traditionalists – just because I'm educated.

🐦 Ex told me white guys'll only date me to annoy their parents.

It's exhausting just to read about. Imagine what it's like to live it every day.

And all this is before even going into the stigma and double discrimination faced by women with mental-health issues...

🐦 Have been told I'm lucky to have found someone who'd marry me, because of mental illness/disability.

🐦 'What have *you* got to be depressed about, you silly girl?' 'What's *wrong* with you? Stop crying and pull yourself together.'

Or larger women...

🐦 Fat girls can get away with it if they've a pretty face like you.

Or those suffering even more intersections of prejudice...

🐦 **Because I'm blind & disabled, guy tried convincing me blowing him would be good for me. Not that desperate!**

There are far too many complex issues and experiences that fit into this area of multiple prejudice ever to be able to do them justice in a single chapter. Entire books could be dedicated to each of these types of 'double discrimination', but I hope I've given an introductory sense of the enormity of the issues here while being acutely aware that there is so much more to say.

But, while there is so much more to cover to adequately portray the issues faced by each of these groups, two things are certain. The first, as Ali eloquently explains, is that they all have extremely similar roots:

One of the main reasons inequalities exist is because we're scared and one of the things we have to overcome is the fear of 'what do I have to lose if someone is as equal as I am?'

The second is the importance of working, as feminists, to include these varied priorities and experiences within the movement for equality.

When I interview Elms, she describes this with beautiful simplicity:

It baffles me when I see people saying, 'I don't focus on racism. I focus on sexism.' It leaves me saddened when I hear people

saying, 'You're OK, but you're not.' It makes people, in my opinion, guilty of the same crimes of thoughtlessness that lead to these problems [...]

Because that person on the bus being harassed is still being harassed whether she's being harassed for being religious or for being an atheist or being black or being a woman or because of her clothing or because of her body-language or because of her appearance or because of her handbag or because of her accent.

That's all the same problem.

It's not recognizing the basic humanity of a person [...]

That's the problem.

Chapter 10

What About the Men?

'Firstly as a man of 28 why is it that I'm incapable of washing my own clothes? Secondly, why should my wife be expected to do it?'

Everyday Sexism Project entry

Vital Statistics

Male suicide rates are on average 3 to 5 times higher than female rates
Samaritans, 2013

The suicide rate for males in the UK is at its highest since 2002
Samaritans, 2013

30 per cent of men have heard someone refer to their 'beer belly' and 19 per cent have overheard talk about their 'man boobs'
University of the West of England, 2012

63 per cent of men think their arms or chests are not muscular enough
University of the West of England, 2012

Over 1 in 10 men said they would trade a year of their life for the ideal body weight and shape
University of the West of England, 2012

A quarter of men aged 18 to 24 are worried about the amount of porn they are watching on the internet
BBC/TNS, 2011

🐦 Being laughed at by my guy friends, being called a male nurse, not just a nurse.

🐦 I find the #ShoutingBack timeline is like being at the window onto a previously unknown world that's happening all around under my radar.

🐦 My husband is taking paternity leave and his colleagues mock him for it.

🐦 Mother to toddler son at nursery this morn, 'Don't cry, you're not a girl are you?'

🐦 I became a single parent 30 Jan 99, my youngest was 5. Often people were shocked I had custody. Men can raise children too!

🐦 Guys like me get an insight into what women have to put up with. I had no idea it was so bad.

There are some people who tweet using the hashtag #KillAllMen. I hate it. It's offensive, distasteful and not conducive to progress, particularly when used by those who identify themselves as feminists. It doesn't matter if they choose to describe it as 'ironic' – we wouldn't accept that as an excuse for a trending #KillAllWomen hashtag. It's frustrating when people bring this hashtag up in discussions about feminism, and use it to criticize all feminists – like it's 'proof' that we really do hate men, or are trying to take over the world, 'mwah ha ha haaa'-style. It's annoying to be automatically discounted, and not listened to, on the basis of something you'd never support or subscribe to. So I am, by the same token, extremely sensitive to the unproductive tarring of all men with a single brush. The idea that half the world's population (give or take) have the same strengths and flaws, characteristics and beliefs is the ridiculous notion I spend most of my time debunking and combatting on behalf of women. I'm certainly not going to advocate its application to men!

I say this because it's so important to make it clear that tackling sexism in no way translates to a suggestion that all men are sexist. Men have been some of the project's greatest supporters, and have also used it to share their own experiences of sexism. Often the stories we receive relate to sexism as perpetrated by women, not men, or by a particular company, or by society at large. The project is by no means intended to vilify men in general. Against the wider backdrop of structural gender imbalance, however – economically, politically, socially and historically speaking – I feel it's important for the focus of this particular venture, at least, to remain on women's experiences as the disproportionate casualties of sexism. Hence the crowding of all these very different men, and male attitudes, into a single chapter. This is not to underplay the importance of men to the movement, or to dismiss the problems disproportionately faced by men – which are many and varied.

Why are you ignoring men's experiences – isn't that sexism? Do you hate all men? Do you want women to rule the world? Haven't you ever heard of the draft? Don't you know men can face sexism too? HAVE YOU SEEN THE DIET COKE ADVERT??? And so on.

I hear these questions a lot. One of the things that interests me most about them is that, when they're posed by men, there's almost invariably no personal story or evidence to support them. It's rarely a case of 'I think you're wrong to focus on women's experiences of sexism because here are five things that have happened to me...' (or even '...one thing that's happened to me...'). Instead it seems to be the concept of the project in itself that theoretically offends. Those men who do write in about experiences of their own don't tend to be the ones who have any issue with the project and its aims.

And, in a way, I think that might explain a lot of the issue here. And the hostility. This is the invisible problem rearing its head again. For some men – usually those who haven't experienced prejudice themselves – the idea of protecting women from sexism feels akin to offering 'special treatment'. If you honestly don't think men are treated any differently than women – if you see a catcall as such a rare and 'inconsequential' event that it happens no more frequently than a man is called a 'girl' for crying or stumbles across the Diet Coke ad (yes, more on that later) – then it sort of makes sense that focusing on women's experiences of sexism might seem biased and unfair. And, if you come to it from a very self-centred perspective, you might not be able to see the ironic truth that insulting a man by calling him a 'girl' and many, many more examples of 'everyday sexism' are actually equally offensive to both men and women.

Really the first thing to say about men is that they're brilliant. They have been, in the main, utterly, fantastically, vocally supportive of the Everyday Sexism Project. This goes for my endlessly supportive partner, whose nights and days for the last three years have been filled with endless Twitter shifts, and harrowing reading, and journalists' phone calls, and dealing with death threats, and taking over the website moderation so I wouldn't have to read those graphic threats, and genuinely making it possible for the project to exist at all. It goes for my wary-but-proud dad, and my bravely-exploring-completely-new-ideas-he's-never-been-exposed-to-before little brother. It goes for our ever patient and supportive web developer, Jim. It goes for the men who wrote in to say that they had no idea what women were dealing with...

▶ Reading your Twitter feed has really opened my eyes. I knew sexism existed, but to this extent? It's like there's a world in which women are constantly threatened, and I've suddenly discovered not only that it exists [...] but that it's the world *I* live in too.

And the men who promised they'll be doing something about it from now on...

🐦 Definitely think the awareness is useful from a male point of view. Has definitely led to me thinking more about what I say and do.

The men who've reported rethinking their own behaviour, and those who've challenged others...

🐦 Without even realizing, some posts have helped me change my ways a little now to be more empathetic.

The ones who've publicly championed us – like Simon Pegg, Hugo Rifkind, Chris Addison, James Corden and Ed Miliband. And the thousands who follow the project on Twitter, turn up to events, participate in the Facebook group, ask questions and provide insights and discuss and love and learn with and alongside women everywhere. The brilliant men mentioned in project entries, who are standing up and fighting beside us...

▶ As a student nurse I get a lot from guys who are intoxicated. I was assisting the doctor stitch up a drunk guy's face and the patient started stroking my arms (he had also previously asked me for a kiss 'cause I was 'a bit of alright') I didn't know how to react, I'm a young girl and being in the professional capacity I wasn't sure how to deal with it professionally so I ignored it. The doctor however after a few minutes raised his voice and very firmly told the guy to stop and behave himself because I 'was there to assist him, not to be cuddled'. I was really shocked that the doctor addressed it, but thankful, I thought he would have just ignored it. The world needs more people like that doctor.

🐦 Group of drunk lads shouted 'get yer tits out' to a woman a few yards ahead of me so I lifted my T-Shirt and showed them mine.

This is not a men vs women issue. It's about people vs prejudice.

So let's talk about the men. Can men experience sexism? I think they can. To me, sexism means treating someone differently or discriminating against them because of their sex. If a boy is laughed at for being 'soft' or unmanly because he gets upset, or because he chooses to rock a particularly awesome shade of nail varnish, I'd consider that sexist. If a man is penalized for or prevented from taking paternity leave from work because his bosses don't consider it his role to play a central part in the care of his newborn, I think that counts as sexism too. If we're going to challenge sexism, we should acknowledge and stand up against those kinds of problems. And the Everyday Sexism Project does: we welcome men with open arms and share their experiences on both the website and Twitter feed.

🐦 People who don't trust my ability as a parent without my partner there just because I'm a man out with my daughter.

🐦 Colleague left work early to collect his son from child care b/c he was sick. Our boss asked him 'Can't your wife go?'

🐦 Took 2yr old son to barbers, 'pls leave long but tidy up'. Reply 'hmm you don't want him to look like a girl'.

▸ I'm a male doctor. On numerous occasions I have received comments from female patients about my youth and good looks. One drunk patient said to her friend as I walked past 'I'd love to f*** him'. A few days ago I was in my office and a patient knocked on the door. A nurse opened the door and asked if the patient needed help and was told 'no, I just wanted a better view of the nice young doctor'.

🐦 My husband is never given the same consideration for family policies as female colleagues.

And many of the stories we have received from men suggest that they experience an added stigma against reporting sexism, because of strong stereotypical ideas about men being strong and manly and 'not making a fuss':

▶ As a male nurse I have received endless quips from my female colleagues and patients. From 'show us your pelvic thrusts' while working with new mothers helping with pelvic-floor exercises after giving birth to slaps on the backside. Men dare not speak out due to ridicule from other men 'what are you complaining about?' or losing their employment.

This is, of course, yet another form of silencing.

But it is also important to acknowledge three things that make men and women's experiences of sexism, in the main, quite different. Frequency, severity and context.

In the UK and around the world, most women face disproportionately far greater sexism than most men do – in terms both of individual incidents and the general cultural climate. The incidents themselves are (again, in general) more severe. And within the framework of a patriarchal social structure – that is, taking into account the wider context of social, economic, professional and political gender imbalance – sexist incidents will often have a far greater impact on women's lives than they have on men's, both individually and in combination.

Consider, for example, a 'minor' sexist remark being made in the workplace. A woman and a man both go off sick for a week. When the man returns to work, jibes and comments are made about 'man-flu'. This is sexist. But it is unlikely to have wider ramifications for his position within the company. When the woman returns to work, people speculate that she might be pregnant and have taken the time off for morning sickness. They tease and joke about the possibility. This is sexist. And within the wider context of professional inequality and gender bias relating to women and motherhood, such a rumour – or even the idea that she is of childbearing age – could potentially have a serious long-term impact on her career.

Then there are other issues, closely related to sexism, like sexualization and objectification, about which we once again hear the cry of 'What about the men??' Take, for example, *that* Diet Coke advert. Yes, let's talk about it. It is tweeted to the Everyday Sexism Project Twitter account at least once a week. Yes, it objectifies men. The nudity isn't related to the product. It gratuitously involves a man being manipulated into taking his top off by a group of women and then focuses in on his torso. IT IS SEXIST. But, in the broader context, the very fact that this advert is so often cited as a 'Ha! Men get it too!' trump card during discussions on sexism is also, ironically, proof that it differs from adverts objectifying women. Because actually it highlights the undeniable truth that such examples of the sexualization and objectification of men are much fewer and farther between than those involving women. And so, while the advert in itself may demean and objectify men, its impact on most men is not equivalent to the impact on women of an entire lifetime's narrative of images in which they are dehumanized, objectified and sexualized at every turn. The ad is the exception rather than the rule. Neither the cumulative impact on the individual nor the knock-on effect on social and cultural norms and mores follows in the same way.

Compare the odd Diet Coke advert with the utter debasement of women in advertising. Consider the Belvedere vodka advert showing a shocked-looking woman being forcefully held from behind by a man with the caption 'Unlike some people, Belvedere always goes down smoothly'. Consider the PlayStation Vita commercial featuring a woman with two pairs of breasts but no head – because, after all, once you've got double the tits who needs a face or a brain or a mouth? Remember the adverts showing women on their knees covered in shoes and bags, like clothes horses, or the reams of pseudo-violent adverts showing them stumbling to the floor as their clothes rip, or bound and gagged in the boot of a car, or wearing a neck brace to extol the great virtues of a high-energy diet for their boyfriend, or prone on the ground with a man's foot firmly on their throat? All real and recent examples.

Additionally, within a society that accepts men on their talents and merits, and regards them as a politician or businessman, etc., first and as a man second, the sexual objectification or portrayal of a man in a non-professional light is less potent. Articles have been written about the sexual attractiveness of Barack Obama, for example. But they would come low on the reading list of anybody interested in his career. Articles about Julia Gillard's childlessness, on the other hand, are extrapolated and interpreted as direct indicators of her unsuitability for the role of prime minister. Pieces about Harriet Harman's shoes often come *in place of* rather than in addition to column inches that might have been devoted to her policies. That female politicians are considered first and foremost as women and *then* as public figures means that the effect of similar puff pieces on their careers is far more severe than it is for their male peers.

The sexualization and objectification of men and women differs not just in frequency but also in the specific points at which it occurs. Yes, many male actors have been hailed as 'hunks' in steamy *Cosmo* centrefold spreads that leave little to the imagination and mention scarce little of their filmography. But at the juncture when a Prince of Hollywood becomes notable for his career, or receives an award for his craft, the attention tends to remain largely on his credentials. Compare this to the spectacular achievement of Anne Hathaway, taking home the Best Supporting Actress Oscar for her role in *Les Misérables*. Was the coverage the next day representative of her wide and varied career, or the talent she displayed in the part? No. It focused almost exclusively on her nipples, and the *burning* question of whether or not they'd been visible through her Oscars dress. They even got their own Twitter account, for Pete's sake. (The same dubious honour was granted to Angelina Jolie's leg after she wore a dress with *stop the press* a *slit* at the side – can you see a pattern here?) See also Jessica Ennis's bum being the most discussed aspect of her Sports Personality of the Year nomination and appearance. Or Marion Bartoli's great Wimbledon triumph, forever overshadowed both in memory and column inches by the commentator's proclamation that she'd 'never be a looker'. Yes, of course, as people clamoured to point out at the time, hurtful things have been said about Wayne

Rooney's appearance over the years. But not when he's just raised the championship trophy, or scored a match-winning goal. At those moments his tactics, technique and skill are quite rightly at the fore; he isn't reduced, at the very moment of his crowning glory, to his physical attractiveness and the sum of his body parts, viewed through a female lens.

The rule of frequency, severity and context holds true for sexism in pretty much every form. Take street harassment, for example. Men have written in to the project to describe being harassed and assaulted by women:

🐦 I work in a bar, and I am constantly getting groped by women.

🐦 Girl walked up to me and groped me, then after I said what the hell she said take it like a man. Not cool.

▶ A group of drunk women on a hen night shouted 'keep moving gorgeous' when I passed them in a train compartment. Followed by 'he's going to go home and cry about that tonight'.

That last account is doubly frustrating because it combines harassment in a public space with a sarcastic, sexist jibe aimed at silencing objection. And of course such incidents are just as serious and just as deserving of action as anything comparable experienced by women.

But the overall problem of harassment in public spaces affects women far more regularly than it does men. While such experiences are likely to be relatively rare for men, a 2012 YouGov survey found that 21 per cent of women of all ages had experienced unwanted sexual attention, with 43 per cent of young women aged eighteen to thirty-four having experienced sexual harassment in London in the past year alone and 5 per cent of all women reporting unwanted sexual touching on public transport.

The severity of incidents is also likely to be higher when the victim is female. Project entries concerning men's experiences most frequently describe comments on appearance and unwanted sexual attention, while women far more regularly report angry threats of violence, physically being grabbed, dragged, or picked up, or being pursued, followed or, in many cases, physically attacked upon refusing to respond.

And, finally, context is important here too. Because we face, in the world, a pandemic of violence (both domestic and sexual) against women, so women's experiences in public spaces are coloured by a very different background appraisal of their own safety, which may give them a greater impact. Women are more likely to feel seriously afraid for their welfare when a strange man shouts at them in the street than vice versa. This doesn't mean that men won't also sometimes fear for their safety, or that those instances are in any way less important and awful. But if we're looking at tackling the wider picture, then yes: there are clear reasons to logically conclude that this is an issue affecting women disproportionately. This is something often recognized by men who report to the project, who contextualize their experiences within an awareness that these things happen to women all the time:

🐦 Had a girl in a van shout 'hey there, sexy' as she drove by. Had no idea how to react. A glimpse into what women deal with.

🐦 Unfollowed @EverydaySexism, weary of the constant barrage of
horror. Then it clicked. That's what it must be like being a woman.
#refollowed

Sexism against men is not good. And it's not non-existent. But it's
also not the same thing.

There are, of course, exceptions. There are men who experience
other forms of discrimination that combine with sexist attitudes
and rigid gender norms to cause them to suffer deeply. Men too are
subject to double discrimination: male members of the LBGTQI
community, for example, or disabled men, or men of colour, may
see sexism intersect with other forms of prejudice – and they may
suffer far worse sexism than some women face.

🐦 Being told I can't be trans because I'm 'not manly enough' or I
'don't act like enough of a guy'.

▶ My seven-year-old son likes nail varnish and frequently asks to
wear it, I put it on him and my father-in-law said to me in front of
my son 'He'll get called a poof.'

Of course, wonderfully, some women don't face sexism. That is
fantastic. And, yes, some women can be sexist, which is sad and
frustrating – just as it is when men are sexist. The structural and
ingrained societal elements of gender inequality mean that the
problem is deeply complex – certainly not about simply vilifying men.
Nor is it about suggesting that all women are victims. Rather it is
about giving a voice to victims who have never been heard before

because their oppression has become so normalized as to be accepted.

Also, of course, there are some issues that affect men disproportionately. We know that rates of male suicide, and workplace death and injury are far higher than those for women. We know that men are not given the same amount of parental leave as women are. We know that fathers sometimes struggle to be awarded the same amount of contact with their children as mothers after a divorce.

🐦 At my place of employ: 6-16 weeks maternity leave. Paternity leave? 3 days. And management must be informed 'well in advance'.

🐦 I was going to fight for custody of my two kids but my lawyer told me I don't have a chance because I'm not a woman.

But these are not issues that feminists glory in, or don't care about. Far from it. Many of the issues impacting on men are rooted in the very same gender imbalance that negatively impacts on women. The irony is that we are on the same side here. Feminists would *love* fair, shared parental leave: it would shift patriarchal assumptions about women's careers being the ones to be compromised by having children and create a much more equal professional playing field. Part of the reason why men are the victims of the majority of workplace accidents is that women have found it very difficult to break into professions requiring physical labour, which are considered stereotypically 'male jobs'. The fact that seeking help for depression and mental-health issues can be seen as a 'weakness', and is therefore incredibly difficult for men to do – which perhaps impacts on the male suicide rate – is an aspect of sexist gender norms that paint men as strong and manly and women as weak and in need of protection. We hate those norms! Men fighting harder for child custody or having to pay child support are issues rooted in the idea that women are the 'natural' caregivers and domestic homemakers, while men must bring home the bacon. These are sexist assumptions that feminists are fighting every day.

But one of the most frustrating things about trying to get on board with and support issues specifically affecting men is that so many men's-rights activists (MRA's), with whom we should have so much in common and so much to work towards, set themselves up stubbornly and angrily in direct opposition to feminism. That's a really great shame, given that so many of the issues we are dealing with are simply different sides of the same coin.

It is difficult to understand the unmitigated hatred of feminism that flows from many men's-rights groups – often to such an extent that the true aim seems to be not the righting of wrongs affecting men and boys at all, but rather the demonization and petty abuse of women's campaigners.

Looking at the blogs of many men's-rights activists, the articles seem to follow roughly a 10:90 split, with 10 per cent mentioning specific issues impacting on men and 90 per cent – the vast majority – devoted entirely to trivial, spiteful attempts to insult and discredit feminists. Such attacks are based on everything from criticism of their looks to issue taken with their tone of voice. Rarely are the women's arguments constructively engaged with. One particularly imaginative piece about me, for example, attacks my future children on the basis that my name is Bates – cue childish sniggers about the potential for a son to be named Master. Aside from the pause this gave me to smile at the MRA's rather uncharacteristic assumption of a matrilineal nomenclature, such pathetic pieces can hardly avoid undermining their entire movement.

I asked Ally Fogg, a journalist who writes about gender issues from a male perspective and has explored the men's-rights movement considerably, why it is that so many of its 'activists' focus so relentlessly on demonizing feminism. His assessment is that:

MRAs actually adhere to a fairly coherent and simple political ideology. It holds that a primary (or even *the* primary) political dynamic within society is between feminists and everyone else. They see feminist influence everywhere and as almost entirely negative. To ask why MRAs focus on feminism is rather tautological; the Men's Rights Movement would be more accurately named the Anti-Feminist Movement. Issues which affect men severely but which don't involve women and feminism are largely ignored – look at how the MRM focuses so heavily on male victims of female violence and female sexual abuse, when the overwhelming majority of violence committed against men is committed by other men. This is of zero interest to MRAs.

How brilliant it would be, indeed – given that feminism means not female supremacy but very simply equality for all regardless of sex – if feminists did indeed hold the quite hilarious level of political and social influence MRAs so generously give us credit for!

Fogg continues:

The Men's Rights Movement has a lot in common with old-fashioned conspiracy theorists. They have constructed an apparently simple and seductive explanation for how the world works which depends upon joining disparate dots to create a pattern, while ignoring all evidence to the contrary. In their minds, something like the Fawcett Society (or National Organization for Women in the US) becomes a secretive cabal that is pulling the strings of government; and any time politicians introduce a policy that is vaguely pro-women, it is taken as proof of their domination. MRAs fail to recognize that there are hundreds of other lobby groups and interests with similar limited influence, and, more importantly, ignore that there are huge capitalist, corporate and financial lobbies with levels of influence that are, by any rational measure, vastly more powerful. And no, of course it is not productive!

Looking at men as a whole more widely, it is a sadly undeniable truth that there are some men who feel either a deep and vitriolic rage or a genuine, unquestioned superiority towards women. I have received too many long, specific, intricate emails from men detailing their fantasy of my rape and murder to believe those who say that it's always just a bit of harmless fun. And many of them have clearly never read anything I've written about gender and the importance of including men in the movement before sending me messages like:

▸ Fuck you stupid slut.

▸ You're just another delusional feminist who hates men.

▸ Fucking women should know their place, fucking skanks.

▸ If you'd just stuck to the kitchen, none of this shit would have happened.

▸ You experience sexism because women are inferior in every single way to men. The only reason you have been put on this planet is so we can fuck you. Please die.

🐦 Laura Bates will be raped tomorrow at 9pm... I am serious.

🐦 Anyone involved in a feminist movement today needs to have a penis put in their mouth and shoved up their arse.

🐦 LAURA BATES... I am seriously going to RAPE and KILL you TODAY at 8pm near your house... Are you ready to get FUCKED?

It is often suggested that these men are angry at something else – that they are probably unpopular teenage boys transcending the frustration of their own powerlessness by terrorizing innocent strangers across the net. But this seems too convenient a theory to fit the coordinated gang attacks and entire message-board threads religiously devoted to persecuting female 'targets' (quite apart from being inexcusably offensive to nice teenage boys). And, as Fogg points out:

It could be that some of this is general anger with their lives, relationships or circumstances which is then being redirected onto random women online, but that doesn't seem especially relevant to me – as even if that is true there is something leading them to focus it, primarily, on women.

Instead, he suspects:

[...] it comes down to defence of privilege. A lot of it seems to stem from the feeling that something which is rightfully theirs is at risk of being snatched away – whether that is the right to see Page 3 or lads' mags, the right to make rape jokes, the right to sexually proposition women or whatever.

There is also a sense of tradition – of men's entitlement and expectations being handed down from one generation to the next – which is accepted unthinkingly as just the way that men are 'supposed' to behave. This is an idea many project entries corroborate...

▸ It's been quite a hot summer here (London), and I was wearing a mid-thigh dress. I got on the bus on my way home from school, and, as I passed him, a man looked, pointedly, down my legs and back up again. Reckon his son was sitting next to him, and the teenager looked to be about my age. For the record, I'm 17.

▸ On the bus to a friend's house, father and son sat next to me [...] Father looks at son and points to me and says very loudly 'Have you checked that THING out?' He repeats this statement 4 or 5 times with the son nodding and saying 'Yeah, I've checked IT out.'

And this is important, because those vitriolic, hate-filled emails aside, the vast majority of those men who are occasionally sexist, just like the vast majority of women who sometimes are, are not deliberately, hatefully trying to hurt women or put them down. They've simply grown up in a world that teaches them that this is the way things are. All the same tiny cultural signifiers and media messages and behavioural norms that affect young girls impact on their male peers too. Teaching them that it is their job to be strong, and macho and masculine, that women should be treated as objects, and that putting girls down, or harassing them, or making sexist jokes, is a way for men to prove their manliness, particularly to one another. So, if we are to rightly be aware of the huge impact of these subtle influences on women, we must also, fairly, acknowledge that much of men's sexist behaviour is not intentional, or deliberately prejudiced, but simply the result of being immersed in a very patriarchal culture.

This comes out strongly in many of the project entries, which paint a clear pattern of boys receiving these messages from a very young age. Like the father who told his son, when he threw a tantrum on the bus, 'Would you stop behaving like a little girl already?' Or the mum who described this litany of sad restrictions and social 'rules':

▸ At three my son couldn't play with a pushchair because it was for girls. My friend's five-year-old son was teased for wearing colourful wellies. At seven he couldn't have a pink water bottle or luminous-pink football socks. At eight he shouldn't go to dance because it's girly. My fourteen-year-old can't accept a hug or a kiss from his family especially in public.

And the idea of peer pressure and masculine expectations only increases as boys get older, with countless stories of lad culture and teenage sexism including heavy elements of coercion.

One female university student told me:

The over-the-top type of culture is particularly apparent in sports teams and with reference to lad culture I've noticed it mostly in the rugby and football teams. An ex-boyfriend who played in a university rugby team often told me about the 'banter' that flew around and it seemed that the worse you treated a female the louder the applause, whereas any respectful behaviour or indeed any indication of liking a female as opposed to just using her body has a means to an end was met with ridicule. I was told about certain acts that earned 'lad points' such as slapping your 'conquest's' face with your penis. Other 'games' like 'pulling' the ugliest girl they could find were pretty commonplace and certainly not isolated incidents. There is a big emphasis put on humiliation.

It's important not to underestimate the degree to which our young men are affected by the cumulative force of normalized misogyny. Such pressure doesn't only come from friends and peers, as one heart-wrenching project entry revealed:

▸ I'm a 17-year-old boy and started following Everyday Sexism and was shocked by what women go through all the time. I started noticing it more and pointing it out. I think some friends listen but the most opposition I've had is at home. My mum tells me to 'man up' when I try to discuss sexism and that there's 'something wrong with me' when I pull up my older brother (who's very into all that lad culture) on sexism. She said I'll never get a girlfriend because they want 'real men' not ones who 'act like girls' and said I shouldn't be bothered about sexism because it doesn't affect me and to 'stop being such a whining girl'. My dad ENCOURAGES me and my brother to harass women on the street and so my brother now does all the time. I'm not letting it stop me because all the stories I've read are terrible and talking to girls at school they all say they experience sexism regularly, but I can't believe how much my family and especially my mum hates me caring about it.

It is absolutely right and important not to demonize men for learned behaviour, nor for the invisibility of a problem that they may genuinely have been oblivious to. But what we *can* hope is that, once they *are* made aware of it, they might join the ranks of those other men who stand voluntarily alongside us in the fight for change. This is quite possible. Already a vast number of men have written to the project to express their shock and anger upon reading about women's experiences. Their determination to help make a difference is brilliantly clear:

🐦 As a guy this Twitter feed has definitely opened my eyes and changed my behaviour.

▸ When I was a teen I probably said a lot of sexist things I remember telling and laughing at rape jokes. Looking back at it I see that it was abhorrent and that I was allowing rape culture to run rampant. I did not go to a normal college but film school in Canada, I then had the honour of meeting a bunch of women from all over the world, and that helped me and changed me for the better. As I grew close to these women as friends I heard countless stories about not just sexual harassment but assault. It filled me with rage, but made me realize that I was part of that culture. I wanted to be part of a solution; the Dad that tells his son 'Don't rape' instead of putting the onus on women. I slowly got turned to feminist thought and I can now proudly say I am a Feminist.

And of course, with the support of those many wonderful men who are willing to assist the move towards equality, we are also far better equipped to tackle the issues that those truly concerned about men's wellbeing rightly raise. Fogg, interestingly, prefers not to describe these as 'men's rights':

Because the issues are rarely or never about legal rights and entitlements. There is not a single legal or civil right that men, as a gender, are systematically or structurally denied. The closest one could get to that would be fathers' rights. Personally I don't use that term, I think family disputes should hinge upon children's rights and welfare, not parents'. That said, I do think children have the right to a sustained and ongoing relationship with the natural father, where appropriate, and I do have concerns about the

ability and willingness of family courts to ensure this happens. The Children and Family Act currently going through Parliament may help.

Most of the real issues, from my point of view, are not of men's rights but of men's welfare and wellbeing. There's a pretty long list of issues which disproportionately or exclusively impact upon men: socialization into violence (the willingness to both inflict and accept it); disproportionate suicide rates; different patterns of physical and mental-health problems; drug and alcohol abuse and addiction; underachievement in education; homelessness; criminal offending and the workings of the judicial and penal systems.

Many of those issues are connected, and I believe a lot of them can be traced back to a relative overemphasis on men (and especially boys') personal culpability and agency. We really struggle as a society to see men's problems as products of social forces, preferring to attribute them to individual failings. And yes, all of this is attributable to patriarchy, in feminist terms, but I don't think that means the victims shouldn't matter.

There should never be any victims who don't matter, because this simply isn't about men vs women. It's not about taking away men's rights, or about failing to focus on the issues that affect them, but about working, together, towards a more equal society in which both men *and* women are inherently protected and able truly to fulfil their natural potential.

Chapter 11

Women Under Threat

'I'm crying and it's not just for these women but for all of us women. It is so rare to know a woman who hasn't been abused in some way'
Everyday Sexism Project entry

Vital Statistics

603 million women live in countries where domestic violence
is still not a crime
UN Women, 2003

The annual worldwide number of so-called 'honour killing'
victims may be as high as 5,000 women
United Nations Population Fund (UNFPA), 2000

In the UK over 2 women per week on average are killed
by a current or former partner
Coleman and Osborne, 2010, Department of Health, 2005

85,000 women per year are raped in the UK
Ministry of Justice, Home Office for National Statistics, 2013

Women aged 15 to 44 are more at risk from rape and domestic
violence than from cancer, car accidents, war and malaria
World Bank, 1994

Worldwide over 3 million girls have been estimated to be at
risk for female genital mutilation annually
World Health Organization, 2014

1 in 3 women on the planet will be raped or beaten in her
lifetime
UN, 2008

🐦 laura bates... YOU BETTER WATCH YOUR BACK... I'M GONNA RAPE YOUR ASS AT 8PM AND PUT THE VIDEO ALL OVER THE INTERNET.

🐦 My neighbour raped me when I was 16 – he said I was a slut and was asking for it and no-one would believe me if I told anyone.

🐦 I was told by a school support worker to 'just sleep with' the boyfriend who was pressuring me for sex that I didn't want.

🐦 I walk with my keys between my knuckles, even in broad day light. I am scared to be in a city alone. I should not have to feel this way.

🐦 14yrs old: Boys liked to play the 'rape' game when we were at friends' houses for parties. Would take girls in turn and dry hump and grope them for fun – despite the screaming.

🐦 I don't want to live in a society that told ME not to get raped, but when it does happen, don't expect to get much help for it. I think that's the worst part.

The first thing is that there are two different worlds. I've talked to children who are not yet sixteen but understand a woman's place. They're used to being groped and grabbed on their daily commute in their uniform to school. I've spoken to teenagers who all know a girl who has been raped, or assaulted, or had intimate photographs of herself circulated until she feels desperate and suicidal. I've listened to the women who have been assaulted and abused and then rejected by an asylum system that – irony of all ironies – refuses to believe their story because it is too awful to countenance. I've heard from elderly women who are grateful for the invisibility of age in a society that deems them worthless because at least it is better than their earlier life, full of harassment and assault.

The effect of living in a world where people of one sex are treated – in myriad tiny, indistinguishable, invisible ways – completely and utterly differently from people of another sex is enormous. You don't need to directly experience each individual component for this level of combined violence and oppression and prejudice to have a huge impact on you – on your life and your lifestyle, your ideas and ideals, and your fundamental perception of yourself and of the world around you.

Men and women inhabit two entirely different worlds.

At a recent meeting I was seated next to a brilliant and inspiring teacher. She pointed out to me that it would be a natural cause for concern if, when they lined up for lunch, the young children in her class ordered themselves by race – grouping themselves together with others of the same ethnic background; this would be something she'd take action to resolve. And yet, she said, every day, in classrooms across the country, children are lining up in strictly segregated groups of boys and girls and nobody bats an eyelid. In her classroom, for example, she told me there's a free-play area for 'golden time' – when the boys go without fail to one corner, complete with toy cars and sports equipment and trucks, and the girls go to another, a pink procession of dolls and miniature shopping trolleys and pretend plastic cookery sets. And so it begins.

And, just as surely as millions of tiny messages such as these shape and mould our children's earliest perceptions, so thousands of tiny pinpricks also serve, as our girls become women, to initiate them into a world in which their understanding of their own freedom and safety is completely different from that of men.

> ▶ Male friends do not understand the problem and do not understand the way I hold keys in my hand as a weapon when walking alone just in case.

We think of men and women as living and working in the same world, and experiencing it similarly. But in very many ways the manifestation of an identical event or activity by one might be entirely unrecognizable to the other.

> ▶ On nights out it has become the norm to have my arse grabbed, but the worst is when they grab for my crotch then disappear into the crowd so I don't even know who has done it (yes this has happened more than once and it hurts). I've also been threatened by men and pushed into walls for resisting or for standing up for friends they were trying to grope.

For most women, a night out means hassle and harassment, groping and unwanted advances, wolf whistles and catcalls. Most men's experience of going to a club or bar is manifestly different – though physically they are in the same space. This leads to a knock-on difference in our own behaviours. For many men, the countless routine steps women take to protect themselves – going out in groups and keeping tabs on one another, taking taxis to avoid badly lit routes, holding keys between their fingers on darkened pavements, standing protectively together to avoid groping – are difficult to conceive of.

My experience of walking down the London street on which I live is completely different from my partner's, even though we live together, have similar schedules and both travel the route daily. He doesn't tense at the approach of a car in a distinctive shade of dark green, because it once slowed to a crawl while the driver told him, in chilling detail, how he'd noticed exactly which streets he regularly walked down and at what time. He doesn't cross the road to avoid the fishmonger's, where the men stand in the doorway making comments under their breath about his body as he walks past. He doesn't have to go to the coffee place that's a bit further away and without convenient Wi-Fi because the waiters at the closer place harassed him and asked him for his number and made bets about who would get it the last time he went in. He doesn't duck into a shop doorway when he spots the man who followed him off the bus that time and down the street asking insistently and aggressively whether he knew how beautiful he was until he ran into the supermarket to get away. None of this crosses my partner's radar. When he walks down the street he just walks down the street. But my experience of walking down the street is coloured by every one of these experiences and more, not just on the day they happen but every day after that.

When men write online, they might experience hostility, opposition and arguments. They're unlikely to experience a torrent of death and rape threats detailing exactly how they should be abused and disembowelled. The first flood of these messages that I received were such a shock that I just sat very, very still and quiet for a while. The impact of reading something so very personal and so very violent while sitting in your own living room makes it feel as if something absolutely terrifying is hovering directly overhead; your first instinct is not to move a muscle in case it drops. Not to rock the boat in case you attract that kind of vitriol again. When the words go round in your head at night and the images of what they describe dance against your closed eyelids, you start to think quite seriously about how to avoid this happening again. Then the police say there's nothing they can do and your twitchy jumps at every movement become so great that you actually leave home for a while. That's when you start to consider whether it's really worth writing any more articles, or continuing to talk about the issues you care about any more. And later you find yourself in a late-night bar writing your book with your laptop perched on your knees because there was a noise in the garden and your partner was out and you suddenly felt a choking terror thinking of all the threats and wondering… just wondering. Worst of all, they eventually decide the rape threats aren't getting to you enough and start threatening your family instead. It's a trade-off between your personal mental health and safety and your ideals and career that most men never even have to consider.

Different worlds. It's what lets half the population laugh at something the other half lives in constant fear of.

▶ A co-worker who I considered a good friend at a new workplace came up behind me, wrapped his arms around my waist, and whispered in my ear 'Hey, mate, you know how I know we're having sex tonight? Because I'm stronger than you.' And fell over laughing because I instantly burst into tears.

▸ I was raped by my father as a child. When I first told this to someone I felt comfortable with, my current boyfriend, he made a rape joke and said, 'Well, you shouldn't have led him on.' This just shows that rape is not taken seriously in today's society.

▸ He raped me. I was a virgin. He thought that was hilarious. His friend sat in the back and told me I'd be a nymphomaniac after. That was 20 years ago. Sometimes, while I'm doing dishes, or waiting for a train [...] I think about it. Why I wasn't strong enough to try to leave [...] What I'd do in the situation if it happened again. Trying to remind myself it wasn't my fault. I'm still really angry. And not just at him, but at me.

All these differences in perception and behaviour also shape our more basic, foundational ideas of our own human rights and boundaries – our fear of assault, our assessment of our safety and our judgement of our own culpability.

▸ Until I heard you on Woman's Hour just now I thought it was all my fault. I have had experiences of sexual harassment all my life – the uncle who fondled my breasts as he comforted me when my father was dying in the next room; the supermarket manager who commented on my short skirt during my Saturday job and who said 'You shouldn't wear a short skirt if you don't want comments.'

Then, as an 18-year-old civil servant, I was pushed against a wall and kissed and groped.

And all this time I thought it was my fault for sending out the wrong signals.

The world around us sends us messages about ourselves as women – about our guilt, and our difference, our accountability and our flaws. It gives us endless reminders of the vulnerability and victimization of women. It lets us know that it is normal and common for women to experience assault and harassment and rape. And it tells us that we deserve it. And all the while we are conditioned to be passive and pleasant, not to make a fuss – to be ladylike and compliant and socially acceptable. Before we ever experience violence we are conditioned to expect it – and to accept it.

▶ After a row with an ex-boyfriend about standing me up as he was still in the pub with his mates, he told me 'You should be thankful that I treat you the way I do. Loads of men are at home beating their partners.'

You want to know how early it starts?

▶ I was first molested when I was 8 years old. The same man waited until I was 9 to rape me. He raped me every morning before school for my whole 3rd grade year. I didn't tell anyone. He forced his son to do things to me. It was the most awful and brutal thing that has ever happened to me. But it wasn't the last.

▶ My first experience of groping was when I was 11 years old and was at a baseball game with my best friend and her dad. I was walking up a crowded staircase and someone behind me or beside me, not sure who, goosed me. It was horrifying feeling some strange man's finger groping my entire private region from my vagina to my anus. I was in shock and I felt very violated. That experience was the beginning of my indoctrination into sexism and the idea that because I am female my body does not belong to me.

Vitally, it is impossible to separate these shocking accounts of violent assault from the stories we have received of harassment and verbal sexism, or those of abuse and rape. One may not necessarily lead directly to another, but they are composite parts of the same problem. The daily, normalized suggestion that women are 'other', second-class, inferior beings, the overwhelming sexualization and objectification of them, and the structural sexism that means that news, politics and crime alike are all seen through a default male gaze... These are all contributing factors to the crisis of sexual violence we face.

I don't mean to alarm you, but we are in the middle of an international *epidemic*. One in three women on the planet will be raped or beaten in her lifetime. According to the World Health Organization, 38 per cent of all women murdered are killed by their partners. Around the world, women are subjected to forced marriage, stoning, trafficking, female genital mutilation, childhood pregnancy, acid attacks, 'honour' killings, corrective rape, lives of slavery and servitude because of their second-class citizenship. In some countries they are pushed towards enlarging their breasts to satisfy male demand. In others their breasts are painfully flattened with hot stones to deter male lust. In some places their vaginas are painfully stuffed with dry cotton to make them swell with discomfort so they will tighten for men's pleasure. In others their sexual organs are decimated just to be sure that they – the women – will not experience sexual pleasure.

Actually, I do think you should be alarmed. I think we should all be alarmed.

This is by no means a 'foreign' problem.

According to figures released in 2013 by the UK Ministry of Justice, Office for National Statistics and the Home Office, on average approximately 85,000 women are raped every year in England and Wales. More than 400,000 are sexually assaulted. An average of two women per week are killed by a current or former partner and in any one year there are 13 million separate incidents of physical violence or threats of violence against women from partners or former partners. One in five women in the UK is the victim of a sexual offence and it is estimated that one in four will experience domestic violence in her lifetime.

In 2012, the UK government Forced Marriage Unit dealt with nearly 1,500 cases, of which 82 per cent involved female victims, though the number of unreported cases is likely to be much higher. More than 20,000 girls are estimated to be at risk of female genital mutilation in the UK every year. According to a recent report by UK-based charity Women for Refugee Women, based on female asylum-seekers in the UK, '48 per cent had experienced rape, and two thirds had experienced gender-related persecution, including sexual violence, forced marriage, and female genital mutilation.

Almost all of the women had been refused asylum.'

Were any other crisis to cost the lives of more than two people every week in the UK – or to threaten *one third* of the entire world's population – it would be considered an international emergency. But the rape, assault and murder of women by men is enshrined in our international history. It is so common that it has become an accepted part of the wallpaper.

Women are under threat from this epidemic of sexual violence and equally endangered by public attitudes towards it, which enable and encourage perpetrators, blame and silence victims and even have a serious, damaging impact on the justice system designed to tackle the problem.

There is a massive anomaly inherent in the UK public and media perception of victims of rape, domestic violence and sexual assault. What was she doing there? What was she wearing? Had she led him on? Didn't she know what she was getting herself into? Maybe she was winding him up. Men can't get raped – what's he talking about? Had they been drinking? Have you heard how many people she's slept with before? And so on.

Each of these horribly common reactions relates to the misapprehension that a victim can somehow influence their own assault or be partially to blame for what happens to them. And most are steadily reinforced by the myths and misconceptions about rape and assault that flow through our culture.

Myths about the responsibility of the victim make women and girls feel unable to report...

▶ I was 16. We had spoken on the internet several times before

I agreed to meet him, and he persuaded me to go to his home, where he proceeded to rape me and take my virginity [...] But because of things I have read on the internet about how you 'can't change your mind,' I have never talked about this before.

Hence, according to UK government statistics released in January 2013, 28 per cent of women who are victims of the most serious sexual offences never tell anybody about it. Hence, according to Rape Crisis, only around 15 per cent of women and girls who experience sexual violence ever report to the police.

Myths about what a rapist looks like blur the boundaries of consent...

▶ I'm 38 and reckon between the ages of 11 to the present day I've been sexually assaulted at least 20-30 times. Of course, never thought about going to the police. I had never been held at knifepoint in a dark alley after all [...]

▶ I was raped by a girl. When I told my friends, they said it didn't really count because girls can't rape each other.

Myths about male strength and female vulnerability prevent male victims from feeling able to come forward, or receive support...

▶ Been put in a situation where saying 'No' to a Lady who was older, bigger and stronger than myself didn't count for anything. But of course being that I'm a guy you wouldn't class that as rape would you now?

Myths about dark shadowy strangers make girls think they 'owe' their boyfriends sex and boys think it's not possible to rape a girl you know, even if she's drunk, or semiconscious. They make men think it's not 'abuse' if it's your own wife...

▶ 6 years of rape, sexual assault, physical and emotional abuse because 'I can do what I want to you – you are my wife'.

▶ My boyfriend raped me [...] He got drunk and I tried to leave, but he pinned me down and forced me to have sex. Then he acted like nothing happened [...] He said boyfriends couldn't rape girlfriends. He told me that no one would believe me because I was a big slut.

Myths about women asking for it – secretly enjoying rape – lead to blame and excuses...

▶ My rapist blamed me for his violence: 'You are a slut, you want it!' and later I blamed myself.

▶ At 16 I was raped, and at 17 I was raped. To this day even though I'm 20 now I get told that I probably liked it.

Myths that a rape victim must have struggled and shouted and screamed in order for the rape to have been 'real' leave the many victims who freeze in fear feeling doubted and blamed. Like the rape survivor who told me her story of rape at the hands of a housemate, who had entered her room as she slept in the middle of the night. The Crown Prosecution Service told her they wouldn't take her case to court because there was no evidence of a struggle that was likely to convince a jury. In the weeks that followed, when she went out and had her drink spiked and was raped again – a proper, legitimate, believable, official, respectable STRANGER rape – she never dreamed of going back to report it to the police. Because, she asked simply, what was the point?

And cultural myths are used to sweep violence against women under the carpet, as Nimko Ali explains:

FGM for me is the same as any other form of oppression that women face [...] these things happen to girls because they're female – because they're girls, not because of the colour of their skin or their faith – it's patriarchy that's actually the foundation of all these things.

FGM has been overlooked, and we've put it in this cultural cul-de-sac, because we're uncomfortable talking about what it actually is [which is] a form of violence against women that happens because women are unequal in the society in which they live. I remember it quite vividly. It happened when I was on holiday in Djibouti [...] It didn't make any sense. I was 7 and we were on holiday in Djibouti and I had the FGM – I remember the whole thing very clearly and for me it just did not make sense. And what did not make sense was everybody pretending it didn't happen the day after [...] And then I came back to the UK and I went to my teacher and I said, 'Why did this happen? It's really silly, it's really stupid.' And she said, 'That's part of your culture.'

FGM was criminalized in the UK more than two decades ago, but there has not yet been a single conviction.

Worst of all, these myths are peddled not just by misinformed individuals but also by our national and international press and even our own judiciary, members of government and police forces. And this is where you start to see the real impact they have on justice, and on perpetuating the whole violent cycle...

While running for Governor of Texas in 1990, Clayton Williams compared rape to bad weather: 'If it's inevitable, just lie back and enjoy it.'

In 2008, while sentencing a rapist, Orange County Superior Court Judge Derek Johnson dismissed the prosecutor's call for a sixteen-year sentence and instead sentenced the defendant to just six years. He said: 'I'm not a gynaecologist, but I can tell you something: if someone doesn't want to have sexual intercourse, the body shuts down. The body will not permit that to happen unless a lot of damage is inflicted, and we heard nothing about that in this case.'

In 2010, Colorado District Attorney Ken Buck, who would later run for Senate, failed to prosecute an alleged rapist because the victim had invited the perpetrator to her room. He told her it sounded like a case of 'buyer's remorse'.

When CBS reporter and journalist Lara Logan was sexually assaulted in Tahrir Square while covering the Egyptian revolution, US media pundits criticized her for taking such high-risk assignments and for daring to do her job when she had a young family at home. In a column entitled 'Women with young kids shouldn't be in warzones', one writer asked, 'Should women journalists with small children at home be covering violent stories or putting themselves at risk? It's a form of self-indulgence and abdication of a higher responsibility to family.' Another commentator asked: 'Why did this attractive blonde female reporter wander into Tahrir Square last Friday? What was she thinking?'

In March 2011, the *New York Times* reported on the gang-rape of an eleven-year-old girl in Cleveland, Texas. The article described how two of the suspects were members of their high-school basketball team. It reported that the child victim 'dressed older than her age, wearing makeup and fashions more appropriate to a woman in her 20s. She would hang out with teenage boys at a playground, some said.' It suggested that local residents would be left asking 'how could their young men have been drawn into such an act?' Interviewees were quoted saying: 'These boys have to live with this the rest of their lives.'

At Caernarfon Crown Court in December 2012, a forty-nine-year-old man was found guilty of raping a teenage girl. As he jailed the rapist, the judge said: 'She let herself down badly. She consumed far too much alcohol and took drugs, but she also had the misfortune of meeting you.' The implication was clear: the silly girl put herself in harm's way. The rapist was a 'misfortune': something natural, something to protect yourself from – something that just happens. The agency was all hers.

After the conviction of nine men for the systematic grooming and sexual abuse of a group of young girls in Rochdale in 2012, one of the victims told BBC's *Woman's Hour*: 'Quite a few people rang social services: school, the police [...] even my own dad [...] basically they told my mum and dad that I was a prostitute and it was a lifestyle choice. And because I was only six months off turning sixteen they weren't [*sic*] going to do anything.'

In October 2012, a former Metropolitan Police detective constable was jailed for sixteen months consequent to his failings relating to rape cases, which included falsely claiming that a rape victim had dropped charges. In February 2013, an investigation by the Independent Police Complaints Commission revealed that the Metropolitan Police's specialist Sapphire Unit had 'encouraged' rape victims to withdraw allegations in order to boost detection rates.

In 2012, Republican Senate candidate Todd Akin said that in cases of 'legitimate rape' women rarely fall pregnant, because 'the female body has ways of shutting that whole thing down'.

Stating that abortion should be illegal even in cases of rape, Republican presidential candidate Rick Santorum said in 2012 that rape victims must 'accept what God has given to you' and 'make the best of a bad situation'.

In August 2012, UK MP George Galloway publicly said that the allegations of rape against Julian Assange, who was accused of raping a sleeping woman who had previously consented, were simply 'bad sexual etiquette [...] not rape as anyone with any sense can possibly recognize it'.

In Italy in 2012 a priest posted a notice at his church about domestic violence and the murder of women by men. It read: 'The core of the problem is in the fact that women are more and more provocative, they yield to arrogance, they believe they can do everything themselves and they end up exacerbating tensions [...] How often do we see girls and even mature women walking on the streets in provocative and tight clothing?'

In August 2012, a sixteen-year-old girl was subjected to repeated sexual assaults and raped in Steubenville, Ohio. The incidents were captured on video via mobile phones and posted on social media. When two boys were convicted of the rape, the CNN reporter covering the story said: 'I've never experienced anything like it [...] It was incredibly emotional, incredibly difficult even for an outsider like me to watch what happened as these two young men that had such promising futures, star football players, very good students literally watched as they believed their lives fell apart.'

In the wake of the Egyptian revolution, as female protesters took to the streets alongside their male peers, they experienced wave after wave of sexual violence, sexual harassment, groping, serious assault and rape. But, as the problem persisted in August 2013, the *Egypt Independent* newspaper reported that the human-rights committee of the Shura Council, part of Egypt's Parliament, declared female protesters responsible for the harassment and attacks. One politician, a member of the committee, was reported to have said: 'By getting herself involved in such circumstances, the woman has 100 per cent responsibility.'

At Snaresbrook Crown Court in 2013, a forty-one-year-old man admitted engaging in sexual activity with a thirteen-year-old girl. The judge spared him jail time, instead handing down an eight-month suspended sentence. He said: 'I have taken in to account that even though the girl was thirteen, the prosecution say she looked and behaved a little bit older [...] On these facts, the girl was predatory and was egging you on [...]'

In August 2013, a Montana judge handed a sentence of just one-month imprisonment to a man who raped a fourteen-year-old girl. The girl later committed suicide. The judge said that the girl was 'older than her chronological age' and declared her 'as much in control of the situation' as her rapist.

Does this list of situations in which women and girls are blamed for their own assaults seem endless? Then it mirrors the reality.

In 2012, Alison Saunders, head of the UK Crown Prosecution Service, warned in an interview with the *Guardian* that 'myths and stereotypes' about rape victims may give jurors 'preconceived ideas' that could affect their decisions in court. When victims are 'demonized in the media', she said, 'you can see how juries would bring their preconceptions to bear'.

And yet – while even the head of the Crown Prosecution Service is able to see the connections between a culture awash with victim blaming and the potential miscarriage of justice – it is incredibly difficult to talk about the connections between other forms of latent misogyny within our culture and the epidemic of sexual violence faced by women on a daily basis. This is often because of the enormous imbalance of power in this scenario, between the music moguls and media magnates profiting from our misogyny-drenched culture and its vulnerable, silenced victims.

Talk about the impact of the *Sun*'s Page 3 and you're immediately asked to provide any evidence that it leads men to rape, or you're banned from mentioning the rates of sexual assault and domestic violence in the context of your argument. Criticize Robin Thicke's 'Blurred Lines' video, with its references to splitting a girl in two, and you're shut down because the song is 'ironic' and therefore beyond reproach. But why *can't* we have an open, serious, mainstream conversation about this? Why can't we discuss the fact that we have a society in which 400,000 women are sexually assaulted every year and 85,000 raped, while our culture – from music and magazines to adverts and films – constantly blares out the crystal-clear message that women are submissive, disposable sex objects? Why can't we have a conversation that doesn't suggest a direct cause, but nonetheless takes into account the context that inextricably links them?

In December 2012, the *Daily Mail* journalist Richard Littlejohn wrote an article about a primary-school teacher who happened to be transgender, with little apparent reason why the case merited national news attention. Repeatedly referring to the woman as 'he', Littlejohn claimed to have sympathy with those who required gender-reassignment surgery – yet said her transition would have a 'devastating effect' on the children at the school where she taught. Littlejohn even attacked the school for its supportive stance, in a paragraph dripping with sarcasm: 'the school is "proud of our commitment to equality and diversity". Of course they are.' But when Lucy Meadows, the teacher at the centre of the article, committed suicide three months later after being hounded by the press, the *Daily Mail* slammed anybody who dared to bring up the article. As they told the *Huffington Post*: 'Those criticizing Littlejohn might do well to consider today's words of media commentator Roy Greenslade: 'it is important to note that there is no clear link – indeed any link – between what Littlejohn wrote and the death of Lucy Meadows.'" That is perfectly true. (Though the *Daily Mail* immediately removed the article from its website, which seems a strange step if it genuinely considered it to be utterly unrelated to Meadows's death.) But in any case why should this preclude us from considering the article, and the wider press bias in reporting on stories involving trans people, within the context of this important debate?

A woman died, not in isolation, not in a bubble, but within a world that was utterly hostile to her; utterly unable to respect her personal choices. At the inquest, the coroner exclaimed: 'And to you the press, I say shame, shame on all of you.' But for goodness sake let's not risk hurting the feelings of the privileged acid-tongued reporter who made money from mocking and turning the world's eyes on this vulnerable woman at the most difficult period in her life, because there's no reason to think he had anything *directly* to do with her decision.

Women are being raped, assaulted and murdered every day, but for heaven's sake let's not upset anybody by worrying too much about what might be contributing to it in an 'indirect way'. Let's not worry about connecting these cases, though the murder of a five-year-old girl and the abduction of a teenager and the sexual assault of another teenager and the rape and imprisonment of three women for more than a decade are reported consecutively, one after the other, on the evening news. We don't want to make anybody feel *uncomfortable*.

Best not to talk about porn, either, since that's another freedom-of-speech issue. Although ironically the issue isn't necessarily the medium itself – the idea of sharing filmed sex – but rather the violent misogyny inherent in so much of the mainstream porn available. Can we have a conversation about that? Are we allowed to ask not why there's porn online, or why it's available, but simply what it is about the world that means that so much of its most accessible presence focuses on humiliating and degrading women, making them hurt and cry, forcing them to submit and ejaculating over their faces? Can we ask why little girls are writing to me in tears because they've seen it and they think that's what sex is and they're afraid? Just as a necessary discussion about the deep misogyny in many men's magazines isn't an attack on all print journalism, so the issue with porn isn't the medium but the way in which it's being used.

Can we look at life from the point of view of a thirteen-year-old girl and stop to acknowledge that it looks like a fucking obstacle course? Can we ask why her every move is a tactical manoeuvre as she navigates sexting and porn and body image? Because those girls are the ones who lose out when we tie ourselves in knots trying not to say anything that might force some multimillionaire media mogul to pause for five minutes and defend the extent to which his empire is built on the backs of naked teenage girls.

Better for us women to put up and shut up than to risk offending anybody. Better we stop going for runs, like the 24 per cent of American women surveyed by Stop Street Harassment in 2008 who choose not to exercise outside for fear of harassment or assault. Better we just reconsider our route home, or buy a car, or change our outfits, than piss people off by questioning how unsafe we are made to feel on our own neighbourhood streets. Better we teach our teenage girls to carry whistles, and alarms, and travel in packs than question why the world allows them to be walking, talking prey.

Because after all, this is normal. This is the world that we live in. This isn't something that's gone wrong; it's just the way things already are – it's the point we started from. Don't forget that 'women are equal now, more or less'.

We immerse young people in a world of sex and sexualization, but we don't stop to talk about consent, or relationships, or their right not to be touched or coerced or assaulted.

▶ I didn't know any of it was wrong until when I was 17, about six months after I was raped. I almost reported it but didn't, because I thought it was my fault and I shouldn't have talked to the guy who did it.

When we end up justifying and normalizing and getting used to everything, telling young women that this is the world they will have to navigate and the way they should expect to be treated, we leave them with nowhere left to go. When we tell them that everything they are is what they look like – that their bodies and their sexuality and their sexiness comprise their sum value – and then bully, repress, criticize and censure them *for* their bodies and their sexuality, we create a society that has no place for them in it. When we introduce them to a world in which they're seen as sexual prey and have a one in three chance of being raped or beaten, without stopping to question that status quo or trying to fix the culture that enables it to continue, we have already robbed them of their right to belong. And so we lose them.

We lost Amanda Todd, pressured into exposing her teenage breasts to a stranger on the internet and blackmailed and bullied for the photographs for the rest of her short life until she hanged herself. We lost teenager Rehtaeh Parsons, who hanged herself after she was gang raped and labelled a slut when photographs of her rape were published online. We lost twelve-year-old Gabrielle Molina, who committed suicide after being taunted by school bullies who called her a slut and a whore. We lost Felicia Garcia, fifteen, who jumped in front of a train after enduring bullying and taunts about being a slut because of sexual activity at a party. We lost nineteen-year-old Lizzy Seeberg because when she tried to report her rapist she received threatening texts from his friend telling her, 'Don't do anything you would regret', and campus security failed to interview the alleged perpetrator for ten days, by which time she had committed suicide. We lost Audrie Pott, fifteen, who hanged herself after her brutal sexual assault was photographed and shared online and led to vicious sexual bullying. We lost Rachel Ehmke when she committed suicide, aged just thirteen, after she was taunted by bullies who called her a slut and scrawled the word across her locker.

And we will keep losing them, as long as we're prepared to continue living – as if this is simply *normal* – in a world where the threat of rape or beating hangs over one third of women's heads.

Chapter 12

People
Standing Up

'I don't feel
intimidated
any more.
I feel strong'
*Feminist
interviewee*

🐦 'I said have a nice day BITCH!!' Wow thank you SO much, genuine gentlemen on the streets of nyc.

🐦 You have to wonder what a guy who is quietly cat calling women in a Starbucks at 6am is doing with his life.

🐦 Man called me an Opinionated Lesbian Cunt! Thank you I'm proud of being Opinionated, Lesbian & having a Cunt.

🐦 I never realised I could speak out against these daily experiences. I haven't even discussed these with my boyfriend of 10 years.

🐦 Thank you for telling me I'm beautiful, 14-year-old boy, but no, I won't be sucking your cock.

🐦 Had an experience a few years ago I've never told a soul about. Your video made me realise I'm not alone. Thank you.

Women everywhere have had enough. We've reached our tipping point and we're not afraid to say it. We're not afraid to be dismissed, or belittled, or laughed at any more, because there are too many of us. There's no silencing someone who has tens of thousands of others standing right behind them. We can't be silenced when we're all saying the same thing.

A storm is coming. It didn't start out as a full-blown hurricane. It started with almost imperceptible whispers of 'Is it just me?' and 'Hang on a minute...' and 'Maybe I'm overreacting, but...'

But those whispers became a voice, fuelled by the bravery of Malala Yousafzai and the buoyancy of Caitlin Moran and the fearlessness of Lena Dunham, underpinned by the solidarity of social media, sharpened by the wit of Jezebel, spurred on by the incorrigible positivity of No More Page 3, the outrage of Julia Gillard, the legacy of Jyoti Singh Pandey, the strength of Zerlina Maxwell and Anita Sarkeesian, the fearlessness of Janet Mock, the courage of Mona Eltahawy and Nihal Saad Zaghloul. This is the voice of thousands and thousands of women and it's saying:

Enough is enough.

And if you think the storm has reached its peak, you haven't seen anything yet. This is just the beginning. What we have witnessed so far was just an overture. In late 2012, the video of Australia's then prime minister Julia Gillard decrying the misogyny she suffered in office swept virally across the globe. In India, protesters lined the streets after the horrifying gang rape and murder of Jyoti Singh Pandey in December and the subsequent death of a five-year-old rape victim in April. In Bangladesh, protest swelled into a human chain after the rape of a teenager by four men, the latest in a series of violent rapes of young women to which another teenager lost her life. In Nepal, demonstrators swarmed Kathmandu after a gang rape case involving police and immigration officials. In Sri Lanka, protests in solidarity with the Delhi rape victim intensified after details of another gang rape near Colombo emerged in January. At Eve Ensler's call to action, one billion people in 193 countries marched on 14 February to protest against the rape and violence that will affect one in three women on the planet in her lifetime. And in America, at the peak of the war on women's bodies, Senator Wendy Davis stood for eleven hours against a Republican bill that would severely limit access to abortion.

Feminism being, purely and simply, the notion that people of all sexes deserve to be treated equally, this movement looks very different in different countries – it has widely varied goals and aims, and very different means of achieving them. But, thanks to the rise of social media, there is a sense of cohesion and solidarity growing ever stronger between women and across borders and boundaries that enables us to stand alongside our sisters and solicit for them as never before.

It's got power, this storm, and its power is in its immediacy, its vitality and its pragmatism, as women around the world are united with the force of pressure that has been building for centuries. Enough is enough. It's the power of a generation of young women coming to the world and finding it wanting, and a generation of women who've fought this fight already rolling up their sleeves to get stuck back in and finish it for good. It's the power of a movement that is spreading like an epidemic; that sees injustice in its path and will not be silenced as we've been silenced before. A movement so strong that its international outrage provoked a commitment from Pakistan's president to work with the United Nations to ensure education for all children after Malala Yousafzai was shot in the head by the Taliban for no greater crime than making the journey to school. Enough is enough. A movement that stood up and screamed when Egyptian protesters were assaulted and raped in Tahrir Square just for fighting for their freedom alongside their brothers. A movement that threatened to devastate the Maldives tourist industry when a fifteen-year-old rape victim was sentenced to 100 lashes, until the president stepped in to overturn the court sentence. A movement that demanded justice and pardon for Marte Deborah Dalelv when the Norwegian national was jailed for extramarital sex after being raped in Dubai. It was a movement that would not stand by in silence when the devastating case of the teenage girl raped in Steubenville, Ohio, was reported by CNN in a way that seemed to imply sympathy with the perpetrators rather than with the victim. A movement that forced one of the biggest social-networking sites in the world to admit that it was wrong about rape and domestic violence. Enough is enough.

Davis's now legendary filibuster succeeded in part because of the stories from real women that poured in from around the world, enabling her to keep talking and stay on topic as the hours wore on. It was a feat of unity that simply wouldn't have been possible before social media and this new digital wave of feminism. Women from Texas, from other US states and from around the world began sending their stories, like ammunition passed along the lines as she stood, fighting a fight that was coming to represent so much more than opposition to a single bill.

And no, we haven't won yet. For the sentence of a fifteen-year-old rape victim to be overturned because of international pressure remains a travesty for the hundreds of thousands of nameless, faceless victims whose fate is not elevated into the spotlight. A public outcry to help to raise awareness of certain human-rights abuses for the first time cannot be glibly interpreted as a happy solution for their victims. Of course there are millions of women for whom the tools to directly access the online elements of this burgeoning movement are not accessible. But there is a great power in collective action, and in collective awareness, and every judgement or decision that incites international condemnation will have a knock-on effect on the likelihood of such a decision being taken again in the future. This might not be the end of the line, but it is the beginning of change. The old systems that have oppressed and belittled and dismissed women for so long are under attack and their archaic joints and scaffolding are creaking in the heat of the battle.

This is a battle that we will win. Because women are wittier, brighter, stronger and braver than a misogynistic and patriarchal world has given us credit for. The mass of hundreds of thousands of stories that we've collected does not represent a cluster of cowering victims. It is an outpouring of passion, borne of the frustration of being silenced for too long. And it is strong.

These women's voices are funny, mocking, shrewd and wise – do they sound like victims to you?

🐦 I'm tired of debating comfy mid-class white guys about what sexual oppression is. I talk facts, they talk unicorns.

🐦 'NICE, nice,' said the man just behind me, nodding his head approvingly. 'I like the way you walk. Boyfriend?' It took all the strength I had to keep my clothes on, I was so flattered and aroused.

🐦 "But what's in it for me?" is what I just asked the kind man who said he'd be willing to shag me if I lost some weight.

🐦 I'm in fancy dress for a hen party and a man shouts 'you skank' at me. The worst thing about it was that I was dressed as Andrew Ridgeley from Wham at the time.

🐦 Thought I'd torn my coat when 'lady got a hole' was shouted at me. No, just one man's shrewd observation that I have a vagina.

🐦 I'm a mechanical engineer, got told at an industry function 'you don't look like an engineer'. I asked him if it was the breasts.

Modern feminism is strong. It's not a movement that has to apologize for its priorities; but one that is marching forward, tackling every obstacle in its path one by one and not taking any crap about which jobs are too small or irrelevant, or which issues too 'lightweight'. People of all ages are rallying: schoolgirls who've had enough of being told to 'get back in the kitchen', graduates finding themselves a step behind their male peers, mothers sick of the rigid categorization of their children, grandmothers not ready to disappear. The husbands and boyfriends and fathers and brothers, the bosses and colleagues, the friends and the lovers. The victims of sexism and assault and the perpetrators who've realised the impact of their actions; the boys who've been as bullied and bruised by societal norms and expectations as our girls.

As Hayley Devlin, a nineteen-year-old student working on the No More Page 3 campaign, rather brilliantly puts it:

Women are bored of it. Bored of being told to 'get our tits out for the lads', bored of double standards and bored of being belittled by the media. It's 2013! We should be equal by now and won't give up until we are.

It's all really just quite overwhelmingly simple.

In the UK the movement is marked by its sense of purposeful pragmatism – from Imkaan, the black-feminist organization with its campaign against sexism and racism in music videos, to East London Fawcett, with its audit of the gender diversity in London's art galleries, to Let Toys be Toys and their onslaught on gendered supermarket aisles. It's a movement in which anyone and everyone is welcome, whether or not they want to wear lipstick and high heels, whether or not they choose to crack jokes or debate the issues, with leagues of supportive men and boys standing proudly alongside. Given that feminism simply means thinking everybody should be treated equally, regardless of sex, the entry criteria is refreshingly wide.

We can tackle sexism any way we like. Sometimes we'll get angry about it; sometimes we'll demand legislative change, or lobby the government; sometimes we'll write a poem, or go on a march; sometimes we'll sing, or scream, or shout; and sometimes... Well, sometimes, we'll just laugh...

🐦 A guy kept harassing me for my phone number so I gave him the number of another sexist, figured they'd have a lot in common.

🐦 Man: "Nice tits". Me: "If you're going to be a sexist pig at least be accurate. I have fantastic breasts." Silence...

🐦 Managed to stop white van full of men mid-catcall by shoving a big powdery donut into my mouth then smiling with mouth full.

🐦 'A woman's place is in the kitchen' you know what you're right. Lemme grab a knife.

🐦 Guy on train after I asked him to move his bag off seat: 'Why don't you grab my cock?' Me: 'I didn't bring any tweezers.'

And women are signing up to it in droves – with new feminist societies springing up at schools and universities across the country, social-media groups like the brilliant Twitter Youth Feminist Army providing online communities, and a plethora of women taking on their own battles without necessarily even having to feel that they are part of some wider, sacrosanct cause. When students at Cambridge University stood up against an annual jelly-wrestling contest because it was archaic, sexist and just downright sad, they weren't necessarily taking on a doctrine and a banner. But they were, nonetheless, part of a growing movement of women matter-of-factly putting their foot down to sexist rubbish and not taking no for an answer.

As Jo Cheetham, a writer, art historian and feminist told me:

Seeing Page 3 in the newspaper, being shouted at by builders, men saying sexist things when I worked in bars [...] it used to make me feel vulnerable, upset, weak. I don't feel like that anymore. Now there are so many amazing and supportive social networks where we can discuss all this stuff, so many brilliant women coming together and looking out for each other that I

don't feel intimidated any more. I feel strong. Women are taking ownership of the internet and using it as a platform to stand up to sexism. This has been the turning point for me.

She was right about women using the internet to take control. When Jaclyn Friedman, Soraya Chemaly and I decided to take on Facebook over graphic content depicting and encouraging rape and domestic violence, people told us we were crazy. Others had tried before – there had been high-profile campaigns and a 200,000-signature petition. Images of women bloody, battered and beaten remained live on the site, alongside groups about killing 'sluts' and forcing women to miscarry by punching them, or throwing them down flights of stairs. Facebook had refused to budge. We knew it was a long shot, but we also knew that we could draw on this incredible, burgeoning feminist spirit growing around the world. Instead of taking on Facebook directly, we launched a campaign aimed at the companies whose vast coffers were financing its content and, crucially, whose logos and adverts were appearing emblazoned alongside the rape jokes and images of women's bruised, bleeding faces.

The sheer, international energy of digital feminists sent the campaign viral, using our hashtag 60,000 times in the first day alone and clocking up 6,000 emails to advertisers as the international press picked up the story.

But the most surprising and moving thing was the outpouring of creativity and effort from women and men, around the world, who had their own ideas to offer and their own talents to help drive the campaign forward. It got personal. One woman began to make an art form out of what she called 'brandalism'. She took the famously recognizable adverts and logos of companies who had refused to respond to the campaign or declined to withdraw their advertising from Facebook, and digitally altered them to include components of the horrific images their logos had appeared alongside.

While Dove scrambled to make placatory statements after refusing to withdraw their ads from Facebook, global followers of the campaign made their feelings about the company – supposedly built on an ethos of female empowerment – very clear indeed. When Dove posted inane pictures on its Facebook page asking women 'What do you dedicate most of your getting ready time to? A. Hair B. Nails C. Skin Care D. Makeup?' protesters answered with witty, angry replies, visible to all on the viral images...

I dedicate most of my time to hoping that one day women will be treated as equals in society [...]

Dear Dove, I spent most of my 'getting ready time' this morning wondering why you are comfortable with your ads showing up next to pictures of women getting raped [...]

None of the above. I spend most of my time NOT patronizing companies that allow their ads to be shown on Facebook pages that make fun of violence against women [...]

Another artist created a composite version of one of the awful images Facebook had refused to remove – a picture of a little girl with two black eyes – using the avatars of Dove's own Twitter followers. He sent it back to them, with the simple message: 'Dove, these are your customers.'

Messages demonstrating the strength of public feeling began to pour in, as small businesses around the world threw their hats into the ring. Completely unbidden, companies we never targeted or contacted as part of the campaign voluntarily joined us, withdrawing their adverts from Facebook in solidarity with our cause. Granted, their ad budgets were peanuts compared to the big fish we were focusing on, but the gesture was incredibly powerful and it brought me to tears in those fraught, twenty-four-hour days of trawling through images so graphic and abusive I felt like I wouldn't ever be quite the same again.

And their messages summed up something much wider than their own small acts: they encapsulated the spirit of the whole campaign and of this fledgling new feminism.

A small sweet shop said: 'We understand we're a small company at the moment and that our stance will have little impact on this subject singly, but we hope that we might encourage others to do the same and that together we may be able to stop this from happening.' Another tiny start-up, Down Easy Brewing, wrote: 'Our measly few dollars a month will not make a dent in the Facebook bottomline, but our conscience as a corporation and as human beings will rest a little easier [...] Stand up to the bullies. Stand up for those who cannot or will not stand for themselves. We may never rid the world of hate, but we sure as hell should try.'

And that was the moment that I knew we were going to win. Not just this campaign, but the battle for hearts and minds that would take us towards gender equality afterwards too.

In a landmark victory, Facebook responded to the campaign within a single week. The company promised to update its policies and guidelines on rape and domestic violence, and to train its moderators to recognize and remove images of violence against women. The battle had been won. The media hailed it as a triumph for online campaigning and social media. But really it was a testament to the growing strength of feminist feeling around the world.

Now, because of that strength of feeling, every one of the thousands and thousands of people who might post an image of a battered woman on Facebook just for 'lolz', will receive a simple message from a platform that is such a large part of their culture that it serves to frame the world around them. They'll get the message that it's not OK.

The success of that campaign exemplified why this movement is so strong. It is because of the bond women and the men who love them form, across countries and cultures and borders – the incredible, moving, heart-warming, strengthening solidarity of the feminist community. This is a community that lets women know that they're not alone. It lets them realize that they don't have to put up with prejudice – and that if they choose to take a stand there will be others right behind them, every step of the way.

▶ I've never told anyone this story before, and it feels amazing to finally let it out.

A schoolgirl wrote to tell me that previously when the boys in her year had shouted sexist jibes and told her to get back in the kitchen she'd never felt able to say anything – she'd felt so alone. But, after discovering the project, she showed it to several of her female friends and, with each other's support, they started to stand up to the sexist bullying. Later, together, they showed it to the boys.

One of the seventeen-year-old girls I interviewed said it was hard to talk to her family about how she felt, because every time she mentioned women, or feminism, they would immediately cry, 'Oh, she's off on one again!' But now she has the strength that comes with knowing that hundreds of thousands of women feel exactly the way she does, and she's less likely to be silenced.

To others it has given the courage to report a crime they had suffered the consequences of for years. One woman wrote:

▶ I was violently raped by a boy that I knew when I was 13 years old (he was 17). I told my parents and we went to the doctors the next day. My recollection is that I was so shamed by what had happened, particularly as it was my first 'sexual' encounter, that I didn't want to either name the boy or go to the police. Years later I read the doctor's notes from the appointment: he had written that I had 'gone a bit too far with a boyfriend' and I was pretending that I had been raped. He didn't even examine me, even though I was bruised quite badly [...]

I am going to make an appointment with the surgery manager when I feel strong enough and demand a formal apology for their appalling and criminal mismanagement. I will possibly also go along legal channels. Thanks to this site, I know I have a mass of women who support me and understand why this can't be left.

And for others still, the kindness of strangers and the realization of belonging to a worldwide community are invaluable. A woman in Mexico tweeting us her experience might receive hundreds of responses from people she has never met, from Canada and Pakistan and Singapore, expressing their sympathies and concern, sharing stories of their own and exchanging tips and advice: simply letting her know that she's not overreacting and she's not alone.

🐦 The few times I've offered my experiences to @EverydaySexism I've found myself crying with gratitude from people's kindness. I needed that.

🐦 I just found out about @EverydaySexism and I am so thankful that I am not alone in this journey. That all women are not alone.

And, simple though it sounds, for many girls and women the project is their first exposure to the idea that they have the right not to be subjected to prejudice because of their sex.

▶ I think we're all taught subconsciously to be sexist to ourselves. Wish I'd stumbled upon this site earlier in life. It would have saved me all the hard lessons I had to learn on my own to realize what is right. When unpleasant things have happened to me, I'd always find me blaming myself first – not the man who's at fault. Always making up some sort of excuse thinking 'maybe it's me' and 'it probably is me'. Or upon hearing something sexist I'd laugh it off [...] but really, it's not funny.

One woman wrote to me after hearing about the project online and seeing the Chime for Change video. She said:

I went to your Twitter page, and started reading the tweets that women were posting, and I couldn't believe it. I've been experiencing these exact same things ever since I was a child, really. I was so moved by the bravery of these women to speak out like this [...]

I feel like FINALLY someone is recognizing this and doing something about it, and openly acknowledging that it really *is* sexual harassment, and that it's *NOT* okay.

And then, she took the single, simple step that has become the hallmark of today's feminism. She told everybody she knew.

I felt so moved by this 9 minute video, that I sent this email out to everyone I know. It's very personal, but somehow after watching your video I felt like I needed to share my story and yours, and to let people know about this important movement and that we no longer have to live in silence. I'm 29 years old, and I suffer from PTSD from early childhood trauma and abuse. This movement has started a healing process in me already that I can't explain. And I only learned about this a couple of hours ago.

And that single email made me aware, suddenly and overwhelmingly, of the power of individual, grassroots activism. Because when the message comes from your friend or your sister, your loved one or child it has such powerful impact. And normal women and men being the ones stopping, thinking about this, and then taking the time to chat to their friends and families about it, to let them know what a big problem it is and ask them to help stop it, is possibly the most effective way we can make real change.

When we worked on the Chime for Change film, a lovely, supportive young guy in his twenties was part of the film crew. Attending the early meetings, he listened to the story of the project and the women's experiences I related, clearly understood the issue and was extremely supportive. But when I saw him a week later his face was ashen as he told me he'd been asking his female friends about their experiences. 'Every one of them has so many stories,' he told me. '*Four* of them have been *ejaculated* on…' he trailed off, aghast. Even though I'd told him all this, even though he'd heard and cared, it took the harsh reality check of realizing that it was happening to those he loved to really make him grasp the true horror of what was happening. It got personal.

And, just like the problem that caused it, this revolution *is* personal. Across the country and around the world, women and men are standing up to sexism in their own personal, dignified and beautifully unique ways…

Tired of cold callers asking to speak to the 'man of the house', now I put them on to my 6-year-old son… he sings them 'Sexy and I Know It'.

You don't *look* like a lesbian… 'But since I am a lesbian, I *must* look like one!' is my answer.

▶ I used to purposefully jam the copier so people would stop asking me to make photocopies for their meetings. I'm an engineer.

A woman working in the City wrote to tell us that after experiencing sexist jibes and insults at work she simply printed off her employer's sexual-harassment policy and firmly placed a copy on every desk in the workplace. A waitress found her own way to get around the boss who turned a blind eye every time the chef groped her at work... She took a loaded tray full of glasses next time she walked past him and dropped them, shattering all over the floor, forcing the manager to come over and take note of what had happened. An engineer realized a TV-repair man was trying to take advantage of her presumed lack of technical knowledge when he told her 'TV needs a new tube, love, pricey'. Quick as a flash, she replied: 'That's a split capacitor; fix it for free or I'll report you.' He fixed it for free and threw in an apology too. A man described running after another man who he saw shouting at two women in the street, tapping him on the shoulder, and asking him, simply, 'Why did you do that?'

It's personal. Change is happening in a million different ways. Strong women are providing thousands of kick-ass role models for a new generation of fearless girls...

🐦 Aged 10: mocked mercilessly at school cos I said I was going to be a scientist with a lab with loads of cool stuff in it.

🐦 Aged 41: I'm actually an engineer (semiconductor failure analysis), and I DO have a lab with loads of cool stuff in it :)

🐦 Part of mostly female research group working in coding/ physics/fieldwork heavy area. Love it.

🐦 Careers teacher said he'd eat my indentures if I became engineer. Took them & salt to school 5 years later.

And, as one mother told me, we should not underestimate a burgeoning tribe of fierce parents who will not let their daughters grow up to be cowed by sexism.

My daughter is clever, inquisitive, determined, strong, confident, imaginative, understanding, exuberant and bursting with the promise of all the achievements and experiences that await her. She could rule the world. Yet already and daily from here on in she will be slowly, gradually, insidiously told that she should be good, not make a fuss, make way for men, not expect too much from a career, have children, get married, look after a man and be thin and pretty.

I see it as my maternal duty to guard her against all of this. If it takes my last breath I will use it to tell her that she can be as great as she wants to be, that she should never accept less because she is female and that she is equal to any man that she ever meets. I will not allow her glorious nature to suffer because the world cannot accept that she is a girl and a woman.

So this is it. It's happening everywhere. Don't think that you can hide, because you can't. Don't think you can opt out either. You're either with us or you're against us. There is no in-between, because it's the in-between that has been the problem for so long. The people who discriminate against us, who scream at us in the street, who grope us at work, who attack us and abuse us and assault us: they're bullies. And bullies flourish only in an environment where their victims are weakened by isolation. Where there's no supporting ourselves because there's no support to be had. But a bully loses his strength like a candle being snuffed out when the rest of the school stands up and links arms with the victim. There's no sitting on the fence, because sitting on the fence is turning a blind eye – even if you don't mean to, or didn't realize you were until now. It doesn't make you bad or wrong if you just hadn't noticed sexism before. It doesn't mean that you're part of the problem. It means you're part of the solution. We need you. We need you to stand with us. And we can't do it without you. You can't achieve a victory that requires a culture shift from a whole society without half of that society on board – it's just simple maths. But more than that: this is for you too! It's for everybody who wants to live in a fair society – for the men who want fair paternity leave and hate the Diet Coke advert and the aunts and uncles and mothers and brothers and grandpas of all those little girls who deserve to grow up in a world where their horizons aren't limited and stunted and constrained to the number of inches around their stomachs. It's for the boys who deserve to cry when they need to, without being reprimanded and masculinized and forced into muscular, angry strait jackets.

The thing about sexism is that it is an eminently solvable problem. Unlike so many of the other major issues facing our society, which demand huge amounts of money, or medical research, or legislation to fix, the answer to this is already within our reach. The Everyday Sexism Project didn't set out to resolve the problem, but to force people to recognize that it was real. I can't point to a single, practical political change, or a missing law that will make everything right, because it's just not that clear-cut anymore. But again and again in the past three years, I've seen change happen. I've seen what success looks like. And it's really very simple. Because all the different issues that the project has exposed – sexism, harassment, assault, rape – are so closely connected, so too are the methods of resolving them. By creating a cultural shift in attitudes and behaviours towards women we would take a huge step towards tackling each of those problems. Whether it's the professional, media, domestic or social sphere, by making it unacceptable to disrespect and belittle and dehumanize women in one world, we immediately shift their status in another. But it really, truly does have to be a team effort. It's sort of like recycling – it's something every single person can make an active, practical contribution to, starting today if they choose. But, just like recycling, a few well-meaning people going all out and doing everything in their power to make it work won't make a jot of difference overall if everybody else carries on shrugging their shoulders and tossing the milk carton into the bin.

So be the person in the meeting who objects to an application being dismissed because the interviewee is a 'maternity risk'. Be the aunt or uncle who buys their niece a chemistry set and their nephew a toy stove. Be the picture editor who doesn't illustrate every article with a pair of women's legs. Be the teenager who challenges his friends when they're calling girls sluts. Be the colleague who points out inappropriate behaviour for what it is. Be the TV exec who commissions a programme with five female leads. Be the guy who tells his mate it's not cool to shout at women in the street. Be the advertising director who thinks outside the box. Be the person at the bus stop who steps in to stop harassment. Be the parent who teaches their son about consent.

It isn't sweeping reform or mass changes of the law that we need now, but a change in ideas and inherited assumptions. And that is something everybody can contribute to. Enough is enough.

▶ Prior to reading the posts/tweets from the Everyday Sexism project, I would have been filled with doubt about whether I was making a mountain out of a molehill [...] I probably would have left it alone and thought, 'Well, that's just how it is. There's nothing we can do.' Fortunately, the E.S. project shows us all that it is the insidious nature of small, everyday occurrences which erode an individual's confidence and freedom, and society's integrity and fairness; and that it IS worth rearranging even the smallest stone in order to re-direct the flow of the river.

For me, that one entry sums up what's happening with feminism now, and with this pragmatic, welcoming, simple wave of activism. We might be moving small stones. People might sometimes find it hard to accept. They might point out that there are boulders elsewhere, or remark that they're used to seeing the bed of the stream littered with pebbles – that's just the way it is. But it doesn't have to be. And if you will pick up just one stone, then together we *will* redirect the flow of the river.

A Note on Statistics

The Vital Statistics sections included at the beginning of each chapter of this book are intended as a statistical snapshot of the inequalities referred to in each section, but they by no means represent the beginning and end of the available data on any given issue. I am quite aware that readers might have questions about the methodology and selection criteria of different studies; and, while I have made every effort to include only statistics from reliable sources, I absolutely acknowledge that there may be other, occasionally conflicting data to be considered elsewhere. These statistics do not directly inform the conclusions of each chapter, but nonetheless might provide a helpful general idea of the available research in each area.

Acknowledgements

This book would not exist without the thousands of people who found the strength to speak out about often deeply personal and painful experiences. I am immensely grateful for their courage. Enormous thanks are due to so many people without whom it wouldn't have been possible to begin at all. To Elinor Cooper, who truly 'got it' from the start and was the best guide and friend I could have hoped for, and everybody at Rochelle Stevens for their wonderful help and support. To Abigail Bergstrom, for her infectious enthusiasm about the project and her passion in championing it, and all the brilliant team at Simon & Schuster.

And to Monica Hope for her great clarity and sense of calm.

To each inspiring interviewee who gave so generously of their time and energy, and to those (in particular Harriet Walter) whose insights were invaluable even if their words do not appear directly in this book. To each of the schools and universities that so kindly welcomed and accommodated me.

To James Bartlett, whose patience and charity enabled the Everyday Sexism Project to come about in the first place, to every one of the incredible volunteers who keep it running; Emer O'Toole, who was my saving grace at the exact moment when it all could have fallen apart and Beryl-Joan Bonsu, who never stops offering to help more. To Peter Florence, for his enormous generosity, kindness and support of the Project and this book. To Aisha Mirza and Aileen Bintliff for their compassionate and intelligent guidance as trustees.

To Natasha Walter, Chitra Nagarajan, Ceri Goddard, Holly Dustin, Sarah Green, Stella Creasy, Lauren Wolfe, Soraya Chemaly, Jaclyn Friedman, Josh Shahryar and all the other people, too numerous to name, who welcomed me and the project into the feminist movement with open arms and made us at home. To Lucy Anne Holmes, for her endless support and boundless generosity even while climbing Everest and taking on the biggest newspaper in the country.

To Anna, who first showed me how to break gender boundaries and still inspires me daily, and to Nick, without whose tireless help, support, listening ear and love none of it ever would have happened. And finally to my mum, who showed me what compassionate social justice looked like before I even knew what it meant.